THE WORLD'S GREAT BALLETS

THE WORLD'S

HARRY N. ABRAMS, INC., *Publishers, New York*

JOHN GRUEN

GREAT BALLETS

La Fille Mal Gardée to *Davidsbündlertänze*

Project Director: Darlene Geis
Editor: Margaret Donovan
Designer: Judith Michael
Picture Researcher: Mary Whitney

Page 1: Marie Taglioni in La Sylphide, 1832
Pages 2–3: The Snowflakes from George Balanchine's production of The
Nutcracker. New York City Ballet
This page, above: A scene from Jean-Georges Noverre's Médée et Jason,
1763; below, Gaetan Vestris in Ninnette, 1781
Page 5: The original cast of Giselle, 1841

Library of Congress Cataloging in Publication Data

Gruen, John.
The world's great ballets.
Includes index.
1. Ballets – Stories, plots, etc.   2. Ballet –
History.   I. Title.
GV1790.A1G78   792.8'45   80-39921
ISBN 0-8109-0725-9

CONTENTS

INTRODUCTION

The great dance critic and poet Edwin Denby has said, "The first taste of art is spontaneously sensual, it is the discovery of an absorbing entertainment, an absorbing pleasure. If you ask anyone who enjoys ballet or any other art how he started, he will tell you that he enjoyed it long before he knew what it meant or how it worked. . . . You don't have to know about ballet to enjoy it, all you have to do is look at it."

Indeed, setting all intellectual profundities aside, Denby's statement pinpoints the essential element in the enjoyment and appreciation of the art of dance. To look at dance is to be exposed to the widest spectrum of human expression, but it is, even more, to be swept away by the visual impact of the harmonious interaction of bodies in motion. It is an entertainment and an experience that stirs the soul even as it educates the eye. It is a spectacle that takes what is most natural to us, movement, and exalts it into something that illuminates our very existence.

What makes ballet such a soul-satisfying revelation is its synthesis, over a period of more than four hundred years, of every aspect of organized human movement—from folk dance of primitive and ethnic origins to the rarefied elegance of court dance; from the Renaissance spectacle of the masque to the bawdy farce of the *commedia dell'arte*; from the codification of classical dance to the contained abandon of the ballroom; from the liberated earthiness of modern dance to the exuberant rhythms and low-down undulations of jazz; from everyday modes of human locomotion to the startling experimentations of minimal dance. This book offers the reader an entry into all the various elements of ballet through a description of sixty-two outstanding works culled from the vast repertoire created during the last two hundred years. Old and new, all are among the best-loved ballets performed today.

Although *La Fille Mal Gardée* (1789), the ballet that begins this survey, does not represent the dawn of classical ballet, it is one of the two earliest extant works in the modern repertoire, the other being the rarely performed *Whims of Cupid and the Ballet Master* (1786). Actually, ballet as we know it began two hundred years earlier in France with the production, in 1581, of the spectacular *Ballet Comique de la Reine*, commissioned by Queen Catherine de' Medici. France remained the stronghold of the art for the next two centuries, especially during the reign of Louis XIV, himself a dancer of note. In the seventeenth and eighteenth centuries, ballet reached an esthetic, technical, and pedagogical peak in France under such dancers, choreographers, and teachers as Marie Sallé, Marie Camargo, Jean-Georges Noverre, and Gaetan and Auguste Vestris.

La Fille Mal Gardée, choreographed by Jean Dauberval, represents the climactic development of eighteenth-century ballet— the *ballet d'action*, an artistic breakthrough credited to the great French choreographer Noverre. The idea that technical mastery, pageantry, or operatic display was the sole purpose of ballet was rejected by Noverre, who, in his treatise *Letters on Dancing and Ballets* (1760), also demanded a dramatic veracity in which action, gesture, and expression flowed into one cohesive narrative whole. The plot or story line became the motivation for the steps and gestures; music was commissioned to suit the subject matter of the ballets and the movements that conveyed it. Noverre also called for a reform in costuming, pointing out the need for less cumbersome attire to permit greater expressiveness and freedom of movement. He thought it especially important to do away with masks, allowing for naturalistic facial expressions. The innovations represented by the *ballet d'action* paved the way for the rise of the Romantic ballet.

In the nineteenth century, students of the early French masters spread across Europe to establish schools of classical ballet that would soon emerge with their own national identities: Salvatore Viganò in Italy, Charles Didelot in Russia, and the Bournonvilles, Antoine and his son August, in Denmark. In France, the Romantic ballet flowered in such works as *La Sylphide, Giselle*, and *Coppélia*. In this glorious age arose the cult of the great Romantic ballerinas, including Marie Taglioni, Fanny Elssler, Carlotta Grisi, Fanny Cerrito, and Lucile Grahn, and the choreographers who created vehicles for them, Filippo Taglioni, Jules Perrot, Jean Coralli, and Arthur Saint-Léon.

The romantic image of these ballerinas was enhanced by the development of the *pointe* shoe, which allowed them to rise magically on their toes, ethereal creatures creating an illusion of weightlessness. When it first appeared, in the 1820s, the *pointe* shoe was merely a soft silk ballet slipper reinforced by heavy darning on the tip of the toe. It was in such a slipper that Marie Taglioni thrilled audiences in *La Sylphide*. By mid-century, there

Varvara Nikitina and Enrico Cecchetti in the Bluebird pas de deux *in the original production of*
The Sleeping Beauty, 1890

had developed the concept of a boxed toe, reinforced by layers of hardened glue inside a satin slipper. This structural advance fostered hitherto unimagined technical virtuosity, particularly in the performance of pirouettes and sustained balances. Taglioni also introduced the Romantic tutu, a skirt consisting of airy layers of tarlatan that reached only to mid-calf, thus revealing her *pointe* shoes and legs clad in maillots, or tights—the close-fitting leg coverings developed in the early years of the century by M. Maillot, the hosiery maker for the Paris Opéra.

With the passing of the great Romantic ballerinas and choreographers in the latter half of the century, the center of classical ballet shifted from France to Imperial Russia. There the French School was transmuted into the classically pure Russian School under the tyrannical influence of French-born choreographer Marius Petipa and the equally despotic pedagogy of the Italian Enrico Cecchetti and the Danish-trained Christian Johansson. It was Petipa, working in St. Petersburg's glamorous Maryinsky Theater, who almost single-handedly defined the Imperial Russian style, with its gilt-edged classicism, its poetic lyricism, its systematized and psychologically motivated miming, its folk-inspired character dancing, and its superbly structured *divertissements*. Indeed, Petipa's prodigious choreographic inventiveness transformed the rather languid and fragile art of the early Romantic ballet into one possessed of exuberant dramatic impact and dazzling virtuosity.

Oddly enough, until the late 1890s, the greatest exponents of the classical Russian style were virtuoso ballerinas of Italian birth—Virginia Zucchi, Marie Giuri, Antonietta Dell'Era, Carlotta Brianza, and Pierina Legnani. Their technical brilliance profited from the improved toe shoe and was exposed by the shorter tutu, which allowed greater freedom for demanding legwork and other technical feats. Among the ballets created for these Italian ballerinas were the masterpieces choreographed by Petipa and his assistant, Lev Ivanov, to the music of Peter Ilyich Tchaikovsky—*The Sleeping Beauty, Swan Lake*, and *The Nutcracker*. Then, in the century's final years, there arose a generation of Russian dancers who would surpass their Italian predecessors and set the highest standards of refinement in the art for the next century. Technical virtuosity was now matched by individuality of execution, dramatic expressiveness, and personal charisma. Dancers such as Mathilde Kschessinska, Olga

Preobrajenska, and Nicholas Legat produced ever more astonishing technical feats and flourishes and etched indelible characterizations in ballets by Petipa and other choreographers.

At the turn of the century, the Maryinsky Theater School gave rise to a second generation of Russian dancers whose names are now legendary: Michel Fokine, Anna Pavlova, Tamara Karsavina, and Vaslav Nijinsky. At the same time, however, the tradition of great choreographers such as Petipa and Ivanov grew stale through repetitiveness of thematic and choreographic pattern. In reaction to this decline, the young Fokine began to formulate his revolutionary approach to choreography which, in its principles of free-style movement and dramatic integrity, was as innovative as the principles of Noverre had been more than a century earlier.

Disenchanted with the stagnant academic approach to choreography, Fokine formulated several radical new precepts. He insisted that the style of movement for each ballet should be determined by its subject and period and by the character of its music; that both dancing and gesture must fully serve as vehicles of dramatic expression; and that a dancer's *entire* body must become an expressive instrument and that this expressivity must be communicated and flow into the bodies of all the dancers in the group, thus imparting a unified mood to the dance as a whole. Fokine was especially inspired in the earliest development of his ideas after having seen the visionary American dancer Isadora Duncan in her first appearance in Russia in 1905.

Also dissatisfied with the static condition of the arts in Russia was Serge Diaghilev. In 1899, with artists Leon Bakst and Alexandre Benois, Diaghilev had founded the magazine *Mir Iskusstva* (*World of Art*), which championed modern art in Russia as exemplified by the ideas and work of its three cofounders. In 1906 Diaghilev, enlarging his scope, organized an exhibition of Russian art at the Salon d'Automne in Paris, and, in 1907, produced a series of concerts in Paris to introduce to the Western world the finest examples of Russian music. That same year Fokine created *Le Pavillon d'Armide* for the Maryinsky Theater and, soon after, the first version of the ballet that would be called *Les Sylphides*.

Upon seeing Fokine's new works, Diaghilev recognized that the choreographer's approach to ballet was compatible with his own artistic credo of novel and free expression. The following

year, when Diaghilev returned to Paris with his own company of Russian dancers, Fokine's works formed the core of its repertoire. On May 18, 1909, Diaghilev's Ballets Russes made its debut at the Théâtre du Châtelet with a program that included Fokine's *Le Pavillon d'Armide* and *Polovtsian Dances* from Borodin's *Prince Igor*. The response by the Parisian public was nothing short of ecstatic. Within a month, the Ballets Russes had introduced the West to other Fokine ballets (*Les Sylphides* and *Cléopâtre*), the dancers Pavlova, Nijinsky, Karsavina, and Adolph Bolm, and ballet sets and costumes designed by artists

such as Bakst, Benois, and Nicholas Roerich. The age of modern ballet had begun.

Diaghilev's company was soon deprived of the high artistry of Anna Pavlova, when in 1910 she embarked upon what would become a career of pioneering world tours; for the next twenty years, Pavlova brought ballet to audiences who had never even heard the word before. But the Ballets Russes hardly missed the great ballerina. Returning to Paris for the next several years, Diaghilev introduced a series of stunning new ballets by Fokine, including *Le Carnaval, Schéhérazade, The Firebird, Le Spectre de*

Anna Pavlova in Michel Fokine's The Dying Swan

Jeux and the scandalous production of Stravinsky's monumental *Le Sacre du Printemps* —he married, fell from favor, and was dismissed by Diaghilev. Although Fokine returned to create a few more works for the Ballets Russes, it was another young dancer, Léonide Massine, who rose to the position of chief choreographer. Between 1915 and 1920 Massine created some ten works, notably *Parade, La Boutique Fantasque, Le Tricorne* (*The Three-Cornered Hat*), and *Pulcinella*; all, except *Boutique*, with decor by Pablo Picasso. Inevitably, Massine also fell out of favor and, between 1920 and 1925, the Ballets Russes relied heavily on the choreography of Nijinsky's sister, Bronislava Nijinska. The crowning achievements of Nijinska's tenure were her ballet set to Stravinsky's *Les Noces*, her ultrachic *Les Biches* to music of Francis Poulenc, and *Le Train Bleu* to music of Darius Milhaud.

By 1925, the repertoire of the Ballets Russes was defined by the contributions of some of the most brilliant creative personalities of the time. Its dancers included Lydia Sokolova, Lydia Lopokova, Leon Woizikowsky, Stanislas Idzikowski, Lubov Tchernicheva, Vera Nemchinova, Felia Doubrovska, Olga Spessivtseva (who starred in the ill-fated 1921 London production of *The Sleeping Princess*, which nearly bankrupted the company), Pierre Vladimiroff, and Anton Dolin. Among its composers, in addition to Stravinsky, were Sergei Prokofiev, Georges Auric, Erik Satie, Ottorino Respighi, and Manuel de Falla, while artists such as André Derain, José-Maria Sert, Natalia Goncharova, Juan Gris, Marie Laurencin, and Georges Braque designed costumes and sets that awoke the eye to modern art. It was a confluence of talent that would place Diaghilev's Ballets Russes in the forefront of twentieth-century ballet.

In 1924, Nijinska became incensed over Diaghilev's interest in the choreographic talent of a young Russian dancer who had recently been taken into the company with other members of a small group that had left the Soviet Union to tour Europe. His name was George Balanchine and with him came Tamara Geva and Alexandra Danilova. When Diaghilev assigned Balanchine the choreography of a revival of Stravinsky's *Le Chant du Rossignol*, Nijinska withdrew from the Ballets Russes. Balanchine's rise as chief choreographer was swift, and in ballets such as *Barabau, La Pastorale, Jack-in-the-Box, The Triumph of Neptune*, and *La Chatte*, he redefined the choreographic character of the

la Rose, Narcisse, Petrouchka, Le Dieu Bleu, and *Thamar*, most of which were created for the exquisite talents of Karsavina and Nijinsky. But the impresario's passion for his protégé Nijinsky soon brought about a rift between Diaghilev and Fokine, especially when Diaghilev encouraged the young dancer to try his hand at choreography. Nijinsky's first ballet, *L'Après-Midi d'un Faune*, had its premiere on May 29, 1912, and it shocked *le tout Paris*. Diaghilev's enthusiasm for the work enraged Fokine, who left the company after the premiere of his own *Daphnis and Chloe* ten days later.

Nijinsky's controversial career as choreographer for the Ballets Russes was short-lived, for soon after his next two works—

Tamara Karsavina and Vaslav Nijinsky in Le Spectre de la Rose, *1911*

Ballets Russes. In these earliest ballets, which had narrative allusions, Balanchine created a choreography that could convey a plot line yet stand alone as a pattern of intriguing dance abstractions. From the first, a sign of his ineffable genius was his ability to produce works that were startlingly innovative and modern without resorting to the quirkiness of individual eccentricity and while retaining the purity of classicism.

In 1928, Balanchine created his version of Stravinsky's *Apollon Musagète*, and the age of neoclassicism in ballet was born. The work was also a vehicle for the talents of Diaghilev's latest favorite, Serge Lifar, and in 1929 Balanchine revealed the intensely dramatic side of his own choreographic gifts, as well as Lifar's performing skill, in *Le Fils Prodigue* (*The Prodigal Son*), with music by Prokofiev and evocative sets by Georges Rouault. The future of Diaghilev's Ballets Russes seemed to hold endless promise, but, on August 19, 1929, it was cut short by the impresario's death in Venice.

With Diaghilev's demise, the Ballets Russes disbanded and modern ballet fell into chaos. But the seeds of growth had already been planted. In England, two former members of Diaghilev's company, Marie Rambert and Ninette de Valois, had taken the first steps toward the establishment of a British ballet. Rambert's efforts were concentrated around the intimate Mercury Theatre in London, and her Ballet Club would encourage the first choreographic efforts of Frederick Ashton and Antony Tudor. Tudor remained with Rambert throughout the 1930s, developing his dramatic, deeply psychological approach to ballet, while Ashton soon joined forces with De Valois in her newly formed company, the Vic-Wells Ballet. Appearing in ballets created by Ashton and Tudor for both Ballet Rambert and the Vic-Wells Ballet was a young dancer, Alicia Markova, whose talent and ethereal style had brought her to the attention of Diaghilev and into his company at the age of fourteen. Markova soon teamed with her British compatriot, Anton Dolin, also a former protégé of Diaghilev. Together they formed their own troupe—the Markova-Dolin Company—and, especially in *Giselle*, the two became the outstanding balletic partnership of their generation. When Markova left the Vic-Wells, Ashton centered his attention on a young dancer named Margot Fonteyn. The magical chemistry of their collaboration, supported and guided by De Valois, eventually resulted in one of the

world's cultural treasures—the company known today as the Royal Ballet.

For their part, the numerous Russian artists of Diaghilev's Ballets Russes, stranded in 1929, ultimately banded together in the early 1930s. Throughout the decade they carried on the tradition of Russian ballet in various companies which bore such vaguely grand and often confusing names as Ballets Russes de Monte Carlo, Ballets Russes du Colonel W. de Basil, René Blum Ballet de Monte Carlo, Educational Ballets Ltd., the Original Ballet Russe—all of which somehow emerged in the 1940s as the Ballet Russe de Monte Carlo of Sergei Denham. Despite the organizational chaos, these companies boasted a veritable gal-

Serge Diaghilev and Léonide Massine

axy of brilliant stars, including Lifar, Danilova, Markova, Dolin, the "baby ballerinas" Irina Baronova, Tatiana Riabouchinska, and Tamara Toumanova, André Eglevsky, David Lichine, Yurek Shabelevsky, Igor Youskevitch, Nathalie Krassovska, Vera Zorina, Mia Slavenska, and Frederic Franklin, performing in outstanding ballets by Balanchine, Fokine, and Massine. Though international in scope and character, the Ballet Russe de Monte Carlo, after the advent of World War II, became in essence an American company.

In 1933, Balanchine was invited by a young and highly perceptive esthete of means, Lincoln Kirstein, to come to the United States to establish a school and company that would champion a uniquely American style of ballet. Balanchine accepted Kirstein's offer and, in 1934, under the choreographer's direction, the School of American Ballet opened in New York. This academy would be the foundation of various small compa-

nies of American character—Ballet Caravan, the American Ballet, American Ballet Caravan, and Ballet Society—which, in 1948, finally coalesced into the realization of Kirstein's and Balanchine's vision, the New York City Ballet. In the ensuing years, the New York City Ballet gave definition and resonance to Balanchine's concept of the American style and dancer—a style deeply rooted in the Petipa esthetic of pure classicism and technical virtuosity but brilliantly transmogrified by the choreographer into works which were marked by diamond-etched clarity, profound musicality, and windswept speed, performed by dancers with tall, long-limbed, loose-jointed bodies.

In the late 1930s, the company of a former Maryinsky dancer and partner of Pavlova, Mikhail Mordkin, was transformed through the vision of the American Richard Pleasant into Ballet Theatre, a company that offered an American approach to a repertoire of international scope. In its early years, following its debut in 1940, and through the financial support and artistic direction of former Mordkin ballerina Lucia Chase, Ballet Theatre brought together numerous talented choreographers, among them Fokine, Lichine, Bolm, Tudor, Agnes de Mille, and Eugene Loring. The company fostered the careers of dancers such as Patricia Bowman, Chase, Karen Conrad, Nana Gollner, Nora Kaye, Hugh Laing, Annabelle Lyon, Alicia Alonso, Donald Saddler, Nina Stroganova, John Kriza, and Jerome Robbins. Robbins, a young New York–born dancer, was given his first choreographic opportunity by Ballet Theatre; *Fancy Free*, created by him in 1944, was a milestone in American ballet, launching a career that would extend from Ballet Theatre to Broadway to the New York City Ballet.

In later years, Ballet Theatre would continue to produce original works by both established and new choreographers (most notable among the latter were the first ballets of Eliot Feld). Its primary repertoire, however, consisted of the ballet classics, along with the masterworks created by Tudor in the 1940s. Serving as a showcase of ballet stars of international stature, Ballet Theatre (renamed American Ballet Theatre in 1957) attracted such dancers as Toni Lander, Lupe Serrano, Carla Fracci, Erik Bruhn, Ivan Nagy, Natalia Makarova, Rudolf Nureyev, Mikhail Baryshnikov, and Alexander Godunov. At the same time, artists from within the ranks were not ignored: dancers like Royes Fernandez, Bruce Marks, Sallie Wilson,

Bronislava Nijinska and Anton Dolin in Nijinska's Le Train Bleu, 1924

Eleanor D'Antuono, Ted Kivitt, Marcos Paredes, Martine van Hamel, Fernando Bujones, Marianna Tcherkassky, and Cynthia Gregory rose to stardom. In 1980, after forty years under the direction of Chase and, since 1946, Oliver Smith, Ballet Theatre was placed under Baryshnikov's artistic direction, and a new era began.

In addition to the two major American companies, smaller companies, like those of Ruth Page, Robert Joffrey, Alvin Ailey, and Arthur Mitchell, have gained stature. Almost every leading American city boasts a successful ballet company, including Philadelphia (with a company which evolved from Catherine Littlefield's dance group of the 1930s), Houston, Boston, San Francisco, Salt Lake City, and Atlanta.

The story of American modern dance begins with its pioneer, Isadora Duncan. Faced with the stagnation of American classical dance at the turn of the century, Duncan was the first to explore a free and indigenous dance form. She was followed by Ruth St. Denis and Ted Shawn, who together founded the first school of American modern dance, Denishawn. Out of this group emerged three major figures who broke away to form their own companies and explore their own concepts of movement: Martha Graham, Doris Humphrey, and Charles Weidman. Along with modern dancers who did not come from Denishawn—Helen Tamiris, Lester Horton, and Hanya Holm (a disciple of the German expressionist dancer Mary Wigman)—these pioneers spawned wave upon wave of American modern dancers who would give their own individual expression to the myriad possibilities of dance. Some, like Ailey, José Limón, Merce Cunningham, Alwin Nikolais, Murray Louis, Pauline Koner, Paul Taylor, Anna Sokolow, Pearl Lang, Glen Tetley, Erick Hawkins, John Butler, Louis Falco, Bella Lewitzky, Lar Lubovitch, Twyla Tharp, and Pilobolus,

Above, left: The original cast of Apollo, *1928: Alice Nikitina, Felia Doubrovska, Lubov Tchernicheva,*
and Serge Lifar
Above, right: Serge Lifar and Felia Doubrovska in the original production of The Prodigal Son, *1929*

have left an indelible imprint on the world of contemporary dance.

Also in the postwar years, the dance world became aware of several emerging European ballet companies distinctly different in character from the venerable ones in London, Paris, and Copenhagen. These new groups, all working out of a classical base and offering a wide variety of choreographic styles, from the purely abstract to the full-length story ballet, included the companies established or transformed by such dancer-choreographers as Roland Petit, Maurice Béjart, John Cranko, Hans van Manen, Rudi van Dantzig, Birgit Cullberg, and, most recently, Jiří Kylián.

Although the Russian ballet continued to celebrate the great classics in opulent productions, during the 1950s the West was also introduced to the style that Russian ballet had acquired

Above: The original Ballet Rambert production of Jardin aux Lilas, *1936, with Hugh Laing (center) and Maude Lloyd (right)*
Below: The 1935 Vic-Wells production of Frederick Ashton's Façade *with Robert Helpmann (front row, far left), Margot Fonteyn (front row, third from left), and Ashton (front row, reclining)*

under the Soviet regime. While the "Socialist Realist" character of the choreography left something to be desired, no one could dispute the magnificence of the artists of the Kirov and Bolshoi ballet companies. Galina Ulanova, Maya Plisetskaya, Irina Kolpakova, Maris Liepa, Ekaterina Maximova, Vladimir Vasiliev, Yuri Soloviev, Natalia Bessmertnova, Nina Sorokina, Vyacheslav Gordeyev, Ludmilla Semenyaka, and Nadezhda Pavlova have stunned audiences with their technical and expressive brilliance. Such dancers have engendered the hope that an innovative choreographic esthetic and style, recently hinted at in the works of Yuri Grigorovich, will emerge to do justice to their talents. (The dissatisfaction of many searching artists with the limitations of Soviet balletic expression has been made amply clear by the defections or departures to the West of Nureyev, Makarova, Baryshnikov, Godunov, Valery and

Above: Anton Dolin and Alicia Markova in Giselle
Below: Jerome Robbins's Fancy Free, *1944, with Robbins, Michael Kidd, and John Kriza as the sailors*

Galina Panov, and Leonid and Valentina Kozlov.)

The events of this dance history are reflected in the analyses of the sixty-two ballets discussed in this book. The universally acknowledged classics are, of course, included, but with the proliferation of choreographers and ballets in the twentieth century, it is impossible to encompass every major work. Among the missing are certain undeniably important ballets by Fokine, Massine, Nijinska, Balanchine, Tudor, Ashton, De Mille, Robbins, Joffrey, Petit, Cranko, Gerald Arpino, and by various other masters of American modern dance.

The art of dance is a continual exploration of the limitless possibilities of emotional expression achieved through movement. It is hoped that this volume will at least approximate for the reader what can only be fully and palpably experienced by watching dancers moving in space and responding to the experience with one's own sense of movement. Only then can dance unfold its wondrous powers of communication. And so it may be that the real object of this book is to arouse in the reader the desire to share the experience of dance firsthand, and thus to be placed directly in touch with one of the glories of human achievement.

Martha Graham in her Letter to the World, *1941*

Above: Pilobolus in Monkshood's Farewell: *Robby Barnett and Martha Clarke (left), Jonathan Wolken (right)*
Below: Ric McCullough and Jeanne Solan of the Netherlands Dance Theatre in Jiři Kylián's November Steps
Overleaf, left: Edward Villella in The Prodigal Son. *New York City Ballet*
Overleaf, right: Peter Martins in Apollo. *New York City Ballet*

THE WORLD'S GREAT BALLETS

LA FILLE MAL GARDÉE

1789 ◆ *Music: various traditional French songs* ◆ *Choreography by Jean Dauberval*

La Fille Mal Gardée (*The Unchaperoned Daughter*) has the distinction of being one of the two ballets that come to us directly from the eighteenth century. (The other, *The Whims of Cupid and the Ballet Master*, is danced only infrequently, in the repertoire of the Royal Danish Ballet.) *Fille*, as the ballet is affectionately called, has been restaged by many ballet companies throughout the world and after almost two hundred years still serves as a delightful vehicle for the great ballerinas of our day. It remains a comic masterpiece and is most probably the work that paved the way for the great Romantic ballets of the nineteenth century. Blending classicism with everyday life, it brought ballet down to earth from Olympus.

Fille is all sunlight and smiles, with only a fleeting hint of clouds and none of the Gothic elements that were to follow in the Romantic ballet. Hidden beneath its comic charm are two wise themes: love conquers all, and bounteous nature is man's master. The work provides almost continuous virtuosic dancing; its characters are clearly defined and each acts according to a particular psychological motivation. In spirit and in action, *La Fille Mal Gardée* is pure pastoral poetry in dance.

Of the many versions now performed, one of the most engaging is in the repertoire of England's Royal Ballet; it is choreographed by Sir Frederick Ashton and uses John Lanchbery's arrangement of the score composed by Ferdinand Hérold for the 1828 Paris Opéra staging. Ashton's *Fille* is described here.

THE BALLET

After a charming overture, the curtain rises on the farm of the wealthy Widow Simone. Madame Simone is the mother of Lise, an adorable but rather willful young girl who, against her mother's wishes, is in love with Colas, a rambunctious young farmer. At her mother's insistence, Lise reluctantly sets to work.

The amorous Colas reappears several times during the scene, and each time Lise deserts her chores and happily joins him in a dance. Thomas, a wealthy landowner, arrives with his simple-minded son, Alain. Lise is briefly sent off while her mother and old Thomas plan for the union of their children —and their land holdings. Coming to an agreement, they joyfully call Lise back. Realizing what has happened, Lise is dismayed, especially after seeing Alain, befuddled and far more interested in his red umbrella than in anything else. She protests the intended marriage but is cut short when everyone is called to the harvest.

The next scene opens in a cornfield, where Colas leads the harvesters in an exuberant dance. Lise reluctantly dances a duet with Alain, but when Colas joins the pair she is elated. Alain soon becomes the object of the harvesters' ridicule, and his father leads him away, leaving Lise and Colas free to dance an inspired *pas de deux*. The Widow Simone then performs a merry clog dance, and all join hands for a whirl around the Maypole. A sudden rainstorm sends everyone scurrying for cover.

Act II opens with the rain-drenched mother and daughter rushing back into the farmhouse. Locking the door, Widow Simone sets Lise to work, this time at the spinning wheel, and then nods off to sleep. Still in pursuit of Lise, Colas appears at the locked half-door and begs her to join him. An eager Lise unsuccessfully tries to spirit the key away from her sleeping mother, waking her in the attempt. Widow Simone, unaware of Colas's presence at the door, picks up a tambourine and asks her daughter to dance for her. Sleep soon overcomes her again, leaving Lise to dance for her lover.

The arrival of the harvesters interrupts Lise's dance. Carrying large sheaves of straw, they have come to be paid by Widow Simone, who lets them into the house. Simone again orders her daughter to work and, after locking her safely in the house, leaves with the young farmers for some refreshment. While Lise, alone at her spinning wheel, muses over the joyous prospect of married life with Colas, she is jolted from her revery as he suddenly springs from one of the sheaves. In delight, she dances with him and they exchange scarves as tokens of their love. When they hear Widow Simone approach, Lise pushes Colas into her bedroom and locks the door. Simone immediately notices Colas's scarf around Lise's neck. Furious, she banishes her disobedient daughter to the bedroom.

The time for the signing of the marriage contract has come. Thomas and the ever-distracted Alain enter, accompanied by a notary. After Simone and Thomas sign their agreement, Alain is given the key and told to release his bride-to-be from the bedroom. Torn between his father's wishes and his private fantasies, he reluctantly unlocks the door, exposing the shocking sight of Lise in the arms of Colas. All of Widow Simone's precautions have been in vain! After a few angry moments, she relents and resigns herself to the inevitable. She finally blesses Lise's marriage to the man she truly loves, and all rejoice, including Alain, who hugs his beloved umbrella in relief.

Opposite: Frank Augustyn in Frederick Ashton's version of La Fille Mal Gardée. *National Ballet of Canada*
Overleaf: Jacques Gorrissen and Karen Kain in Ashton's Fille. *National Ballet of Canada*

LA SYLPHIDE

1832 ◆ *Music by Jean Schneitzhoeffer* ◆ *Choreography by Filippo Taglioni*

Among the many great ballets of the nineteenth century, *La Sylphide* must be considered the most important. A perfect blend of naturalism and fantasy, this work heralded the arrival of the Romantic ballet. Moonlit woodland glades inhabited by unearthly creatures dressed in gossamer white would appear in ballets for the rest of the century, the age of the *ballet blanc*.

La Sylphide gave immortality to the ballerina Marie Taglioni, daughter of the choreographer, who originated the title role. It was Taglioni's ineffable sense of the ethereal that inspired the glorification of the Romantic ballerina and the consequent de-emphasis of the male *danseur*, who had reigned from the time of Louis XIV, the original *dieu de la danse*. Not only did Taglioni transport audiences with her artistry, but she heightened the aura of otherworldliness by dancing on *pointe*—the first to realize fully the expressive potential of this technique. So great was Taglioni's success in *La Sylphide* that her name became synonymous with the title role, and to this day ballerinas try to recreate if not surpass that original vision of magical perfection.

La Sylphide is the Romantic ballet as poetry. Its events are motivated by the imagination of James, who strives to grasp a world that only *he* perceives. The sylph represents his romantic ideal, the unattainable quest for a dream of poetic perfection. Although fantasy and reality coexist in the work, we are never quite sure if they overlap except in the mind of James. The other characters in *La Sylphide* are clearly delineated: the sylph, though capricious, is innocent; Madge represents the dark elements of the imagination; Gurn, Effie, and the others are real people, untouched by James's romantic visions. Later ballets would also blur the distinction between fantasy and reality, but with dramatic rather than poetic impact.

The version of *La Sylphide* described here is the American Ballet Theatre production first staged in 1964 by Harald Lander from August Bournonville's 1836 version, and later restaged and partially revised by Erik Bruhn (1971). The music is by Herman Løvenskjold, with additional music by Edgar Cosma.

THE BALLET

Dawn is breaking through the high, arched window of the manor house of a farm in the Scottish Highlands. Beside the fireplace, illuminated by the dying embers, James, the young scion of the house, sits sleeping in a high-backed wing chair. We know he is dreaming, for we see the image of his dream kneeling serenely at his side. She is a sylph—a translucent winged creature whose misty white costume shimmers mysteriously in contrast to the dark, richly colored tartan of James's kilt. Suddenly she rises and darts about the room. She is clearly enthralled by the handsome young mortal still dreaming in his chair. The sylph concludes her dance by playfully kissing James. Startled, he rushes to capture his dream, only to be eluded by the flirtatious creature, who magically escapes through the hearth.

Still dazed by the apparition, James is unaware that he has been observed by Gurn, who, like several other young Scotsmen, has been asleep in the huge room. Before Gurn can confront James about his actions, it becomes clear why he and the other young men are there. It is James's wedding day and his betrothed, Effie, enters with his mother. A small retinue of bridesmaids also comes to offer wedding gifts to Effie.

Among the girls, unseen at first, is a sinister, stooped figure leaning on a cane and dressed in rags. She is Madge, an old hag with the gift of prophecy. Seeing her warm her hands at the fire, James instinctively senses that her presence is an evil omen for his wedding and he attempts to eject her from the house. The kindhearted Effie is startled by his rage and begs James to allow Madge to remain.

The wedding guests, delighted to have Madge in the house, ask her to tell their fortunes. A stool is placed in the center of the room, and in a brilliant mime passage Madge foretells happy, amusing, or shocking events to members of the gathering. For Gurn, she predicts great wealth and happiness. Effie pleads with James to let her also offer her palm to Madge. When the crone tells Effie that she will share married bliss not with James but with Gurn, James wrathfully pushes Madge toward the door. Madge turns on him, lifts her cane above her head, and ominously raises herself to her full, commanding height. Everyone, including James, is stunned by this menacing gesture. Having demonstrated that she possesses unsuspected powers, Madge leaves.

The household returns to normal. Effie, her friends, and James's mother go upstairs to dress for the wedding, and Gurn and the other young men depart. James is alone, but he soon becomes aware of a presence. The window drifts open, revealing the sylph poised on the sill. She floats into the room. At the

Mikhail Baryshnikov and Gelsey Kirkland in American Ballet Theatre's production of Bournonville's
La Sylphide

Again, Gurn enters in time to catch sight of James and his vision and bolts up the stairs to tell the others what he has seen. The sylph curls up in the wing chair, and James covers her with a large tartan shawl. Gurn rushes down the stairs followed by Effie, James's mother, and the others. Suspecting the sylph's hiding place, he triumphantly flings the tartan from the chair, only to find it empty. The sylph has vanished.

Satisfied that Gurn's jealous accusations are false, Effie turns lovingly to James. After a charming dance by Effie, Gurn and James perform dazzling solos. The joyful mood mounts, as all join in an exhilarating Scottish reel. In the midst of this whirling dance, the sylph flits through the room. Only James catches sight of her, and each time she comes near him he finds it increasingly difficult to concentrate on his surroundings. The dancing ends, and it is time to toast the bride and groom.

As James picks up the wedding ring he will place on Effie's finger, the sylph mischievously snatches it from his hand and flies out the door. James races after her, and as the guests raise their goblets in a toast, they are astonished to discover that he is gone. A frantic search for him fails until Gurn returns from outside and tells them he has seen James distractedly pursuing a mysterious flying creature into the woods. Effie swoons into the arms of James's mother as Gurn rushes to her side, and the curtain falls on Act I.

The dark elements of the supernatural, so essential to the Romantic imagination, dominate the opening of Act II. A large fire under an enormous cauldron eerily lights the night sky. Madge, now in full manifestation as a witch, hovers over her magic brew while three demonic hags cavort around her. Madge is casting a magic spell to poison a long, diaphanous pink scarf, which will be the instrument of her revenge on James. Their evil done, Madge and her companions vanish into the night.

With the dawn, James, carrying his jacket, enters a clearing in the dense forest, still in search of his capricious sylph. All at once, she appears and calls her companions—a circle of sylphs—to greet him. James is enchanted and dances with them, and when the sylphs scurry into the woods, he follows, leaving his jacket behind. Gurn then enters the glade and finds the jacket. He is about to call the other members of the search party when Madge appears. She warns him that if he intends to marry Effie, James must not be found. Gurn hides James's jacket,

reappearance of his fantasy, James is again transported. The sylph tells him how sad she is that his heart belongs to another. Her sorrow is fleeting, however, and soon she dances gaily for him. Entranced, James joins the dance but never once manages to touch the elusive sylph.

Erik Bruhn as Madge. National Ballet of Canada

and when Effie and James's mother arrive, he tells them their search has been in vain; they return home.

A moment later James appears, again desperately seeking the sylph. Madge reenters and offers to help by presenting him with the bewitched scarf. This, she tells James, when wound about the shoulders of the sylph, will keep her on earth with him. Overjoyed, he offers to pay her, but Madge spurns his money and, cackling with glee, returns to the forest.

The sylph reappears and a playful James teases her by hiding the gift behind his back until she begs him to let her see it. He unfurls the scarf into the air to the sylph's utter delight. As the two dance joyfully, James winds the pink scarf around the sylph's shoulders; she suddenly becomes still. Slowly, her wings drop to the ground as she backs away from him. She staggers pitiably, attempts to fly, and then dies. Too late, James realizes he is the victim of the witch's revenge.

The other sylphs enter and sorrowfully carry away their sister while James, helpless, watches in grief. Madge appears and as he rushes toward her in a fury she strikes him down. Wrathfully confirming her prophecies, the witch shows James the apparition of his dead sylph floating to heaven and, moments later, the happy wedding procession of Effie and Gurn. The dark powers of the supernatural have shattered James's reality as well as his fantasy.

Cynthia Gregory as the Sylphide and Ivan Nagy as James. American Ballet Theatre

GISELLE

1841 ◆ *Music by Adolphe Adam* ◆ *Choreography by Jules Perrot and Jean Coralli*

Giselle is the quintessential Romantic ballet as drama: a perfect amalgam of creative elements in which music, story, theme, and choreography combine to produce the ideal vehicle for the artistry of the ballerina.

The ballet was, in fact, created as a labor of love. Théophile Gautier, the French poet and critic, conceived *Giselle* expressly for the talents of a young ballerina whom he adored, Carlotta Grisi. Her dances were created by her lover and teacher, Jules Perrot, the great dancer-choreographer. Their efforts were rewarded, for Grisi's transcendently poignant portrayal of Giselle made her the successor to Marie Taglioni and Fanny Elssler as the great ballerina of the Romantic age.

Although *Giselle* presents several challenging roles—notably those of Albrecht, Myrtha, and Hilarion—the title part requires not only superb technical facility but a dramatic talent that can project Giselle's progression from bucolic innocence through mental derangement to an ethereal spirituality. The ballerina in *Giselle* must be a consummate actress as well as dancer.

With *Giselle* as a perfect example of the genre, one would think that the dramatic Romantic ballet would have flourished. Another half century would pass, however, before *Giselle* would be equaled—by the Petipa-Tchaikovsky masterpiece, *Swan Lake*. (The version of the ballet which we describe here is the 1968 American Ballet Theatre production with choreography by David Blair after Perrot and Coralli.)

THE BALLET

The curtain rises on a peaceful Rhineland village as a group of peasants cross the empty square. Hilarion, a gamekeeper, enters and places a rabbit at the door of a cottage. It is a gift for his love, Giselle. He quickly conceals himself as Count Albrecht rushes onto the scene with his companion, Wilfred. Removing his cloak and sword—trappings of nobility—Albrecht reveals himself disguised as a peasant, Loys. Although Wilfred questions the wisdom of this pretense, he obediently takes the sword and cloak and hides them in a nearby hut before he leaves.

From his ardent approach to Giselle's cottage, it is evident that Albrecht too is in love with her. He knocks on her door, then hides. The door opens and Giselle, the image of girlish simplicity, runs out. She is in love and expresses her joy with a breezily bounding dance. Finding no one about, she is saddened

for a moment until Albrecht surprises her. In the presence of her beloved, she is suddenly demure; to the wistful musical theme that identifies her, she gently resists his tender pledge of eternal love. To test his faithfulness, she plucks the petals from a daisy; her fears are confirmed when they tell her "he loves me not." Albrecht stops her tears by furtively discarding an extra petal, and believing the ruse, Giselle joins him in a blissful romp.

Hilarion disrupts their intimacy to declare that Albrecht is false to Giselle. Albrecht instinctively reaches for his sword. This telling gesture eludes the unworldly Giselle, but Hilarion, with thoughts of exposing Albrecht's true identity, departs.

Gaiety is restored with the entrance of the peasants, who celebrate the grape harvest with a jolly dance. The lovers join them, but at the peak of the dance Giselle falters and clutches at her heart. Albrecht becomes alarmed, but Giselle, recovering, assures him that it is nothing. Berthe, Giselle's mother, urges her to be careful, reminding her daughter that should she die before her wedding day, she will become a Wili, one of the doomed spectres of unmarried girls who have been victims of unfaithful lovers. Giselle returns with her mother into the cottage, while for the moment Albrecht and the others depart.

Next, the hunting party of the Prince of Courland and his daughter Bathilde arrive. Giselle, enthralled with Bathilde's elegance, kneels before her, lifting the hem of the princess's gown to her cheek. Princess and peasant girl soon confide to each other that they are both in love and engaged to be married. Bathilde removes her necklace and gives it to Giselle.

Rested and refreshed, the hunting party returns to the forest. Hilarion emerges from the hut where he has been concealed. He has Albrecht's cloak and sword, final proof of his suspicions. Before Hilarion can reveal his discovery, Albrecht returns and Giselle asks him to dance. Her happiness is so great that she then executes a solo of dazzling virtuosity. The spirit of the gathering mounts ecstatically until Giselle is lifted by her friends and declared Queen of the Day.

Suddenly, Hilarion shatters the idyll by tearing the lovers from each other's arms. He produces the sword and claims that its noble owner is Albrecht. Giselle is incredulous, while Albrecht assures her that the accusation is false. Hilarion sounds the hunting horn, calling back the royal party. To everyone's dismay, the prince and his daughter recognize

Carla Fracci and Erik Bruhn in Giselle. *American Ballet Theatre*

Albrecht. Bathilde asks what has prompted him to dress in this amusing fashion, and Albrecht replies that it was only a foolish fancy. Giselle rushes between Albrecht and Bathilde, insisting that there must be some mistake. No, the princess assures her, Count Albrecht is her fiancé.

The onrush of these revelations deprives Giselle of her reason. With sudden violence, she tears the necklace from her neck and flings it to the ground. Then she becomes strangely still and, with halting, disjointed movements, recalls her former moments of bliss with Albrecht.

Jarred from her revery when she trips over Albrecht's sword, Giselle picks it up by the blade, swings it in a large circle to keep the others away, and then attempts to plunge the tip into her breast. Albrecht rushes to stop her. She does not recognize her distraught lover, her mother, Hilarion, or friends. With a glazed stare, she gestures toward something unseen in the air, something that seems to beckon to her. A flicker of recognition that draws her to Albrecht passes quickly, and in a final burst of strength she rushes to her mother's arms and dies. In despair, Albrecht lunges at Hilarion, forcing him to face the result of his scheming, while Hilarion, equally desperate, places the guilt for Giselle's death on Albrecht. Fearing that the gamekeeper is justified, Albrecht allows Wilfred to lead him from the sorrowful scene. Hilarion kneels beside Giselle, surrounded by the mournful villagers, as the curtain falls.

An eerie musical theme played by harp and strings sets the mood of Act II. In a woodland glade beside a shadowy lake, Hilarion kneels at Giselle's grave. He binds two sticks of wood into a crude cross and forces them into the earth. Looking about him, he catches fleeting glimpses of ghostly creatures; frightened, he rushes off into the forest.

A veiled, spectral figure glides into the clearing. It is Myrtha, Queen of the Wilis. By her commanding, icy presence and bounding leaps, she defines the realm of the Wilis. She then summons her subjects, who, with their gauzy white garb and strictly controlled movements, suggest a battalion of deadly night guardians. The time has come to call forth their new initiate, the ghost of Giselle. Giselle rises from her grave, strikes a pose of obeisance to Myrtha, and then instantly flings herself into frenzied spinning—a brief, dazzling solo at the end of which she and the others vanish.

A dirgelike theme announces the arrival of Albrecht. Dressed in noble attire, he kneels and places some lilies on Giselle's grave. Her ghost momentarily appears, but departs before he can see her. Finally, she reveals herself and they dance: a yearning revery of lost love which, as it unfolds, casts aside its melancholy tone and becomes a celebration of their reunion.

As Albrecht follows Giselle into the forest, a menacing musical theme brings back the Wilis, who are pursuing Hilarion. Trapped, the gamekeeper is forced to dance to his death and is then heartlessly swirled into the lake by the vengeful Wilis. Like a death patrol, the triumphant spectres, in bounding pairs, follow their queen into the night. Moments later, they reappear with Albrecht, and Myrtha announces that he too is doomed.

Still under the spell of her earthly love, Giselle intercedes for Albrecht, but she is forced to obey Myrtha's order to lead him in a dance of death. Tender at first, their dance becomes a highly charged struggle for survival, with Giselle urging the faltering Albrecht to maintain his courage. Finally, Albrecht, pushed to deathly exhaustion by the relentless Wilis, falls to the ground. But the strength of Giselle's love has overcome even the Wilis' dark powers—a distant bell tolls the break of day. Alarmed, the Wilis realize they must retreat, for their nocturnal kingdom is receding with the shadows. Giselle lingers over the prone figure of her beloved, and this last gesture awakens in Albrecht the meaning of everlasting love. Although his life is spared, Albrecht is bereft as he watches Giselle return to her grave.

Dominique Khalfouni and Mikhail Baryshnikov in Act II of Giselle. *Paris Opera Ballet*

NAPOLI

1842 ◆ *Music by H.S. Paulli, E. Helsted, N.V. Gade, and H.C. Lumbye* ◆ *Choreography by August Bournonville*

Under the influence of different choreographers, ballerinas, and ballet masters, the early classics of ballet were altered so frequently that it is now difficult to identify the original choreographic passages. The course of the Royal Danish Ballet, however, has run contrary to this trend. Beginning in 1829, under the creative direction of dancer-choreographer August Bournonville, the Danes developed and closely guarded their own Romantic ballets and choreographic style. Since the vast Bournonville repertoire remained in relative isolation in Denmark until the mid-twentieth century, these uniquely Danish works have been preserved in their original form.

Napoli, or The Fisherman and His Bride is considered the finest example of that scintillating blend of exuberant virtuosity, pantomimic eloquence, elegant choreography, and sunny social commentary known as the Bournonville tradition. In *Napoli*, as in all Romantic ballets, elements of realism are intertwined with the dark forces of fantasy. But Bournonville's fascination with the recreation of authentic folk traditions and his deeply Christian tone render his works unique in the genre. Above all, it is Bournonville's choreography, with its particular sense of skimming fleetness and gentle, cheerful presentation, that makes us grateful that ballets like *Napoli* have been preserved.

THE BALLET

A crowd representing every facet of Neapolitan society fills the Santa Lucia wharf at twilight. Veronica, a widow, enters with Teresina, her daughter. The girl is loved by Giacomo, a macaroni dealer, and Peppo, a lemonade vendor, but her heart belongs to Gennaro, a young fisherman. As Teresina waits for him to return from the sea, a humorous but impassioned quarrel arises between the two rivals. When Gennaro returns, he too takes part in some good-natured bantering, first with Veronica, then with Teresina herself. But all the quarrels are resolved when Veronica agrees to her daughter's match with the fisherman. Fra Ambrosio blesses the young couple, and a group of young men and their sweethearts dance a buoyant *ballabile*.

When Teresina, guitar in hand, departs with Genarro for a moonlight boat ride on the bay, the rest remain behind to be amused by the street singer Pascarillo and a puppeteer. Meanwhile, the bay has slowly become enshrouded by a menacing storm. Amid thunder and lightning, the crowd rushes about, seeking protection from the threatening rains. When the storm

subsides, Gennaro is carried unconscious onto the wharf. Believing Teresina drowned and influenced by Giacomo's and Peppo's slanders, Veronica curses her daughter's lover, but Fra Ambrosio tells him not to despair. He places a medal of the Blessed Virgin around Gennaro's neck for protection and sends him back to sea to search for the lost Teresina.

The spectacular Blue Grotto is the setting for Act II. Teresina is carried into the grotto by two naiads, subjects of the sea god Golfo, who is so enchanted by the girl that he transforms her into a naiad. Gennaro's search soon brings him to the grotto. When he finds Teresina's guitar, he knows that she must be near, but when they finally meet, Teresina, in her altered state, fails to recognize him. Desperate, the fisherman prays to the Virgin to restore Teresina's memory. Golfo has to succumb to the greater power of Heaven: Teresina assumes her mortal form, and the lovers are sent back to Naples with gifts from Golfo.

As Act III opens, the people of Naples have made a pilgrimage to the shrine of Monte Virgine, for they fear that Gennaro's safe return is the work of the devil. When Teresina miraculously appears with her mother, everyone is amazed to see her. Gennaro now enters and Teresina explains that it was he who has rescued her, but the unbelieving friends still feel that evil witches were the cause of her return. To quell their fears, Fra Ambrosio is called for, and when he blesses Gennaro and tells the gathering that it was the power of the Blessed Virgin that saved Teresina, everyone is finally reassured. The act ends with a festive *divertissement* in which Bournonville's innovative choreography shines in all its complex yet crystalline clarity. A *pas de six*, solos, *pas de deux* (sometimes including the *pas de deux* from *The Flower Festival at Genzano*), trios, and an exhilarating tarantella bring the ballet to its rousingly happy finale.

Niels Kehlet and Solveig Ostergaard in Napoli. *Royal Danish Ballet*
Overleaf: Linda Hindberg and Ib Andersen in Napoli. *Royal Danish Ballet*

THE FLOWER FESTIVAL AT GENZANO PAS DE DEUX

1858 ◆ Music by E. Helsted and H.S. Paulli ◆ Choreography by August Bournonville

Napoli (1842) was not the only ballet by August Bournonville to be inspired by the romance of the Mediterranean. So great was the Danish master's love for the charming people and sunny clime of Italy that sixteen years after *Napoli*, still taken by the theme, he created *The Flower Festival at Genzano*. Based on a true story from *Impressions de Voyage* by Alexandre Dumas père, the tale is a simple one. It concerns a band of robbers and the romance of Rosa and her lover, the brigand, Paolo. The action is set against the famous *Infiorata*, a flower festival held in the Central Italian town of Genzano di Roma on the eighth day after the feast of Corpus Christi. While the full one-act ballet is still performed in Denmark, it is the *pas de deux*, considered one of Bournonville's most perfect compositions, that has captured the hearts of audiences throughout the world and is danced in the repertoires of many major ballet companies.

Ballerinas and *danseurs* love this *pas de deux*, but not for bravura tricks, since it does not possess them. Rather, it is the work's gentle sentimentality and exhilarating sense of theatricality that account for its endurance. With wistful grace, the couple first dance together, then in solos, before they reunite for a playfully exuberant conclusion. The technical control required to execute its skimming *batterie* and swift changes in direction proves a challenge for the dancers and a delight for the viewer.

If *The Flower Festival at Genzano pas de deux* were the only work to have survived from the bounteous riches of the Bournonville oeuvre, the ballet world would still have absolute and sublime proof of the Danish choreographer's genius.

Above: Rudolf Nureyev and Merle Park in the Flower Festival at Genzano Pas de Deux.
The Royal Ballet

DON QUIXOTE

1869 ◆ *Music by Ludwig Minkus* ◆ *Choreography by Marius Petipa*

Miguel de Cervantes's *Don Quixote*, the seventeenth-century mock epic of the misadventures of a deluded knight in search of his ideal, inspired choreographers to create ballets as early as 1740. In the twentieth century, the balletic treatment most familiar to audiences comes from the 1869 Bolshoi production created by Marius Petipa. Though not as faithful to Cervantes's philosophical intent as certain later versions—notably that of George Balanchine for the New York City Ballet in 1965—Petipa's succeeds as a grand comic *ballet d'action* which, with numerous revisions by subsequent choreographers, manages still to entertain and delight. For many years, Petipa's *Don Quixote* was known only as the original source of the *grand pas de deux* (a standard showcase piece for bravura dancers), but in recent decades there has been revived interest in the full-length work.

Departing from the Romantic tradition and its obsession with the world of the imagination, Petipa instead chose to portray the very real, earthy people of Spain. His earlier travels to that country had made him an authority on Spanish dancing, and inspired by Minkus's bright, pseudoethnic melodies, Petipa created a ballet that amounted to a series of variations on Spanish themes. When the work was restaged by Alexander Gorsky for the Bolshoi Ballet in 1900, he went beyond Petipa's conception by creating a dramatic *mise-en-scène* that dispensed with balletic formality and followed lines of theatrical realism. Gorsky's production forms the basis for the later version by Rudolf Nureyev and, most recently, for Mikhail Baryshnikov's highly successful staging for American Ballet Theatre.

No balletic version of *Don Quixote* has ever been considered a masterpiece, for it is difficult to capture the philosophic depth and dramatic intensity of the novel. Perhaps this is an impossible task in dance, for even the production originated by Balanchine, which is scrupulously faithful to Cervantes and is admirably spectacular and moving, somehow misses the mark. But when *Don Quixote* is presented in the context of Kitri's wedding, it offers a seamless sequence of brilliant dances in the classical and *demi-caractère* mode, a number of marvelous principal character roles, and a thrilling showcase for the ballerina as Kitri. If the Baryshnikov production (which is the one described here) is any test, audiences will throng to performances of *Don Quixote, or Kitri's Wedding* for years to come.

THE BALLET

A musical prologue introduces the major characters, who are drawn from an episode in Book Two of the novel. In highly stylized poses suggesting the action that will follow, they appear before a front curtain depicting a magnificently decorative Spanish fan. The curtain then rises on a sunny square in Spain, alive with a crowd of spirited townspeople. Kitri, the beautiful and willful daughter of an innkeeper, is in love with Basil, a poor young barber. Lorenzo, her father, intends her to be married to the wealthy fop, Gamache. Although Kitri has not the slightest intention of obeying her father, she flirts with Gamache to tease Basil. The townspeople take turns dancing: two flower girls who are Kitri's friends execute a complex set of variations highlighted by fast jumps and turns in canon; the fiery street dancer, Mercedes, performs a sinuous flamenco-inspired variation; and the dashing toreador, Espada, and his entourage burst into a thrilling series of stabbing steps, accented by strong jumps, leg beats, and pirouettes. Then Don Quixote, a scrawny old knight, and his faithful companion, the rotund Sancho Panza, enter the square. The ridiculous-looking pair are affectionately mocked—but welcomed nevertheless—by the townspeople. Weary of her father's demands and Gamache's attentions, Kitri resolves to run away with Basil. Comic confusion ensues as the lovers rush off, with her father and suitor close behind.

In Act II, Kitri and Basil have taken refuge in a gypsy camp. That night, Don Quixote and Sancho arrive at the camp, and the pathetic Don mistakes Kitri for his beloved ideal, Dulcinea. In a grandiose gesture of chivalry, he attacks a windmill in Kitri's defense, but is knocked down by one of its arms. While injured, the Don has a vision of exquisite wood nymphs dancing in the moonlight. In their midst appear Kitri and Mercedes in idealized form, as well as his beloved Dulcinea, beckoned into the dream by the darting spirit of love, Amour. The next morning, Gamache and Lorenzo arrive at the camp, in pursuit of the wayward Kitri. Sancho Panza foolishly shows them the direction in which the lovers have fled, while the Don ineffectually tries to divert them.

The scene next shifts to a local tavern. Basil and Kitri have joined the revelry, but their cavorting is interrupted by Gamache and Lorenzo. Basil, expressing the hopelessness of his

Cynthia Gregory in Mikhail Baryshnikov's staging of Don Quixote. *American Ballet Theatre*

love for Kitri, feigns a comically melodramatic suicide. Kitri is desolate until Basil furtively reveals his trick. Then, playing along, Kitri sadly entreats her father to listen to Don Quixote's demand that he allow the marriage of the unhappy lovers so that they can be united in spite of death. At the very moment the marriage is performed, Basil springs back to life. Despite initial consternation, Gamache and Lorenzo accept the turn of events, and everyone prepares to celebrate.

As Act III opens, the joyous wedding festivities are already in progress. In a gesture worthy of the Don himself, Lorenzo demands retribution for having been deceived and challenges the hapless Don to a duel. Although Lorenzo defeats the knight, he manages only to incur the scorn of the townspeople and pity for his victim. The celebration continues, culminating in the *grand pas de deux*, a glittering showstopper displaying the virtuosity of the principals, dazzling feats of partnering, such as one-arm lifts, and in the coda Basil's rapid turns *à la seconde* with alternating *ports de bras*.

Suzanne Farrell as Dulcinea and George Balanchine as the Don in Balanchine's production of
Don Quixote. *New York City Ballet*

COPPÉLIA

1870 ◆ *Music by Léo Delibes* ◆ *Choreography by Arthur Saint-Léon*

If the librettists for *Coppélia, or The Girl with Enamel Eyes* had chosen to extract anything more than fragments from E. T. A. Hoffmann's *Der Sandmann* for their story, the ballet might easily have been more tragic than *Giselle*. But they took only the name of the sinister alchemist, Dr. Coppélius, his mechanical life-size doll, and a young man who is torn between his love for the doll and for his betrothed. The librettists, Saint-Léon and Charles Nuitter, set their tale, not in the philosophically oriented bourgeois society of the original story, but against an innocent, bucolic background. By making the heroine, Swanilda, and the hero, Franz, clever and rambunctious peasants, uninvolved in the intellectual maelstrom of German Romanticism, and Coppélius a comically self-deluded alchemist *manqué*, they created a masterpiece of comedy in ballet. The somber Gothic undertones remain, nevertheless; depending on the production, *Coppélia*, particularly in the characterization of Dr. Coppélius, skirts the dark edges of tragedy. And yet the libretto will not allow tragedy to prevail, for its insouciant message seems to say: "Philosophical ignorance is bliss."

Coppélia was created at the very end of the age of the Romantic ballet. The number of great Romantic ballerinas was dwindling, and the male dancer had all but disappeared from the stage. (Indeed, the role of Franz was originally performed by a woman *en travesti*.) The first Swanilda, the sixteen-year-old Giuseppina Bozzacchi, groomed to be the heir of Carlotta Grisi and the hope of French ballet, died within months of the ballet's premiere, during the Prussian siege of Paris. Still, *Coppélia* was a brilliant climax for French ballet —a perfectly constructed work and a magnificent vehicle for the ballerina, who must have a seamless and effortless technique as well as great personal charm to match the silvery éclat of the choreography. What is more, Delibes's prodigious score was an inspiration for Tchaikovsky and helped launch the glorious era of the Russian classical ballet.

THE BALLET

A rich overture unfolding like the dawn breaking over a pastoral landscape is interrupted by an exhilarating mazurka, which subsides as the curtain rises on a quiet village square in Galicia. Seated alone in front of a two-story house at one side of the square is Dr. Coppélius, a curious figure in rumpled clothes. He looks up with tenderness at the balcony, where a young girl sits reading a book, and enters the house just as the door of another opens, revealing Swanilda. She dances to a lilting waltz expressing her love for Franz and also her anger at Coppélia, the girl on the balcony, who is stealing his attentions.

Swanilda hides and watches as Franz, a cheery swain, decides which young girl he will pursue that day. To Swanilda's chagrin, he chooses Coppélia. Coppélia suddenly looks up from her book, stands jerkily, and blows him a kiss. Franz's flirtation is interrupted by Swanilda, who pretends to be chasing a butterfly. When Franz catches the butterfly and pins it to his vest, the horrified Swanilda quarrels with him. She leaves as the square fills with dancing villagers. The burgomaster announces that, in honor of the new town bell, all couples who marry tomorrow will receive generous dowries.

Supported by Franz, Swanilda then dances to a sweetly sad melody. As a final test of Franz's love, Swanilda resorts to the local custom of shaking a stalk of wheat near her ear. When she hears nothing —the sign that her lover is untrue —she runs off in tears. Franz unsuccessfully attempts a reconciliation, as his friends dance merrily. (One of their dances is a czardas, the first appearance of this Hungarian dance on the stages of Western Europe.)

As evening approaches, the villagers depart and Dr. Coppélius emerges for his evening constitutional. He carefully locks the door and wraps the key in his handkerchief, but he is soon playfully set upon by Franz and his cohorts. Shooing them away, Coppélius mops his brow with his handkerchief and then wanders off, unaware that his key has fallen to the ground. Swanilda and her friends come out of her house, bent on confronting her rival, Coppélia. Stumbling upon the key, they all creep into Coppélius's house. Dr. Coppélius returns and sees his door ajar; he scurries in just as Franz places a ladder against the house and cautiously climbs to the balcony. At this crucial moment, the Act I curtain falls.

A stealthy, whispering theme introduces Act II. Tiptoeing into Dr. Coppélius's workshop, Swanilda and her friends are frightened by ominous shadows. Scattered about the room stand strange life-size figures, among them an astronomer, a Moor, a jester, and a Chinese man —the dolls Dr. Coppélius builds in his workshop. The girls also find Coppélia sitting behind a curtain in an alcove.

A little scared of the mysterious girl, they introduce themselves politely, but Coppélia fails to respond. Boldly, Swanilda draws nearer and tugs at the girl's dress. After repeated efforts at rousing Coppélia, Swanilda finally realizes that Coppélia, too, is a doll. Staggering about the room in uncontrolled delight, the girls unwittingly bump into the Chinese man, who springs to life and performs a sprightly dance before collapsing into a heap. The girls then wind up all the figures and join them in an ebullient dance. Suddenly Coppélius bursts into the room; in the midst of the confusion, all the girls escape except Swanilda, who conceals herself behind the curtain of Coppélia's alcove.

The exhausted Dr. Coppélius slumps into a chair, only to be disturbed by a sound at the window. As Franz enters and begins to search for Coppélia, he is grabbed by the toymaker. Franz tells Dr. Coppélius that he is in love with his daughter and wants to marry her. An idea strikes the alchemist, and he invites Franz to join him in a drink. Coppélius plies his guest with liquor until Franz falls into a stupor.

Dr. Coppélius now rises in triumph. He seeks out a large book and consults it for a moment. A bittersweet melody reflects Coppélius's feelings as he approaches the alcove that holds his beloved Coppélia. He pushes her chair into the room and then stands over the unconscious Franz. Motioning as if he were drawing forth the young man's life force, he returns to Coppélia and showers it upon her. Repeating the gestures, he brings animation to Coppélia's feet, eyes, and torso. For a moment, as Coppélius bends over his book, the doll breaks from her rigid stance, revealing that Swanilda has disguised herself as Coppélia. With a final trip to Franz, Coppélius brings total animation to the doll.

In an amusing, mechanical dance, Swanilda /Coppélia performs for her "creator," taking every opportunity to taunt him. Coppélius realizes something is still missing: Coppélia has not yet become human. Drawing forth the young man's most vital possession —his soul—Coppélius bestows it on Coppélia and she blossoms into human form. Coppélius's ecstasy is fleeting, for his image of perfection quickly turns into a willful young girl, who repeatedly attempts to rouse Franz. Trying to divert her, Coppélius gives her a mantilla and a rose and asks her to perform for him. Grudgingly she launches into a brilliant Spanish dance. Before she has time to catch her breath, Coppélius bids her

dance a Scottish reel, which she performs with dazzling speed. Swanilda, weary of the game, then demands that Coppélius wake Franz.

Coppélius forces the unruly girl into the alcove. At that

moment, Franz begins to stir and Coppélius starts shoving him toward the window. Swanilda sneaks from the alcove and begins pushing over dolls, stomping on the magic book, and wreaking havoc throughout the workshop. With Coppélius in frantic pursuit, Swanilda runs to the alcove and pushes out the chair holding the body of the broken Coppélia, disrobed and wigless. Franz, finally aware of his foolish infatuation for a doll, recon-

Coppélia, as staged by George Balanchine and Alexandra Danilova for the New York City Ballet: opposite, Patricia McBride; above, Shaun O'Brien, Helgi Tomasson, and Patricia McBride

ciles with his sweetheart. They rush from the house, leaving a pitiful Dr. Coppélius slumped beside the image of his shattered dreams.

Act III presents the festival celebrating the new village bell and the wedding of the village sweethearts. After the burgomaster dispenses the dowries, Coppélius demands retribution for the destruction of Coppélia. He loses some of his tragic dignity when he accepts a dowry as compensation for his loss. The celebration commences with a *grand divertissement*, including dances for Dawn, Prayer, Work, and Jesters. The *grand pas de deux* for Swanilda and Franz alternates tender duets, revealing their new, mature recognition of their love, with solos demonstrating that their irrepressible natures have not been totally tamed. They are joined by all the celebrants in a joyous coda.

Patricia McBride in Act III of Coppélia. *New York City Ballet*

LA BAYADÈRE

1877 ◆ *Music by Ludwig Minkus* ◆ *Choreography by Marius Petipa*

The creators of Romantic ballet shared with other artists of the time a fascination with the spiritualism and exoticism of the Orient. The most notable early dance treatment of such themes was Filippo Taglioni's opera-ballet *Le Dieu et la Bayadère*, based on a poem by Goethe. Premiered at the Paris Opéra in 1830, the ballet provided the choreographer's daughter, Marie Taglioni, with one of her greatest roles as the Bayadère.

More than forty years later, Marius Petipa conceived the idea for his own Oriental ballet. Together with Sergei Khudekov, the Russian publisher and ballet enthusiast, Petipa wrote a libretto for a work entitled *Bayaderka* or *La Bayadère*. At its premiere in February, 1877, at the Maryinsky Theater, St. Petersburg, *La Bayadère* was a triumph: it catered to the Russian taste for spectacular theatrics, exotic settings, and convoluted, melodramatic plot lines, yet also contained classical choreography of breathtaking purity. Its Kingdom of the Shades scene exhibits, in the words of Mikhail Baryshnikov, "[Petipa's] finely wrought architectural sense . . . in full bloom. Poetically . . . unmatched in the classical repertory."

Although the Kingdom of the Shades scene has been staged in the West in productions by the Kirov Ballet, London's Royal Ballet, and American Ballet Theatre, versions of the complete work have been seen only in Russia until recently. On May 21, 1980, Natalia Makarova, the most brilliant exponent of the Kirov School in the West, mounted for American Ballet Theatre her full-length version of *La Bayadère* (the one subsequently described here). The resulting production was admirable but controversial. There was certainly no question of the enduring value of the Kingdom of the Shades scene (restaged for Ballet Theatre by Makarova in 1974) but, according to some critics, the "turgid" narrative that preceded and followed it seemed an unwelcome return to the worst excesses of Russian classical ballet. Still, it must be said that the lavish decor was a feast for the eye and the melodramatic pantomime and story provided a certain undeniable historical insight. As a result, the Kingdom of the Shades scene was enriched with a dramatic intensity that it lacks when performed by itself.

THE BALLET

The curtain rises on a clearing in a lush Indian forest where a temple stands with a sacred fire burning before it. Warriors enter paying homage to Solor, their noble leader, who has just killed a huge tiger. The moment Solor is alone, he summons a fakir, asking him to find his beloved, Nikiya, a temple dancer. The fakir agrees and Solor departs. Then the curtains at the temple entrance part as a group of Brahmin priests descend the steps; they are followed by the Bayadères, who perform a ritual dance around the fire.

Nikiya, the most beautiful of the Bayadères, is summoned by the High Priest and, with veiled face, comes down from the temple. When he removes her veil, the priest is stunned by her beauty. Nikiya dances an exquisite solo at the conclusion of which the High Priest declares his love. The Bayadère spurns his

Above: Natalia Makarova and Anthony Dowell in Makarova's staging of La Bayadère. *American Ballet Theatre*
Overleaf: Merle Park and Michael Coleman in Rudolf Nureyev's version of the Kingdom of the Shades scene from La Bayadère. *The Royal Ballet*

attentions by telling him that her religious vocation forbids such attachments, and the priest, ashamed, suppresses his passion. But later, when he sees Nikiya talking to the fakir, he grows suspicious.

After the High Priest and the others have returned to the temple, Nikiya dances a solo expressing her yearning for Solor. Solor appears and the Bayadère rushes to his arms; they dance a passionate *pas de deux*, concluding with their pledge of eternal love over the sacred fire. Unbeknownst to the lovers, the High Priest has observed them from behind the temple curtains and vows to take vengeance on Solor.

Scene 2 takes place in a sumptuous hall in the palace of the Rajah Dugmanta who, with his warriors, is drinking a toast to a large portrait of Solor. To reward Solor's heroism, the rajah intends to give him the hand of his daughter, Gamzatti. The girl enters the hall and, seeing the portrait of Solor, she is instantly smitten. Solor himself now sweeps into the hall to greet the rajah. When the rajah announces his decision to give Solor his daughter to wed, the warrior is reluctant at first. But then Gamzatti's veil is removed and Solor, infatuated by her beauty, immediately agrees.

After the couple are entertained by the court dancers, the arrival of the High Priest is announced. Incensed at seeing Solor with Gamzatti, he asks that the hall be cleared and then in private informs the rajah of Solor's duplicity. When the rajah, rather than punish Solor, decides to destroy Nikiya, the High Priest is appalled. He pursues the rajah as he stalks out of the hall.

Gamzatti, having overheard their conversation, has sent for Nikiya. When Nikiya arrives, Gamzatti informs the girl of her betrothal to Solor and reminds her that she can offer him all her riches, while Nikiya is a mere temple dancer. The Bayadère replies that she and Solor have vowed eternal love over the sacred fire. An argument ensues and only the quick action of Gamzatti's nurse prevents the distraught Nikiya from stabbing the princess. Humiliated by her act of passion, Nikiya runs from the hall as Gamzatti vows to destroy her.

Scene 3 opens on a lush garden of the palace, where a *grand divertissement* is danced in celebration of the betrothal of Solor and Gamzatti. The couple perform a brilliant *pas de deux* and variations, accompanied by joyful court dancers. Then, the High Priest enters with Nikiya, and the Bayadère, against her

will, is made to dance. Her movements convey her melancholy, but when the nurse presents her with a basket of flowers, the Bayadère thinks it is a gift from Solor and dances happily with it. Lifting the basket to her face, Nikiya suddenly clutches her throat—she has been bitten by a poisonous snake hidden among the flowers by Gamzatti and the rajah. The guilty parties, feigning innocence, quickly lead the stunned Solor away. Nikiya refuses the antidote offered by the High Priest and succumbs to her mortal wound.

Act II is set in Solor's private quarters, where the fakir urges the repentant hero to smoke opium. Falling under the influence of the drug, Solor is visited by a recurring vision of Nikiya.

Scene 2 is the enactment of Solor's dream state as he sinks more deeply under the opium spell. A legion of beautiful but emotionless representations of Nikiya descend from the darkness of the Kingdom of the Shades in countless repetitions of sustained *arabesques penchées*. There follows a passage of transcendent choreographic construction in which the Shades, with hypnotic pacing, perform a veritable lexicon of classical positions and steps. As the Shades disappear, Solor bursts into the alien domain in search of Nikiya. Her vision appears and they dance a *pas de deux* of tender forgiveness in which Nikiya nevertheless remains aloof. As Solor and Nikiya continue their dance, the Shades complement their movements in symphonic harmony. The dream passes, and moments later the rajah and Gamzatti arrive to summon Solor to his wedding.

Act III takes place within the temple. The Bronze Idol is seated at the foot of the altar, which is dominated by an immense statue of Buddha. The idol rushes down the altar steps and performs a solo of soaring virtuosity. Carrying a small candle in each hand, the Bayadères then begin their exotic dance of the ritual lights, as a prelude to the wedding ceremony.

As Solor and Gamzatti begin their wedding dance, the shade of Nikiya appears to Solor and also dances with him. The princess is frightened by Solor's attention to something no one else can see. But with desperate determination, Gamzatti and the reluctant Solor obey the High Priest's summons to the altar. As the two make their vows, the gods become angry and smoke fills the temple. There is a rumble of thunder before the temple crumbles into ruin, destroying all within it. The aftermath of the devastation is an apotheosis in which the shade of Nikiya leads Solor into a blindingly brilliant vision of paradise.

THE SLEEPING BEAUTY

1890 ◆ *Music by Peter Ilyich Tchaikovsky* ◆ *Choreography by Marius Petipa*

In the history of the performing arts there are those rare moments when an artistic collaboration produces a creation that could only have come about through the magical intervention of fate. For nineteenth-century Russian ballet, that creation was undeniably *The Sleeping Beauty*, a paragon of fantasy in classical ballet which was nevertheless the result of a very practical, though inspired, process.

A ballet based on Charles Perrault's fairy tale was suggested to the choreographer and composer by the enlightened director of the Imperial Theaters, Ivan Alexandrovich Vsevolozhsky. They, in turn, collaborated literally measure by measure to produce a work that would not only capture the universal imagination but also constitute the definitive treatise on classical ballet technique. What is more, this masterpiece was built upon a tale almost entirely devoid of dramatic content, amounting to little more than a contest between the abstract forces of good and evil in which mortals are mere pawns. That such a fragile premise came to be imbued with theatrical grandeur and

Antoinette Sibley in the Rose Adagio from The Sleeping Beauty. *The Royal Ballet*

45

artistic depth attests to the mystery of genius.

Oddly enough, *The Sleeping Beauty* was not a staggering success at its premiere. Before long, however, it was recognized as the masterpiece of choreography, spectacle, and musical delight that it is. It has enjoyed countless productions, and innumerable ballerinas have aspired to dance Princess Aurora. Every major ballet choreographer has acknowledged a debt of gratitude to Petipa for his infinite inventiveness and to Tchaikovsky for his transcendent score.

The description which follows is based on London's Royal Ballet version (1946), supervised by Nicholas Sergeyev, with additional choreography by Frederick Ashton and Ninette de Valois.

THE BALLET

An ominous blast of brasses and percussion is quelled by a lyrically poignant melody; these are the leitmotifs that will set the tone for the ballet and carry along its narrative. The Prologue ("The Christening") is set in the palace of King Florestan XXIV, on the christening day of his daughter, Princess Aurora. Cattalabutte, the royal master of ceremonies, sees to the final preparations as the guests gaze upon the infant in her elaborate cradle. A wistful theme by harp and strings announces the arrival of the six fairy godmothers: the Fairy of the Crystal Fountain, the Fairy of the Enchanted Garden, the Fairy of the Woodland Glades, the Fairy of the Songbirds, the Fairy of the Golden Vine, and, most splendid and commanding of all, the Lilac Fairy. After a thrilling *divertissement*, in theme and variation form, five of the fairies grant their gifts to the child.

Suddenly, a discordant rumbling and stormy flashes of light disrupt the court. The king snatches the guest list from Cattalabutte and realizes to his horror that an unpardonable omission has been made. A moment later, a black coach drawn by monstrous rats careens into the hall. Seated majestically in the coach is Carabosse, the wicked fairy. She dismounts and demands to know why she has been slighted. With contempt, she berates the quivering master of ceremonies and then begins a malevolent dance with her hideous retinue. She tells the gathering that although the royal child will grow up endowed with all the lovely qualities bestowed upon her, on her sixteenth birthday she will prick her finger and die.

But Carabosse's moment of triumph is cut short, for she has not noticed that the Lilac Fairy has yet to give her gift. The good fairy cannot cancel out the curse, but she can mitigate it. Everything foretold will come to pass, even the dreaded day when Aurora will prick her finger. The princess, however, will not die. Instead, she and the entire kingdom will fall into a long, deep sleep until the day when a handsome prince braves the enchanted castle and awakens her with a kiss.

Act I ("The Spell") takes place at Princess Aurora's sixteenth birthday celebration. Among the guests in the palace garden are three crones furtively attending their spindles. Since the king has outlawed spinning, Cattalabutte has the three apprehended. Next, to the melodious strains of Tchaikovsky's most famous waltz, peasant boys and girls execute a swaying, intricately patterned dance. Four foreign princes who have come to ask for Aurora's hand in marriage present themselves to the king and queen.

At that moment Princess Aurora, the image of scintillating youth and beauty, darts into the garden. In one of the most technically demanding dances in all of classical ballet, Aurora performs the Rose Adagio with her suitors. She approaches each prince demurely and accepts a rose from him. As the music and the technical difficulties mount, her shyness fades into regal authority. One by one, her noble cavaliers support her as she turns, lifts her leg effortlessly *à la seconde*, and finally balances on *pointe* in *attitude*.

After a brief *pas de deux* with one of her suitors, Aurora performs a solo which flows into the memorable sequence in which each cavalier offers Aurora another rose. With each consecutive presentation, the same dance sequence is repeated, with the number of pirouettes corresponding to the number of roses in her hand. A marked decrease in the music's tempo then finds Aurora and her suitors restating the *promenades* of the earlier section, which are concluded in ever more ecstatically sustained balances in *attitude*. A musical crescendo brings the variation to its denouement, and Aurora's last spellbound balance is broken as she modestly comes off *pointe*.

Then, as Aurora joins her young friends in more dancing, the hooded figure of a stooped old woman appears. The mysterious figure holds out a spindle to the princess, who innocently accepts the gift and at once pricks her finger. Helplessly showing

Natalia Makarova and Mikhail Baryshnikov in The Sleeping Beauty. *American Ballet Theatre*

her wound to the stunned observers, Aurora launches into a frenzied dance before falling, lifeless, to the ground. Carabosse triumphantly throws off her cape; despite all precautions, her prediction has come to pass.

But hope returns as the Lilac Fairy appears and calmly tells everyone that their long sleep is about to begin. One by one, the people fall asleep where they stand, and layers of thick foliage slowly enshroud the scene. The Lilac Fairy rises into the air, sprinkling glittering fairy dust over the enchanted kingdom.

Act II, Scene 1 ("The Vision") opens on an aristocratic hunting party a century later. Tiring of their games and dances, Prince Florimund, the leader of the hunt, asks the party to leave him. He dances a melancholy solo and then the Lilac Fairy appears. She tells him of Princess Aurora still sleeping in the enchanted kingdom and conjures up her vision. When the enraptured prince pleads with the Lilac Fairy to bring the vision to life, she produces a dancing vision of Aurora. At first eluding Florimund, the vision finally dances a dreamlike, rapturous *pas de deux* with him before vanishing into the forest. Then the prince and the Lilac Fairy embark on a journey to the sleeping kingdom.

In Scene 2 ("The Awakening"), the Lilac Fairy leads Florimund into the palace, now completely enveloped by gnarled vines, layers of dust, and a century of cobwebs. Picking their way past sleeping courtiers and ladies-in-waiting, they enter Aurora's bedchamber. With tender caution Florimund bestows a gentle kiss upon her forehead. To an ecstatic crash of cymbals,

the princess awakens; the two gaze at each other in instant mutual adoration. Immediately, the shroud of foliage, cobwebs, and dust dissolves, and the room is filled with brilliant light. As the court awakens, the king and queen enter and bless the couple. Good has triumphed over evil, and the entire court rejoices.

A brilliant orchestral fanfare opens Act III ("The Wedding"). Guests from all parts of the kingdom and from fairy-tale land have been asked to join the celebration of Princess Aurora and Prince Florimund's wedding. Cattalabutte greets some of those invited: Puss-in-Boots and the White Cat, Little Red Riding Hood and the Wolf, Cinderella and Prince Fortuné, the Golden, Silver, Sapphire, and Diamond Fairies, Hop-o'-My-Thumb, the Bluebird, and the Enchanted Princess. All perform in the *grand divertissement*, offering brilliant variations, with the soaring Bluebird *pas de deux* containing probably the most virtuosic, breathtaking moments in the entire work.

In dazzling attire, Princess Aurora and Prince Florimund then perform the glorious *grand pas de deux*. After an adagio that expresses both profound adoration and elegant nobility, Prince Florimund executes a sweeping solo of heroic passion and Aurora a variation of pristine clarity. Their romping coda is almost mischievous in its mounting delight.

A stately sarabande by the courtiers and a joyous mazurka are capped by the arrival of the Lilac Fairy. In a stirring apotheosis, the entire assemblage forms a spectacular tableau of obeisance to the strains of a majestic theme.

THE NUTCRACKER

1892 ◆ *Music by Peter Ilyich Tchaikovsky* ◆ *Choreography by Lev Ivanov*

The Nutcracker has surely become the most beloved ballet of our time. Its score alone is the most readily recognizable by virtue of countless concert performances and recordings. In the last twenty-five years, the proliferation of productions of the ballet has resulted in a worldwide audience of millions. Despite certain detractors, who dismiss the work as an empty, childish panto-mime with little actual dancing, *Nutcracker* invariably plays to sold-out houses and, in many cases, has even been the financial salvation of a ballet company. The best explanation for this phenomenon is that it speaks to the child in everyone—the child who believes in fantasy and the spirit of Christmas.

The success of *Nutcracker*, though now taken for granted, was long in coming. Only reluctantly did Tchaikovsky accept the commission to compose a ballet score based on an adaptation by Alexandre Dumas fils of the E. T. A. Hoffmann tale *The Nutcracker and the Mouse King*. That he completed the score, which he considered "infinitely worse than *Sleeping Beauty*,"

owed more to mere resignation to the task than to inspiration. The only part of the experience he enjoyed was his discovery in Paris of the celesta, a new instrument which he jealously guarded and used in his score.

As with *Sleeping Beauty*, the music was written to the strict requirements of Marius Petipa, who was to be the choreog-rapher, but Petipa fell ill and the final production was choreo-graphed by his assistant, Lev Ivanov. At its St. Petersburg premiere at the Maryinsky Theater in December, 1892, the ballet was an outright failure. To the first-night audience the children in Act I were deemed irritating; the sets were thought to be cumbersome and too "German middle class"; the balle-rina, Antonietta Dell'Era, was considered ugly and the score banal.

More than sixty years and a few productions of modest success would go by before George Balanchine, with the insight as well as the genius of a master choreographer, mounted a production

Above: Act I of George Balanchine's production of The Nutcracker. *New York City Ballet*
Overleaf: Mikhail Baryshnikov in his production of The Nutcracker. *American Ballet Theatre*

for the New York City Ballet that gave *Nutcracker* new life. Undeniably, it was the extraordinary success of this 1954 production that paved the way for all the subsequent stagings that have made *Nutcracker* not only a staple of the ballet repertoire but a holiday tradition on a par with Charles Dickens's *A Christmas Carol*.

Because of the universality of its story and particularly its elements of childhood fantasy, *The Nutcracker* has been interpreted by many choreographers in their own personal ways. Some, like Rudolf Nureyev and Mikhail Baryshnikov, have mounted productions emphasizing the story's rite-of-passage aspects, making it a more Gothic and less whimsical tale. (Indeed, in such productions, the roles of the children are performed by grown dancers.) Although moderately successful, such versions have somehow failed to capture the essential innocence of Tchaikovsky's score, which consistently calls for the sunlight of the imagination rather than the shadows of psychology. Thus, Balanchine's *Nutcracker* and similar productions—which do capture that quality—continue to attract generations of viewers who return year after year to be refreshed and exhilarated. The Balanchine version (in which the heroine is named Marie rather than the more traditional Clara) is the one described here.

THE BALLET

To the strains of a gossamer overture, the curtain rises on a drop curtain depicting snow-covered rooftops in an early nineteenth-century German town; an angel holding a star-topped wand hovers above the town in benediction. The curtain then rises on a hallway in the home of Dr. Stahlbaum and his wife. Asleep in a chair beside a double door is Marie, the Stahlbaums' young daughter; at her feet is her little brother, Fritz. The children awake and peer through the keyhole into the room beyond, where their parents are trimming the Christmas tree.

Lights come up behind the double doors and illuminate the comfortable living room while guests and children begin to arrive for a party. As the music swells with anticipation, the center scrim rises and the children rush excitedly to the tree, which suddenly bursts brilliantly into light. The festivities begin, first with an energetic children's march and then a sprightly *galop* for everyone. The children are playing with their gifts when a mysterious cloaked figure enters.

The stranger throws back his cape and shows himself to be Herr Drosselmeyer, Marie's godfather. With him is a young boy of princely poise whom he introduces as his nephew. Marie comes forward shyly to greet the boy but, disturbed by the stirrings of adolescent attraction, runs back to her mother. After Drosselmeyer performs some magic tricks, he shows the children his gifts for them: three mechanical dolls, a Harlequin, Columbine, and toy soldier. Then, he furtively removes a curious object from his coat, a wooden figure dressed in military uniform, its face framed by white hair and beard. He presents this toy, a nutcracker, to Marie.

Before Marie has had time to enjoy the present, Fritz jealously grabs it and hurls it to the floor, breaking it. Moved by Marie's sadness, Drosselmeyer ties his handkerchief around the Nutcracker's broken jaw and gently returns it to her. Then, to a sweet lullaby, Marie cradles her beloved Nutcracker, while the other girls also rock their dolls. Later, Drosselmeyer's nephew gallantly gives Marie a little white bed for her Nutcracker, and she accepts it with timid adoration. As the party draws to a close, parents and children alike perform a dance of charm and grandeur, the adults mirrored in their stately measures by the children. The last guests to leave are Drosselmeyer and his nephew. As the lights dim, Marie and the boy part with eyes only for each other.

It is now the middle of the night. Marie, in her nightdress, steals into the living room. Picking up her injured Nutcracker, she climbs onto a sofa and falls asleep with him in her arms. Drosselmeyer mysteriously emerges from the shadows of the darkened room and removes the broken Nutcracker from Marie's arms. Waving a screwdriver like a magic wand, he fixes the broken jaw, and then returns the mended toy to the sleeping child.

Now, the room seems to assume a life of its own. Awakening, Marie is startled to see Drosselmeyer summoning three enormous mice from the corners of the room. The mice scurry around Marie, then disappear as the terrified girl springs back on the sofa. Suddenly, the walls of the room fly away, and its slightest details become gigantic. Marie kneels over her Nutcracker protectively, but as the Christmas tree begins to grow to a monumental height, the tiny bed carrying him is swept away. However, the bed soon reappears full-size, bearing upon it an equally life-size Nutcracker.

Marie is still dumbstruck when a trumpet call summons the Nutcracker to lead a regiment of toy soldiers in battle against a horde of mice. The seven-headed Mouse King is about to vanquish the Nutcracker, but Marie impulsively throws her slipper at the Mouse King. The villain is run through by the Nutcracker before he can reach Marie. The victor severs a crown from one of the Mouse King's heads, and then bids the bed carrying Marie to follow him. The Christmas tree rises magically into the air, the enormous French windows part, and with the bed floating after him, the Nutcracker walks regally into a wondrous winter landscape.

As new snow begins to fall, the Nutcracker's homely guise vanishes, revealing a handsome young prince. He places the crown on Marie's head before, hand in hand, they start on a

magic journey into the forest. The gently falling snow takes on the shape of snowflake maidens. Their windswept waltz intensifies as more and more snow maidens swirl, turn, and leap in their glittering white attire. The Nutcracker Prince leads Marie through this dazzling scene as the curtain falls.

After an enchanting orchestral prelude, the Act II curtain rises on the Kingdom of Sweets, ablaze with light and decorated with every kind of candy and sweetmeat. Like tiny tree ornaments, a corps of white-gowned angels with golden crowns glide by in charming patterns. Then, her movements mirrored by the tinkling celesta, the ruler of this kingdom, the Sugar Plum Fairy, performs her famous dance. Her subjects then rush on the scene in waves of color and decoration to welcome the Nutcracker Prince and Marie, who arrive in a walnut-shell boat with a candy sail.

In a brilliant mimed passage, the prince tells the gathering of the battle with the Mouse King and how Marie saved him. Delighted, the Sugar Plum Fairy commands her subjects to perform a *grand divertissement* in honor of their visitors. First, Spanish dancers, representing Hot Chocolate, perform a swaying, rhapsodic fandango. Coffee, an exotic harem girl, then undulates to a sensuous melody. A bouncing mandarin represents Tea, followed by the Candy Canes, whose leader bounds furiously through his hoop. Marzipan Shepherdesses prance to the charming flutter of their candy pipes.

Next, the outrageous preening Mother Ginger waddles in and pulls a drawstring attached to her voluminous skirts. Out pop a bevy of *commedia dell'arte* clowns, called Polichinelles, who perform one of the most superbly realized children's dances ever conceived. In the beloved Waltz of the Flowers, the corps of flowers weaves, winds, and bends in swirling patterns while the dazzling Dew Drop darts among them with stunning virtuosity.

As if the enchantment will never end, a grand, deeply poignant theme heralds the arrival of the Sugar Plum Fairy and her cavalier. Together, they dance the *grand pas de deux*, emblematic of the love that stirs in Marie for the Nutcracker Prince. After a buoyant waltz brings together all the inhabitants of the Kingdom of Sweets for a brief reprise of each dance, the music melts to a lullaby while Marie and the prince are led to a magic sleigh. The Sugar Plum Fairy and her subjects wave a fond farewell as the sleigh bears the two happy children slowly into the sky.

Adam Lüders and Kyra Nichols in Balanchine's production of The Nutcracker. *New York City Ballet*

SWAN LAKE

1895 ◆ *Music by Peter Ilyich Tchaikovsky* ◆ *Choreography by Marius Petipa and Lev Ivanov*

Swan Lake is without question the greatest, most fully realized Romantic ballet, surpassing even *Giselle* in dramatic scope and depth. The work's enduring popularity is largely due to Tchaikovsky's superlative score, which captures like no other the full range of human emotions—from hope to despair, from terror to tenderness, from melancholy to ecstasy. This crowning achievement of high Romanticism was actually Tchaikovsky's first ballet score, directly inspired by Léo Delibes's symphonic approach to the genre, as exemplified by *Coppélia* and *Sylvia*.

Although it is the 1895 production of *Swan Lake* that has come down to us, Tchaikovsky completed the score, commissioned by V. P. Begichev, in 1876. The first production, in 1877, was choreographed by Julius Reisinger for Moscow's Bolshoi Theater. Although it was considered "too Wagnerian" and in part undanceable, the ballet was performed for the next few years to full houses. A new version by Olaf Hansen in 1880 played havoc with the original, and the ballet went into eclipse for the ensuing decade and a half.

Credit for the revival which led to the ultimate success of *Swan Lake* is a matter of controversy. It may have been I. A. Vsevolozhsky, director of the Imperial Theaters, St. Petersburg, Marius Petipa, or his assistant, Lev Ivanov, who conceived of the idea to remount a portion of the work for an 1894 memorial program for Tchaikovsky, who had died the previous year. What is certain is that Ivanov choreographed Act II for that occasion, and its triumph led to the staging of the complete work the following year, with choreographic credit shared by Petipa (Acts I and III) and Ivanov (Acts II and IV). The complete *Swan Lake* premiered at the Maryinsky Theater, St. Petersburg, on January 27, 1895, and, for the first time, the grandeur of Tchaikovsky's score was equaled by the genius of the choreographic structure and by the virtuosity of the ballerina, Pierina Legnani, in the dual role of Odette/Odile.

The moving story and rich score of *Swan Lake* have inspired countless choreographers to stage their own versions, although most adhere strictly to Ivanov's flawless structure for Acts II and IV, the so-called "White Acts." (The version subsequently described is that by David Blair for American Ballet Theatre, premiered May 9, 1967.) In response to the abundance of brilliant music in Tchaikovsky's original score, choreographers have often rearranged the sequence of dances, sometimes from one act to another, or deleted passages altogether. For example, in certain productions, there is a melancholy solo for Prince Siegfried near the end of Act I, danced to music from Act II. Sometimes there are dramatic departures from the traditional libretto, as in Erik Bruhn's production for the National Ballet of Canada, which finds Von Rothbart transformed into a female role—the wicked Black Queen. Even ideological precepts enter into stagings of this classic. Productions in Soviet Russia and in Cuba, to counter "negativity," have a happy ending in which Siegfried and Odette live on after defeating Von Rothbart.

But whatever changes there are in musical order or dramatic interpretation, the essence of this love story so magnificently rendered in dance remains the same, and at its center stands Odette/Odile. The Swan Queen and her opposite represent the ultimate embodiment of Romantic extremes: one is the vision of purity, nobility, and poetry, the other sinister, corrupt, and destructive. Even more than *Giselle*, *Swan Lake* offers the greatest challenge to the ballerina as dancer and actress.

THE BALLET

A theme of piercing melancholy draws us into the ballet's atmosphere of poetic pathos. The curtain rises on a palace garden where the twenty-first birthday of Prince Siegfried is being celebrated. The prince, with Wolfgang, his old tutor, and Benno, his best friend, joins in the festivities until a fanfare announces the Queen Mother. Clearly disapproving of Siegfried's frivolous behavior, the queen reminds him that tomorrow at the ball in honor of his coming-of-age he will be expected to choose a bride. After presenting Siegfried with his birthday gift, a crossbow, the queen takes her leave. To restore everyone's spirits, Benno dances with two peasant girls in a virtuosic *pas de trois*.

At the approach of evening, the aristocratic couples dance a stately polonaise before they slowly glide from the garden, leaving the prince to his thoughts. For the first time, the famous *Swan Lake* leitmotif is heard. Benno rushes into the garden and points out a flock of swans flying overhead. He suggests a hunt to the prince, and they rush off happily.

Before the curtain rises on Act II, a shimmering reprise of the leitmotif builds to an ominous orchestral statement. The cur-

Ludmilla Semenyaka and Alexander Godunov in Swan Lake. *The Bolshoi Ballet*

swan looks pitifully into her captor's eyes, and he releases her. She then tells him her sad story. She is Odette, the Queen of the Swans. The nearby lake has been created from the tears of her mother, who has wept ever since Odette fell under the spell of the evil magician, Von Rothbart, who transformed her into a swan. Like the other swan maidens on the lake, she returns to human form only at night and will remain a swan until a man pledges eternal love for her. Siegfried immediately offers his vow of love, but Odette questions his sincerity.

Just then, Von Rothbart appears, a dark, helmeted figure who swirls a billowing cape like enormous black wings. Siegfried's first impulse is to fell him with his crossbow, but Odette stops him, for she knows that Siegfried's arrow is powerless against the magician. Von Rothbart disappears and moments later Odette herself departs, with Siegfried after her.

A drift of swans now glide in single stately file onto the shore of the lake. Their preening and poising are interrupted when Benno and the other hunters arrive. As the frightened swans flurry throughout the glade, Siegfried rushes in and commands the hunters to leave. The swan maidens move into a grand waltz of stunning patterns, ending in a picturesque tableau. Odette and Siegfried then begin a *pas de deux* of exquisite tenderness during which she gradually surrenders herself to his love.

Transported by their revery, the lovers move to another part of the forest as four cygnets perform a charming *pas de quatre* with crisp precision, followed by a glorious waltz by two swan maidens. In the next solo for Odette, her melancholy finally gives way to joy and hope. The swans' bounding coda is crystallized by Odette's dazzling *entrechats quatres* and *passés relevés* and by Siegfried's return for an ecstatic conclusion.

With the approaching dawn, the swan maidens must resume their enchanted form. Under Von Rothbart's commanding gaze the swans fly from the glade. To lessen the pain of their parting, Odette tenderly lowers´ Siegfried's head and averts his gaze, then surrenders herself to Von Rothbart's call.

A drum roll building to a jubilant crescendo for full orchestra brings up the curtain on Act III. Among the guests at the ball in honor of Siegfried's birthday are the six foreign princesses who are his prospective brides. A fanfare announces the arrival of the Queen Mother and the prince, who are then entertained with national dances performed by the retinues of the princesses.

tain rises on the moonlit shore of a lake bordered by rocky crags and dominated by a menacing castle in the distance. The hunting party enters, and the prince abruptly tells his friends that he wishes to be alone. Siegfried aims his crossbow at a swan in flight, then, inexplicably, thinks better of it and hides.

Suddenly, a beautiful white creature, half woman, half swan, darts into the glade. Transfixed by this vision, Siegfried takes hold of her before she can escape. Struggling to free herself, the

Maya Plisetskaya as Odile and Mikhail Gabovich as the Evil Genius (Von Rothbart). The Bolshoi Ballet

After each of the princesses dances a floating waltz with the distracted Prince Siegfried, the Queen Mother presses her son for a decision. Just then, the trumpets announce the arrival of unexpected guests.

To a thunderous burst from the orchestra, two strangers rush into the hall — a sinister cloaked knight and a dazzling creature in glittering black attire. Although the woman is introduced as Odile, the knight's daughter, Siegfried sees only his beloved Odette, who has come to him in disguise. Overjoyed, Siegfried indicates that without reservation *she* is his choice.

Siegfried and Odile then begin the famous Black Swan *pas de deux*, which is at once a technical display, a narrative vehicle, and a fascinating study of contrasting passion and deception. At first, they dance with unbridled happiness to a fervent waltz, but soon a disquieting element intrudes as Odile, strangely cynical, returns to the knight as if receiving instructions. Odette's vision appears to warn Siegfried, but the prince does not see her. Odile then deceitfully assumes Odette's gentle quivering and preening motions.

After an exuberant solo by the prince and a delicate, yet coquettish one by Odile, the thrilling coda begins. Siegfried soars around the hall in *grands jetés* and Odile executes thirty-two exhilarating whipping *fouettés*. Although they seem as one in their passion, the prince's turns *à la seconde* convey only rapt ecstasy, while there is a note of triumph in Odile's magically drawn flight backward in arabesque.

Filled with happiness, Siegfried begs his mother and the knight to bestow their blessings on his union with Odile. Although the queen willingly consents, the knight demands that Siegfried also pledge his eternal love for Odile. The prince unhesitatingly makes his vow and, to a crash of thunder and a tragic reprise of the leitmotif, the deception is revealed — Von Rothbart is the knight and Odile his accomplice. With mocking glee the two swirl around Siegfried, then vanish in a cloud of smoke. The prince finally sees Odette's vision and runs frantically from the palace.

Act IV opens at the lakeside, where the swan maidens have resigned themselves to the triumph of their master. Odette, devastated by Siegfried's apparent treachery, tells her sisters that she must die, but they beseech her to wait for the prince. Just then, Siegfried bursts in, seeking Odette. After first resisting

Siegfried's supplications, she finally relents in a dance of heartrending reconciliation. Together, Odette and Siegfried plan to challenge their fate. Von Rothbart appears to separate the lovers forever, but their love is mightier than his powers. In a last gesture of exquisite defiance, Odette rushes to a crag and throws herself into the stormy lake. The faithful Siegfried then follows her.

Siegfried's sacrifice has broken the spell. Von Rothbart's castle crumbles and the defeated sorcerer, overwhelmed by the powerful flutterings of the defiant swans, falls to the ground and dies. In a glowing finale, Odette and Siegfried are seen gliding into eternity as the swan maidens, with each rise and fall of their wings, are released from their enchantment.

Darci Kistler and Sean Lavery in George Balanchine's staging of Swan Lake. *New York City Ballet*

LE CORSAIRE PAS DE DEUX

1899 ◆ *Music by Riccardo Drigo* ◆ *Choreography by Marius Petipa*

The original, full-length *Le Corsaire* (1837; music by Robert Bochsa, choreography by François Decombe Albert) was one of those nineteenth-century ballets inspired by a great work of Romantic literature which, despite its music, choreography, fantastic story line, and stage effects, failed to endure in the popular repertoire. The ballet's complex libretto, based on Lord Byron's poem *The Corsair* (1814), centers on the dashing pirate, Conrad, and his love for the Greek slave girl, Medora. Their heroic adventures, including a spectacular shipwreck, end in the happy union of the lovers.

The only full-length *Corsaire* regularly performed today is the 1899 Drigo and Petipa version presented in the Soviet Union. However, the same version contains a *pas de deux* for Conrad's slave and Medora which has served as a showcase for the dazzling virtuosity of nearly every major ballerina and *premier danseur* in the world. The solos in this *pas de deux* often vary in choreography, since dancers will select the versions that best display their particular virtuosic gifts. Sometimes music from other Drigo ballets or from other composers is interpolated into the dance.

THE BALLET

Rushing energetically onto the stage, the slave, with naked chest, glittering, billowing pants, and a plume affixed to his headband, falls to his knees as Medora enters. To the strains of an impassioned theme, they dance a brilliant duet that reveals the slave's impetuosity and Medora's charm and modesty. His youthful ardor is nowhere more tellingly expressed than in the overhead lift in fourth arabesque which brings the *pas de deux* to a thrilling climax. His solo is a bold, sweeping display that culminates in a circle of flying leaps. Medora's more refined solo exhibits the ballerina's exquisite technical control, highlighted by slow pirouettes and thrilling extensions of the leg *à la seconde*.

The coda, a crescendo of almost circuslike music, brings the dancers together as they ignite the stage with a thrilling sequence of traveling turns for the ballerina and spins in place for the *danseur*. At the peak of their bravura display, the slave flings himself ecstatically at Medora's feet in a final gesture of heroic adoration.

Opposite: Alexander Godunov in Le Corsaire Pas de Deux. *American Ballet Theatre*
Above: Claude de Vulpian and Patrick Dupond. Paris Opera Ballet

LES SYLPHIDES

1909 ◆ Music by Frédéric Chopin ◆ Choreography by Michel Fokine

It is a matter of record that, of the many ground-breaking works Serge Diaghilev nurtured by his visionary genius, *Les Sylphides* was his favorite. In its original version, called *Chopiniana* (1907), the ballet was first performed by members of the Maryinsky Imperial Ballet, with which Fokine was still connected at the time.

To many, this sublime distillation of the Romantic *ballet blanc* is simply a poetic dance revery and nothing more, but it was in many ways more innovative than most of the other original works produced by the Ballets Russes in its twenty-year history. For one thing, except for Alexander Gorsky's *Valse Fantaisie* to music by Mikhail Glinka, there existed no plotless, abstract works in the repertoires of the Russian ballet companies. Fur-

thermore, it was unheard of to choreograph to the revered works of masters, such as Frédéric Chopin, who did not compose for the ballet. At the time, only the revolutionary American dancer Isadora Duncan had dared to dance to Chopin, and it was her visit to St. Petersburg in 1905 that left an indelible impression on Fokine. The young choreographer was deeply struck by Isadora's fluid use of her arms and torso and her loving contact with the floor, and he melded this new freedom of articulation to the basic, almost elementary, technical ballet vocabulary he employed in his choreography. When first performed by Diaghilev's Ballets Russes in 1909, *Les Sylphides* had the additional "audacity" to use Chopin's piano music in full-blown orchestral arrangements (by Alexander Glazunov).

The choreographic structure of *Les Sylphides* is deceptively simple: it is almost impossible to convey by words the subtle shifts in cat's-cradle formations and bowerlike groupings assumed by the corps de ballet as the principals perform their solos and the *pas de deux*. Even more elusive is the aura with which Fokine imbued the work. Every succeeding generation of dancers has attempted to preserve the luminescence of this homage to Romanticism as it was first performed by its original cast, headed by Vaslav Nijinsky, Anna Pavlova, and Tamara Karsavina. It is a tribute to the tenacity of ballet tradition that in many performances of *Les Sylphides* the audience is still transported into its world of nostalgic revery.

THE BALLET

An unabashedly Romantic prelude sets the mood and atmosphere before the curtain rises on a secluded moonlit glade. In a tableau reminiscent of nineteenth-century lithographs, sixteen sylphs in long gossamer tutus surround the *danseur*, who in costume and manner is the embodiment of the Romantic poet. The vision comes to life as the sylphs begin to dance to a nocturne. The poet and two muses remain poised in their silhouette until, in response to the ever-mounting music, they too join the dance.

Then, to a bounding, joyful waltz, a sylph dances alone, accompanied by the movements of her sisters, echoing hers in subdued patterns. In the radiant mazurka that follows, another sylph flies through the glade, disappearing, returning, and repeatedly rising on *pointe*, sustaining the last rise before she bounds into *tours jetés*. In her final statement she turns

Ann Jenner and Barry McGrath in Les Sylphides. *The Royal Ballet*

repeatedly in *relevés*, then, rushing to a back corner, poises for a moment on *pointe*, and vanishes.

The next solo is assigned to the poet, who dances a slow, sustained mazurka. His buoyant leaps and whispered leg beats express his sensitive yearnings, akin to those of James in *La Sylphide* and Albrecht in *Giselle*.

A reprise of the first prelude introduces a third sylph. She pauses softly, lifting one hand to her ear, as if hearing the voice of some woodland deity. In response she rises on *pointe*, *bourrées* in place, and arching slightly backward, lifts her arms in a gesture of ethereal reverence. A brief, soulful cello theme now finds this last sylph attended by the poet. In a tender embrace, the two step softly into the clearing and begin a *pas de deux* that is a revery in waltz time. The poet lifts his weightless muse,

supports her adoringly, and then follows her in delicate *cabrioles* as she flees.

The sylphs have also vanished, but only momentarily. A resounding fanfare calls them back for the concluding *grande valse brilliante*. In response to the lilting pulse of the music, the sylphs fill the glade in sweeping patterns, punctuated by fleeting solos danced by the three principal sylphs and the poet. At its most ecstatic moment, the waltz ebbs to a hush and the dancing stills. As the music throbs gently in anticipation of a poetic resolution, the corps sylphs, joined by the principals, begin to swirl and spring in buoyant *sautés*. Then, as if drawn by a magnetic force, they rush into their original tableau and, to the emphatic concluding chords of the music, the tableau unfolds in a final, dreamlike breath.

Dancers of the Royal Ballet in Les Sylphides

THE FIREBIRD

1910 ◆ Music by Igor Stravinsky ◆ Choreography by Michel Fokine

For his second season of the Ballets Russes in Paris, Serge Diaghilev wanted a new work based on authentic Russian themes. After a series of intense collaborative discussions, a libretto emerged with credit given solely to Diaghilev's principal choreographer, Michel Fokine. When two successive composers failed to produce a score, the third commission went to a young Russian composer whose music had never been heard outside Russia. *L'Oiseau de Feu* (*The Firebird*), as the ballet was to be called, was the first ballet score written by Igor Stravinsky.

Although the title role was intended as a vehicle for Anna Pavlova, the mysterious, innovative score fell uncomfortably on her ears and she declined to dance in the ballet. Curiously, the dancer who most desired to perform the role of the Firebird was the *premier danseur* of the Ballets Russes, Vaslav Nijinsky. Diaghilev thought otherwise, and the role was eventually assigned to the intelligent and luminous Tamara Karsavina. When first presented at the Paris Opéra, *The Firebird* not only stunned the Parisian audience with its aura of fantasy and ritualistic spectacle, but also brought fame to its young star who, because of her electrifying interpretation, was acclaimed the rival of Pavlova. Indeed, the success of this collaboration between Fokine and Stravinsky made another joint effort not only probable but inevitable (*Petrouchka* followed the next year).

Although *The Firebird* was one of the early triumphs of the Ballets Russes, it was perhaps an even greater success in its 1926 revival, which had a new decor by Natalia Goncharova and brilliant performances by Alexandra Danilova and Serge Lifar. With the passage of time, however, the ballet threatened to become an outmoded and static spectacle. Stravinsky's score remains an unquestionable masterpiece, but choreographers and dancers have not always matched its greatness when they have departed from the Fokine original. A few choreographers have risen to the challenge, most notably George Balanchine, with his highly successful 1949 version for the scintillating Maria Tallchief, and Maurice Béjart, whose 1970 production realized Nijinsky's concept by casting Paolo Bortoluzzi as the Firebird.

Still, the Fokine-Stravinsky creation continues to arrest the imagination of traditionalists. There is no question that its music and choreography thrust ballet from a waning Romanti-

cism into modernism. Ballet masters and ballerinas in the title role will always attempt to imbue this work with the stunning and fantastic ambience of the original. One such production (the one described below) is the 1977 staging for American Ballet Theatre choreographed by Christopher Newton from Fokine's original.

THE BALLET

A dark musical theme throbs ominously before the curtain rises on an enchanted garden, at the center of which stands a tree laden with golden apples. A brilliant shaft of light pierces the darkness as into the garden flashes the shimmering, imperious Firebird. She stays but a moment, then flies off before Ivan, a tsarevitch of early Russia, climbs cautiously over the high stone wall and leaps into the garden. An eerie whistling in the air seems to warn the prince that this is a forbidden place. From his hiding place, he sees the Firebird darting about the garden — soaring, turning, and fluttering.

Pausing at the tree, she takes one of its apples and, as she returns for another, is captured by Ivan, who has been mesmerized by the fabulous, seductive creature. Ivan holds her fast in his grasp while she soars, falls to the ground, soars and falls again until, unable to struggle any longer, she slowly sinks to the ground. To a hypnotically sinuous melody, he bends over her and lifts her gently onto *pointe*. The Firebird arches her back and strains away from him, but Ivan pulls her softly back. Arching again, she flutters tremulously, then manages to escape — but only briefly. Finally, he lifts her to his shoulder, where she yields like a sacrificial offering. Ivan, enraptured, makes clear he intends no harm, but the Firebird is still intent on her freedom. She plucks a feather from her plumage and gives it to her captor, telling him that if he releases her, she will return to help him when he is in need. He agrees, and moments later she is gone.

Ivan secures the Firebird's magical gift in his tunic. Suddenly aware of ominous sounds, he picks up his crossbow and conceals himself, watching as a group of beautiful maidens in silken white gowns glide into the garden. These princesses, who are being held captive in the garden, hold hands and form two lines as the most beautiful of all enters. Picking some golden apples from the tree, the maidens enjoy a moment of freedom as they playfully toss them to one another, but they are startled from their game

Preceding pages: Natalia Makarova and Ivan Nagy in American Ballet Theatre's production of The Firebird

64

when the tsarevitch reveals himself. The moment they see each other, Ivan and the most beautiful princess are struck by mutual love. After the group performs a tender, wistful round dance, the enraptured tsarevitch and tsarevna stand together, gazing at each other. Ivan kisses his beloved on the lips, thus sealing their betrothal.

A sudden alarum shatters their revery and the frightened princesses flee into the woods. Before joining them, the tsarevna pauses for a moment to warn Ivan that their captor, the evil and immortal Kastchei, will turn him into stone if he finds him in his garden. The confused tsarevitch, thinking only of pursuing his beloved, rushes to the imposing garden gates and flings them open. A blinding light floods the garden—Ivan has unwittingly released the fearful entourage of Kastchei. Through the open portals come Kikomoras, Belibotchkis, Oriental slaves, and other fantastic creatures who violently prevent the terrified Ivan from escaping. They scatter about the garden, then suddenly cower and prostrate themselves in a circle. To portentous music, Kastchei himself enters.

Crippled but majestic, the evil sovereign slinks about the garden surveying the scene. Seeing Ivan, he beckons the intruder with menacing motions of his skeletal fingers and clawlike nails. The tsarevitch approaches Kastchei boldly and, to everyone's horror, spits at the sinister creature. Kastchei, enraged, commands his slaves to restrain Ivan. When the tsarevna and the other princesses rush into the garden to plead for Ivan's life, Kastchei laughs menacingly and chases them away. The evil one, with three large, heaving motions, begins to turn the captive prince into stone.

Recalling the powers of his magic talisman, Ivan takes the Firebird's feather from his tunic. At that instant the dazzling creature reappears. She leads Kastchei's horde into a large circle and, as if hypnotized, they begin to perform at her command a pulsating infernal dance. In despair, the princesses are drawn into the frenzy. At one side of the garden, the Firebird stands regally overseeing her spell, while Kastchei, at the opposite side, stands powerless. To wave upon wave of surging music, the spellbound creatures continue to hop, spin, and leap frantically. The Firebird repulses Kastchei's attempt to halt the manic dance and orders the creatures to continue, until they finally sink to the ground in exhaustion.

Gliding among the fallen servants, with the impotent Kastchei cowering before her, the Firebird dances to a haunting lullaby until her would-be captors fall into an enchanted slumber. The Firebird then instructs Ivan to go to a hollow tree and remove what he finds there. Everyone awakens as he returns carrying an ornate chest, and a feeling of terror seizes the crowd when they see the contents of the chest—a huge egg containing the soul of the evil master. Lifting the egg above his head, Ivan taunts the supposedly immortal Kastchei and finally tosses it in the air. The egg crashes to the ground and shatters, and Kastchei falls dead. The scene dissolves into darkness.

A dazzling light comes up to reveal the tsarevitch's palace in all its splendor on the coronation and marriage day of Ivan and his tsarevna. All the princesses have found princes, and the couples join with stately figures representing the church and the ancient Russian empire to form a majestic tableau. The tsarevitch lifts his scepter and the music surges into a hymn to the glory of Russia as the curtain falls.

Michael Denard as the Firebird in Maurice Béjart's production for Ballet du XXe Siècle

LE SPECTRE DE LA ROSE

1911 ◆ *Music by Carl Maria von Weber* ◆ *Choreography by Michel Fokine*

The idea for a ballet entitled *Le Spectre de la Rose* was proposed to Diaghilev by the designer Leon Bakst at the suggestion of the French poet Jean-Louis Vaudoyer. A passage in Fokine's 1910 ballet *Le Carnaval*, in which Chiarina gives a rose to the Romantic poet Eusebius, reminded Vaudoyer of Théophile Gautier's poem "Le Spectre de la Rose." He subsequently wrote an article devoted to Diaghilev's 1910 Paris season headed by two lines from the poem: "Je suis le spectre d'une rose /Que tu portais hier au bal." Vaudoyer also suggested the music for the piece, *Invitation to the Dance* by Carl Maria von Weber.

Diaghilev responded immediately to the idea and, intending to make the 1911 Paris season of the Ballets Russes a showcase for his protégé Vaslav Nijinsky, made it clear to Fokine that the title role in *Spectre* would be a vehicle for the dancer. Fokine conceived the ballet as a *pas de deux* for an innocent young girl and the elusive spirit of a rose she has carried with her to her first ball. Bakst's designs set the ballet in the Biedermeier period of 1830 Vienna. Fokine composed the work in a very short time, with Nijinsky as the spectre and the poetic Tamara Karsavina as the young girl. At its Monte Carlo premiere, *Spectre* proved a success that surpassed even Diaghilev's expectations.

To most minds, it is Nijinsky's reputedly sensational final leap that made *Spectre* a legendary ballet. Although with the passage of time the reports of the leap grow more and more extravagant, the fact is that Nijinsky exited over a windowsill that was less than a foot from the ground. In reality, the secret of the ballet lies not in the spectacular pyrotechnics of the *danseur* but in the romantic aura produced by both the spectre and the young girl (who has with few exceptions become sadly relegated to a role of secondary importance). At its premiere, the work was as successful for Karsavina as for Nijinsky, as one can sense today when seeing a ballerina like Carla Fracci perform the young girl's role. *Spectre* should not be dismissed as an old-fashioned vignette, but viewed as a highly demanding challenge for a *danseur* and ballerina to portray, through their artistry, a vision of romance and poetry that is eternal.

THE BALLET

To a wistful introduction by the cello, the curtain rises on a large boudoir. Its furnishings are elegant but spare, and the all-pervasive whiteness of its decor reflects the innocence of the room's occupant. At one side is an alcove containing a bed, while at the other stands a harp. Near the center of the room is a large armchair; behind it, against the wall, is a table on which rests a vase of flowers. In the back corner of the room, a large French window stands open to the summer evening's air.

Dressed in a simple white party gown, cape, and bonnet, a young girl enters the room. Still filled with the memory of her first ball, she dreamily removes her cape and tries to recapture those happy moments, symbolized by the deep-red rose she carries with her. But exhaustion overtakes her and she falls asleep in the armchair; the rose then drops gently from her hand.

Suddenly, the quiet intimacy of the music bursts into a triumphant, sweeping waltz and a beautiful, androgynous creature clad in soft rose petals flies through the window into the room. It is the spirit of the rose the girl has treasured so tenderly. As if grateful for being so cherished, the spectre dances about the room in light, fleeting leaps and pauses behind the sleeping girl's chair, framing his face with soft, sinuously curved arms. He touches the girl and she awakens—perhaps.

Together, they dance a seemingly improvised *pas de deux* of dreamlike fluidity. Their ecstatic waltzing is the image of pure romantic rapture, made the more poetic by the sweet improbability of a young girl dancing with the half-human embodiment of a rose. Before this revery can become fixed in reality, it is over. The girl returns to her chair and to her dreaming; the spectre, in a last gesture of ecstasy, leaps through the window and vanishes into the night air. At that moment, the girl opens her eyes and, gazing about her, realizes that the apparition was a dream. She glances at the floor and sees her rose. Picking it up lovingly, she presses it poignantly to her lips.

Mikhail Baryshnikov and Marianna Tcherkassky in Le Spectre de la Rose. *American Ballet Theatre*

PETROUCHKA

1911 ◆ Music by Igor Stravinsky ◆ Choreography by Michel Fokine

Hoping to equal the extraordinary success of *Firebird* the year before, Diaghilev once more enlisted Igor Stravinsky to collaborate with Fokine. *Petrouchka*, their new ballet for the 1911 Ballets Russes season, was yet another masterpiece, in which music, decor, libretto, and staging combined to produce a vibrant picture of Russian life. In point of fact, Stravinsky had only to expand on one of his previous compositions, entitled *Petrouchka's Cry*, which was inspired by the St. Petersburg Shrovetide Fair puppet shows (Petrouchka was the Punch, or Pierrot, character). Diaghilev also hoped to lure his recalcitrant designer, Alexandre Benois, back to the fold by offering him the opportunity to immortalize on stage the beloved puppet Petrouchka, a vivid memory of Benois's youth. The artist accepted enthusiastically and with Stravinsky wrote a libretto that not only altered the boorish nature of Petrouchka into a sympathetic one, but added a heartless Columbine character, the Ballerina; a bullying Moor; and their puppeteer, portrayed as a conjuring Charlatan.

The production of *Petrouchka* was fraught with difficulties. The score proved to be even more avant-garde than *Firebird*, and the young conductor, Pierre Monteux, had to separate the rebellious musicians into groups so that they could master it. Fokine was faced with the difficult problem of staging crowd scenes as well as choreographing, and the large numbers of dancers he had to manipulate found it nearly impossible to work around the enormous sets. Diaghilev himself added to the complications by asking Leon Bakst, Benois's rival, to touch up the painting of the Charlatan in Scene 2, at which point Benois walked out on the production and the Ballets Russes. Despite all this, *Petrouchka* was an unqualified success for the company and particularly for its stars, Nijinsky, Karsavina, Alexandre Orlov, and Enrico Cecchetti.

Although every ballet masterpiece demands of its performers a supremely subtle artistic intelligence, in *Petrouchka* this responsibility lies not only with the four principal characters, but with every last member of the large supporting cast. Since there is little dancing per se in the ballet; the dancers must rely on their pantomimic talents to give life and credence to the story. Everything the dancers need to find, however, is in Stravinsky's monumental score—the drama, the mystery, the folkloric color, the plaintiveness, the irony and sardonic wit.

The role of Petrouchka is at once the easiest and the most challenging. With the supreme interpretation of Nijinsky as a precedent, the dancer in the title role must convey a pathetic anguish strong enough to break our hearts without falling into bathos. It is easy enough for a gifted dancer to plunge into the histrionics of the role; what is difficult is to retain the dignity and essential purity of the human spirit that the role demands. Almost every major *danseur* since Nijinsky has accepted the challenge of Petrouchka and some—notably, Léonide Massine, Adolph Bolm, Yurek Shabelevsky, Rudolf Nureyev, Erik Bruhn, and Gary Chryst—have succeeded with memorable interpretations.

The following description of *Petrouchka* is based on the 1970 Joffrey Ballet version, supervised by Léonide Massine.

THE BALLET

The curtain rises on a crowded square near the Winter Palace in St. Petersburg. It is late winter in the year 1830 and the Shrovetide Fair is just beginning. In the distance are steeples, festive banners, and a merry-go-round; a puppet theater stands at the back of the square. As they mingle among the *balagani*, or fairground booths, the bustling holiday crowds are bundled up against the cold. At the sound of a tinkling triangle, they all stop to observe two female street dancers who take turns executing virtuoso backbends, kicks, and splits.

Next, the Charlatan suddenly appears from behind the drawn curtains of the puppet theater. In his long robe and sorcerer's hat, the wizened, bearded figure steps forward ominously. He pulls a flute from his robe and plays a tune which mesmerizes the crowd. The curtains magically part, revealing three life-size puppets dangling limply from armrests: a Moor in Oriental garb; a pretty, heavily rouged Ballerina with an artificial air; and Petrouchka, a sad, white-faced puppet wearing a shabby jester's costume.

Still suspended, the puppets begin to move with frantic speed to a wildly rhythmic burst of music. Propelled by the sheer energy of their manic dance, they dash from their places into the square, where they enact a charade in which the Moor and Petrouchka vie for the Ballerina's love. The Charlatan hands Petrouchka a stuffed cloth club, and with bathetic chivalry the

Opposite: Vaslav Nijinsky as Petrouchka in the original Ballets Russes production, 1911
Overleaf: Christian Holder, Denise Jackson, and Rudolf Nureyev in the Joffrey Ballet's Petrouchka, as
seen on WNET/13's "Dance in America"

jealous Petrouchka beats the Moor, despite the coyly arch protestations of the Ballerina. The Charlatan calls a halt to the fray, but commands them to continue their frenzied dancing until they collapse in a heap. The stage goes dark.

Scene 2 takes place in Petrouchka's room, a black and desolate void, with only distorted stars and a sinister portrait of the Charlatan for decoration. Two tiny doors open, and the conjurer's foot heaves Petrouchka into the room. In his isolation, Petrouchka pantomimes his pitiful tale: although a puppet subject to the tyranny of his master, he feels the stirring of a human heart and soul. The Ballerina enters, but stays only a moment, for Petrouchka's awkward gesticulations frighten her off. Alone again, the desperate puppet beats against the walls and, after a last pleading gesture to his master's portrait, thrusts himself through the wall.

Unlike Petrouchka's room, the Moor's quarters (the setting for Scene 3) are bright and sumptuously ornate. In simple-minded bliss, the Moor lies on a couch, tossing a coconut from his feet to his hands. He then attempts to break it open and, finding that neither his teeth nor his scimitar can pierce its shell, he concludes that it must contain the soul of a deity. With reverence he carries the coconut to the center of the room, places it on the floor, and pays it homage. He is interrupted by an unexpected visit from the Ballerina. Playing a trumpet, she prances on *pointe* around the room in a doll-like march. The Moor is drawn to this new diversion and attempts to explore it the same way as he had the coconut—including taking a quick bite into the stiff, unresponsive doll. A ludicrous dance of seduction follows and is interrupted as Petrouchka bursts in and

attempts to save his love from the Moor's clutches. After a comic chase, the Moor ejects the intruder. Returning to his oblivious paramour, he sits her on his lap and mechanically grabs her breast.

In Scene 4, evening is approaching and the cold air, grown bitter, only intensifies the surging of the fairground crowds. To a gloriously swirling melody, a cavalcade of Russian life passes by: a dancing bear; a merchant and two lusty gypsies; stately nursemaids and amorous coachmen. When snow begins to fall, the men clap each other on the back, stomp their feet rhythmically, and launch into a characteristic Russian folk dance. Suddenly, there is a disturbance behind the curtains of the puppet theater. Petrouchka runs into the square, followed by the Moor, scimitar in hand, and the feebly protesting Ballerina.

Before anyone can help him, Petrouchka is struck down by the Moor. The horrified observers stand by helplessly as the quivering puppet dies in agony. The Ballerina and Moor disappear as the Charlatan enters and clears the crowd surrounding Petrouchka. Lifting the inert body, he shows everyone that their concern is over a mere doll—a limp, sawdust puppet. Satisfied with this explanation, the crowd disperses. The Charlatan and the lifeless puppet are alone in the square when the evening's silence is pierced by a shrill blare: it is Petrouchka's cry. Spinning around, the Charlatan sees the ghost of Petrouchka on the roof of the puppet theater shaking his fists at him in mocking triumph. Petrouchka's soul is immortal; the pathetic puppet has prevailed. The Charlatan runs away in terror. Slumping, Petrouchka collapses over the edge of the roof, his arms dangling, as the snow falls silently.

L'APRÈS-MIDI D'UN FAUNE

1912 ◆ Music by Claude Debussy ◆ Choreography by Vaslav Nijinsky

With each new season of the Ballets Russes in Paris, Diaghilev intended to astound the Parisian audience and with each season he succeeded in doing exactly that. Since 1909, the troupe's fabulous success had been founded on Michel Fokine's choreography — in ballets such as *Cléopâtre*, *Schéhérazade*, *Prince Igor*, *Firebird*, *Carnaval*, *Le Spectre de la Rose*, and *Petrouchka* — and, with the exception of *Prince Igor* (a triumph for Adolph Bolm), on Vaslav Nijinsky's supreme portrayals in Fokine's ballets. But by 1912 Diaghilev had started to lose interest in Fokine's work and decided to promote his protégé Nijinsky not only as *premier danseur* but as choreographer.

For quite some time, the impresario had planned to have Nijinsky choreograph a new ballet based on Claude Debussy's 1894 impressionistic masterpiece, *Prélude à l'Après-Midi d'un Faune*. At first, these plans were kept secret, but word soon got out, and so began the first of a series of controversies involving

the ballet. Fokine, always a highly volatile and jealous artist, became incensed upon hearing that Nijinsky was to be his rival, especially because he himself was engaged in creating a similar work, a ballet with a Grecian theme set to Maurice Ravel's *Daphnis et Chloé*. Fokine announced that he would resign at the termination of his contract in June, 1912.

Unmoved by Fokine's ultimatum, Diaghilev proceeded with the plans for *L'Après-Midi*. Tension mounted in the company as Nijinsky required well over one hundred rehearsals for his eight-minute ballet. These demands took dancers and rehearsal time away from the already irate Fokine, whose full-scale work would, ironically, feature Nijinsky in the role of Daphnis.

The premiere of *L'Après-Midi* on May 29, 1912, provoked greater controversy than any previous work staged by the Ballets Russes. Nijinsky dispensed entirely with all suggestion of classical ballet technique — or even of the pseudo-Grecian plasticity represented by Isadora Duncan and Fokine — by creating a ballet performed entirely in two-dimensional profile. The Paris public saw slow, static, highly stylized movements which barely followed in the meter of the music. The dancers were barefoot and seemed to have lost all semblance of balletic form. Even more startling was Nijinsky as the faun. Heretofore drawing ovations for his extraordinary elevation and brilliant technical feats, he now exhibited none of his virtuosity, but rather remained resolutely earthbound, moving in short, rigid steps or posing sinuously upon a rock.

This choreography proved a strange contrast to Bakst's sumptuous, impressionistic decor, which itself stunned Paris by its daring and sensual perspective and coloration. What is more, this celebration of adolescent sexual awakening was climaxed by an act of autoeroticism that had never been suggested, let alone performed, on stage. A *cause célèbre*, which delighted Diaghilev, ensued in the press; artists such as Auguste Rodin championed the ballet, while *Le Figaro* condemned it as an obscene spectacle.

Since that time, the original *L'Après-Midi d'un Faune* has been rarely performed, because its controversial nature has superseded its choreographic novelty. Aside from Nijinsky himself, few interpreters of the work have succeeded in portraying the faun to memorable effect, although David Lichine, André Eglevsky, Igor Youskevitch, Rudolf Nureyev, and George de la

Above: Vaslav Nijinsky and Bronislava Nijinska in the Ballets Russes production of L'Après-Midi d'un Faune, *1912*
Overleaf: Rudolf Nureyev as the Faun in the Joffrey Ballet production of L'Après-Midi, *as seen on WNET/13's "Dance in America"*

73

Peña have captured some of the work's artistic integrity, which survives despite its scandalous reputation.

THE BALLET

The curtain rises on a lush antique glade. Reclining in profile on a knoll is a faun, half human, half beast. Raising a flattened, outstretched palm to his mouth, he echoes, as if on a panpipe, the sinuous tune of the single flute that introduces Debussy's composition. Languorously, he lifts a bunch of grapes and, dropping his head back sensuously, plunges them into his open mouth. Suddenly he senses a disturbance in the glade and alertly flicks his head to see seven nymphs in pleated tunics and long braids approaching the stream at the foot of the knoll. Walking barefooted on *demi-pointe* with angular, flattened arms, they have come to bathe. Intrigued, the faun descends from his resting place to investigate the beauty of these mortals.

Before the nymphs are aware of his presence, one of them removes her scarf. Then, noticing the curious intruder, they are startled and flee. They return with linked arms to retrieve the scarf, but are once again frightened off. Only the leading nymph remains. She lingers, almost as fascinated with the faun as he is with her. But as she links arms with him in a brief moment of melting ecstasy, she too becomes alarmed and flees.

Alone, the bewildered faun looks after the vision; then, noticing the abandoned scarf, he instinctively bends to pick it up. He carries it with great tenderness to his lair on the knoll. The scarf represents his first contact with mortal passion, and he stretches it carefully on the ground. Raising himself at full length, he slowly sinks upon it, sliding both his hands caressingly under his body and pressing his horned forehead against the earth. With a last pelvic thrust, he lifts his head with open mouth in a cry of silent ecstasy.

Vaslav Nijinsky in L'Apres-Midi d'un Faune

LE SACRE DU PRINTEMPS

1913 ◆ *Music by Igor Stravinsky* ◆ *Choreography by Vaslav Nijinsky*

Le Sacre du Printemps (The Rite of Spring) was conceived in a dream. Even before the premiere of *The Firebird* in 1910, Igor Stravinsky was visited in his sleep by a vision of pagan Russia in which a sacrificial maiden danced herself to death.

Enthralled with the idea of this dream, Stravinsky confided it to Nicholas Roerich, the great mystic painter, who was also an authority on Russian folklore from the time of its primitive origins. Very soon, the two informed Diaghilev of their intention to create a ballet, called *The Sacrifice*, based on Stravinsky's theme. Diaghilev, with his artistic vision and daring, gave his enthusiastic support, but more than two years elapsed before *Le Sacre du Printemps*, as it was finally called, was presented. In the interim, Fokine, who was to have choreographed the ballet, had left the Ballets Russes and been replaced by Nijinsky.

Stravinsky's monumental, convention-shattering score was so foreign to everyone's ears, including the rather musically uneducated Nijinsky, that Diaghilev found it necessary to enlist the help of Emile Jaques-Dalcroze, the inventor of eurhythmics, a physical approach to the comprehension of music. At the Dalcroze school in Hellerau, Germany, Diaghilev and Nijinsky met Marie Rambert, an assistant teacher, whom Diaghilev engaged to assist his protégé with the choreography. Although the rehearsals were filled with struggle for Nijinsky and consternation for his dancers, no one was prepared for the scandal sparked by the premiere of *Sacre* at the Théâtre des Champs-Elysées on May 29, 1913.

In the history of dance, theater, and music, there has never been a scene of such pandemonium as the one that occurred that night. It is difficult to understand today the shocking effect the music and Nijinsky's "grotesque" choreography had on the audience. Opinion was violently divided, and, carried away by their fervor, people screamed, whistled, shouted, and assaulted one another; there were even a few challenges to duels. Attempting to pacify the audience and allow the performance to continue, Diaghilev ordered the houselights to be flickered, to little avail. While the conductor, Pierre Monteux, calmly led the orchestra, Nijinsky, standing in the wings, almost went to pieces, shouting out counts that did not even exist in the score to poor Maria Piltz, as the Chosen Maiden, and the rest of the distraught dancers.

In terms of publicity, the *scandale* was to Diaghilev "Exactly what I wanted!" *Sacre*, however, vanished from the stage after six performances, and shortly thereafter Nijinsky was also no longer with the Ballets Russes. Within a year Monteux resuscitated the score for a concert performance, which met with extraordinary acclaim, confirming the work as a monument of twentieth-century music. But Nijinsky's electrifying tableaus of ordered chaos and spastic, "turned-in" positions were lost.

In 1920, Léonide Massine, Nijinsky's successor and principal choreographer of the Ballets Russes, rechoreographed a successful version of *Sacre* that, according to Serge Grigoriev, Diaghilev's *régisseur*, "paid greater heed to the complicated rhythms of the music than to its meaning; and the result was something almost mechanical, without depth, which failed to be moving." The most memorable aspect of this production was the solo for Lydia Sokolova, as the Chosen Maiden, surely one of the longest and most strenuous dance roles ever created.

Since that time, numerous choreographers, including Massine himself (who remounted yet another version in Philadelphia in 1930, featuring Martha Graham), have attempted to create a *Sacre* that equals in strength and power the unrelenting score, which seems to flow and pulsate from a primitive source beyond man's ken. Perhaps Kenneth MacMillan's *The Rite of Spring*, choreographed for London's Royal Ballet in 1962, comes closest to capturing the primordial spirit of Nijinsky's original. Some other notably successful versions include those of Maurice Béjart (1959), who interprets the work as a mating ritual, and Glen Tetley (1974), who features a male as the sacrificial victim. None, however, convinces the viewer that what has transpired on the stage even approximates the essence of Stravinsky's original dream.

THE BALLET

Stravinsky said that the violent awakening of the Russian spring "was like the whole earth cracking," and his score, for large orchestra, is a narrative elaboration of this phenomenon. It is divided into two sections: Section I is entitled The Adoration of the Earth. Its introduction is described by Stravinsky as "...the awakening of nature, the scratching, gnawing, wiggling of birds and beasts." It is followed by Dances of the Young Girls, Harbingers of Spring, The Mock Abduction, Spring Khorovov

Overleaf: Glen Tetley's Le Sacre du Printemps, *with Frank Smith, Richard Cragun, and Charles Ward.*
American Ballet Theatre

[Round Dance], Games of the Rival Tribes, Procession of the Wise Elder, Adoration of the Earth, and Dance of the Earth. Section II is entitled The Sacrifice. Following its introduction are Mystic Circles of the Young Girls, Glorification of the Chosen Victim, Summoning of the Ancients, Ritual of the Ancients, and finally Sacrificial Dance of the Chosen Victim.

Nicholas Roerich described *Sacre* in this manner: "...my intention is that the first set should transport us to the foot of a sacred hill in a lush plain, where Slavonic tribes are gathered together to celebrate the spring rites. In this scene there is an old witch, who predicts the future; a marriage by capture; round dances. Then comes the most solemn moment. The wise elder is brought from the village to imprint his sacred kiss on the new flowering earth. During this rite, the crowd is seized with a mystic terror.... After an uprush of terrestrial joy, the second scene sets a celestial mystery before us. Young virgins dance in circles on the sacred hill amid enchanted rocks; then they choose the victim they intend to honor. In a moment she will dance her last dance before the ancients...the graybeards dedicate the victim to the god Yarilo."

Above: Paul Taylor's Le Sacre du Printemps (The Rehearsal) *with Christopher Gillis, Ruth Andrien, Elie Chaib, and Lila York*

PARADE

1917 ◆ *Music by Erik Satie* ◆ *Choreography by Léonide Massine*

On May 18, 1917, in Paris, Diaghilev's Ballets Russes swept the war-torn world toward the twenties with a ballet called *Parade*. Its origins dated back to 1914 with the young French poet Jean Cocteau, who, after his successful libretto for *Le Dieu Bleu*, was eager to create a new ballet. This work, to be named *David*, would have as its central character the star of a traveling circus (who was never seen on stage). Both Diaghilev and Stravinsky were cool to the idea, and Cocteau, undaunted, looked elsewhere for collaborative support.

The following year, Cocteau was introduced to the eccentric and innovative composer Erik Satie and also to the thirty-four-year-old Cubist painter Pablo Picasso. These meetings would herald a new and highly productive wave of creative collaborations within the Ballets Russes and, by extension, in the world of Western art and music. Still, it was not until Diaghilev himself met Picasso, in the spring of 1916, that Cocteau's project became a serious possibility. Finally, in February, 1917, Léonide Massine, the young successor to Nijinsky in Diaghilev's favor

and, since 1915, choreographer for the Ballets Russes, was assigned *Parade*, and the full artistic collaboration was set.

Although Massine and Picasso worked together with mutual admiration and ease, Cocteau presented problems by insisting on incorporating the sounds of real modern machines, such as typewriters, foghorns, gunshots, and airplanes, into Satie's score. Satie himself was unable to dissuade Cocteau, but when Diaghilev, Picasso, and Massine joined in the objections, Cocteau permitted the young conductor, Ernest Ansermet, to transcribe the sounds for musical instruments. (The typewriter was the only actual machine employed in the final score.) Still, Satie did not care for even the transcribed noises, but resigned himself to them, referring to the insistent Cocteau as "a lovable maniac."

The premiere of *Parade* presented the Ballets Russes with one more *cause célèbre*. How great a scandal there really was is open to question; what remains undeniable, however, is that Cocteau's libretto, Satie's music, Picasso's designs, and Massine's

Preceding page: Gary Chryst as the Chinese Conjurer in Parade. *The Joffrey Ballet*
Above: The Horse in Parade. *The Joffrey Ballet*

choreography combined to produce the first Cubist theater work. Additionally, in his program note "Parade and the New Idea," the French poet Guillaume Apollinaire first used the term Surrealism, thus launching a highly influential esthetic in twentieth-century art.

While the initial shock of *Parade* has waned, its delightful inventiveness remains fresh today. In watching revivals of this work (like the Joffrey Ballet version described here), viewers must suspend their notions of ballet as Romantic and exotic and open themselves to a highly sophisticated rendering of a Cubist canvas come to life.

THE BALLET

A drop curtain depicts one of Picassos's most charming circus subjects in a style that gives no suggestion of the decor of the ballet about to unfold. It shows a group of performers around a table, a horseback rider in Romantic tutu standing atop a Pegasus, and a monkey climbing a striped ladder. This front curtain rises on yet another curtain, on which is depicted a distorted traveling circus booth, so common to the streets of nineteenth-century Paris.

The solemn musical theme that has served as a prelude quickens into a hypnotic whirling, then bursts into a cacophonous rumbling as the French Manager enters. This figure is a quasi-human, eleven-foot-high amalgam of architectural planes and angles, topped by an opera hat and smoking a pipe. This strange apparition stomps across the stage to drum up enthusiasm for his "attraction."

To the clattering of a wheel of fortune, a hand emerges from the curtains of the booth; it bears a placard on which is printed the Roman numeral I. As it withdraws, a jocular Oriental melody introduces the Chinese Conjurer in a spectacular crimson and yellow mandarin robe. He hops around the stage and begins his demonstration of prestidigitation. His grotesquely made-up white face grimaces as he presses an imaginary sword into his scarlet mouth. Resuming his hopping, he returns to the booth.

Now, a new Manager enters. Equally as monumental as his predecessor, this construction is a distortion of New York skyscrapers bearing a sign reading "Parade." As he stomps around, he lifts a megaphone to his "mouth" with his enormous "arm," as

another placard with "II" appears from the booth. Out of its curtains emerges the Little American Girl, dressed in a short sailor dress, white socks, and patent-leather shoes, and with a large bow in her hair. To a frantic pastiche of popular and ragtime tunes (including Irving Berlin's "Mysterious Rag"), she types furiously, gets involved in a shoot-out with imaginary cops and robbers, writhes and struggles on the floor to save herself from drowning on the *Titanic* (whose foghorns sound in the distance), and, finally, with arms outstretched like airplane wings, soars back into the booth.

In silence, the curtains once more part and out prances a horse. It is the old vaudeville gimmick of two people hidden within the form of a comically prancing and bowing horse which occasionally whinnies and rears up on its hind legs. Now the placard reads "III," and a team of Acrobats appears, one male, one female, dressed in white tights decorated with stars and swirls of blue. To a melody which sways like a trapeze, they perform a *pas de deux* of lyrical aerial lifts, tightrope walking, and splits. After the Acrobats return behind the booth curtains, the foghorn sounds again and the first two Managers and the Little American Girl return. In succession, the Horse, the Conjurer, and finally the Acrobats come back, and all the characters reiterate their acts in a last effort to entice an audience. Cacophony returns as together they make frenzied gestures to their public, but to no avail. As the desperate entertainers form a final tableau, the curtain falls.

Léonide Massine as the Chinese Conjurer in the original Ballets Russes production of Parade

THE THREE-CORNERED HAT

1919 ◆ *Music by Manuel de Falla* ◆ *Choreography by Léonide Massine*

Spanish dancing—and, most prominently, the fiery flamenco style—have always been subjects of fascination for dancers and the creators of ballets. However, none of the early attempts inspired by the style, including the *Don Quixote* of Marius Petipa, managed to achieve more than an essentially classical ballet with a Spanish veneer. When, in 1917, the Ballets Russes sought refuge from World War I in neutral Spain, Diaghilev—never one to bypass an opportunity for creative inspiration—decided that this sojourn would produce the first authentic Spanish ballet.

Diaghilev and his choreographer, Léonide Massine, were now part of an inspired quartet which included the Spanish composer Manuel de Falla and a young Spanish dancer, Félix Fernández García. De Falla, who had only recently met Diaghilev and Massine, brought them to a performance of a one-act play for which he had composed the incidental music. This play, *El Corregidor y la Molinera*, a farce by Gregorio Martínez Sierra, was based on *El Sombrero de tres picos* (*The Three-Cornered Hat*) by Pedro Antonio de Alarcón. Diaghilev was smitten by the story and especially by De Falla's vibrant score, which was replete with authentic folk dance themes, and he decided to use this work as the source of his Spanish ballet.

On a brief trip to Granada, Diaghilev and Massine had seen Fernández García and were struck by his "elegant movements and compelling intensity." He was immediately engaged as a member of the company and given the task of instructing Massine in all aspects of Spanish dancing. In addition, Diaghilev, Massine, De Falla, and Fernández García toured the country in an attempt to absorb every facet of the Spanish sensibility.

Throughout 1918, Massine worked on the Spanish ballet, to be called *Le Tricorne*, as well as on *La Boutique Fantasque*, a toy-shop ballet in the genre of *Coppélia* and *Die Puppenfee*. In the summer of 1919, after the Ballets Russes returned to England, these two Massine masterpieces premiered at the Alhambra Theatre in London to overwhelming success. (There was one tragedy connected with *Le Tricorne*. When Fernández García, who had been invaluable in shaping the ballet, learned that Massine, and not he, would dance the leading role, he suffered a mental breakdown and, like Nijinsky, retreated into a life of incurable insanity.)

The triumph of *Tricorne* was due in equal measure to Massine's choreography, De Falla's stunning score, and the magnificent decor of Pablo Picasso, who abandoned the Cubist vision of *Parade* to create a dazzling profusion of rich colors and textures based on themes of his native land. Several years later, Picasso's act curtain, itself a masterpiece of twentieth-century art, would be sold for $1,500 to save the Ballets Russes from financial ruin. (The curtain now hangs in a place of honor in New York's Four Seasons Restaurant.)

Le Tricorne succeeded because it cast away the restrictive classical elements and pseudoethnic musical allusions that had marked previous ballets on Spanish subjects. It was completely authentic in dance, music, decor, and libretto. That future productions of the work featured appearances by María Dalbician, Argentinita, and Vicente Escudero, all masters of Spanish dance, is a tribute to Massine's ability to capture an elusive style. Although his performances as the Miller also established Massine as an inimitable character dancer, *Tricorne* made clear, above all, that he was a masterful choreographer of vast range and style.

THE BALLET

Before the curtain rises, a pulsating drum and thrilling trumpet fanfares give way to an explosion of clattering castanets, stamping feet, rhythmic hand-clapping, and men's voices shouting "*Olé!*" The curtain rises on an eighteenth-century Spanish village with a mill and, beyond an archway, a bridge leading to an esplanade. Standing in front of his house, the Miller is vainly attempting to teach his pet bird to "sing the hour," when his beautiful wife comes outside. After a brief, teasing chase, they embrace lovingly.

The Corregidor (provincial governor) enters next with his beautiful young wife. Theirs is obviously a marriage of convenience, for the Corregidor is a ridiculous, doddering old man stuffed into elegant attire; only his three-cornered hat gives any indication of his important position. When the Corregidor's lascivious eye falls on the Miller's wife, he makes his attraction known by tossing his handkerchief in her direction. She courteously returns his token, but promises nothing, and the Corregidor, his wife, and retinue leave. The Miller, having noticed this exchange, continues *his* playful game by flirting with one of the local peasant girls.

Dancers of the Joffrey Ballet in The Three-Cornered Hat

After the Miller goes into the house, his wife dances a sensuous fandango, observed by the Corregidor. To the strains of a minuet, he attempts to seduce her, and the amused wife leads the old man on with a bunch of grapes. In his desperation to catch her, he trips and falls. Seeing this ludicrous attempt at seduction, the Miller comes out of the house to "help" his wife. The mischievous couple pick the Corregidor up, but the old man's foolish pride has been damaged, and he warns them he will take measures against this insult. The Miller and his wife blithely continue the fandango.

Evening falls, and the Miller, his wife, and their neighbors celebrate the Feast of St. John. After the townspeople perform a haughty *seguidilla*, the Miller dances a solo—a *farruca*, a gypsy dance highlighted by heel-stomping and proud thrusts of the arms. An incongruous interjection of the famous opening theme of Beethoven's Fifth Symphony heralds the arrival of the Corregidor's henchmen, who have come to arrest the Miller. As the Miller is led away, the townspeople desert his wife.

The scheming Corregidor returns, intent on pursuing his lovely prey unhampered. The Miller's wife comes out of the house and walks directly into the villain hiding in the shadows. During their struggle, the clumsy would-be seducer trips again and this time falls from the bridge into the water. The Miller's wife rescues the old man, but is forced to ward him off with a musket before she can finally escape. Leaving his sopping-wet coat and three-cornered hat outside the Miller's house, the exhausted Corregidor goes to sleep. At dawn, the Miller, who has escaped his captors, returns and discovers the telltale clothes and hat. When he also sees the Corregidor in his own nightshirt, he assumes the lecherous fool has succeeded in his seduction.

The Miller assaults the Corregidor, puts on his rival's dry clothes, and runs off to cuckold him after writing on the wall, "Your wife is no less beautiful than mine!" Next, the Corregidor's guards, hot in pursuit of their prisoner, mistake their own leader for the Miller and fall upon him. The uproar soon draws the curious townspeople. When the Miller and his wife, who have found each other on the road, return and relate what has happened, their angry neighbors turn on the hapless Corregidor and his men. Realizing that their leader was indeed treacherous, his own men carry him off to jail. The townspeople, led by the happily reunited Miller and his wife, launch into a lively *jota*, merrily tossing an effigy of the vanquished Corregidor into the air.

John Hart, Margot Fonteyn, and Léonide Massine in Massine's production of The Three-Cornered Hat *for the Sadler's Wells Ballet, 1947*

APOLLO

1928 ◆ *Music by Igor Stravinsky* ◆ *Choreography by George Balanchine*

In 1924, word reached Diaghilev that a group of Russian dancers from the Maryinsky Theater had been given leave to make a brief tour of Europe. The Soviet State Dancers, as they were called, included Tamara Gevergeva, Alexandra Danilova, Nicholas Efimoff, and George Balantchivadze, who was also their choreographer. They were summoned to Paris to audition for Diaghilev at the home of the impresario's benefactress, Misia Sert, and Diaghilev quickly engaged them for the Ballets Russes.

Diaghilev's interest in the choreographic efforts of Balantchivadze (renamed Balanchine) piqued the highly talented but irascible Bronislava Nijinska, who had been acting as chief choreographer of the Ballets Russes since Léonide Massine's dismissal in 1921. Soon after Nijinska resigned, Diaghilev set Balanchine to work on creating the incidental ballets for the Opéra in Monte Carlo (where the company had taken up residence). Balanchine immediately revealed great promise with his sanguine professionalism, his craft, and the speed with which he fulfilled his assignments. Between 1925 and 1927, his role within the company became increasingly important, and his six ballets of that period —*Rossignol*, *Barabau*, *La Pastorale*, *Jack-in-the-Box*, *The Triumph of Neptune*, and *La Chatte* — indicated that the choreographic future of the Ballets Russes would most probably lie with him.

Meanwhile, in Washington, D.C., Mrs. Elizabeth Sprague Coolidge commissioned a new chamber ballet score from Igor Stravinsky. Abandoning the passion and paganism which had characterized his earlier works, the composer produced a score of exquisite refinement and pristine classicism for string orchestra. *Apollon Musagète*, with choreography by Adolph Bolm, premiered at the Library of Congress on April 27, 1928. Although the production attracted little notice, Stravinsky, with fateful foresight, had reserved the European rights to the ballet for Diaghilev.

Thus, in the spring of 1928, Diaghilev handed Stravinsky's score over to the twenty-four-year-old George Balanchine. In a matter of months, the choreographer created a work that, with its purity, classical symmetry, and transcendent invention, marked the arrival of a new genius and changed the face of ballet forever. Balanchine's *Apollon Musagète* premiered on June 12, 1928, with Serge Lifar, Alice Nikitina, Lubov Tchernicheva,

and Felia Doubrovska. When the curtain came down, the stage designer Gordon Craig left the Théâtre Sarah Bernhardt with reluctance, saying he was unwilling to cloud his glimpse of heaven. (In 1979, Balanchine revised *Apollo*, deleting the opening birth scene and the closing march to Olympus.)

Regarding his score, Stravinsky once wrote, "In *Apollo*, I tried to discover a melodism free of folklore.... *Apollo* was also my first attempt to compose a large-scale work in which contrasts of volumes replace contrasts of instrumental colors." He added, "Apollo and the muses suggested to me not so much a plot as a signature, or what I already have called a manner." It was George Balanchine's ingenious insight into Stravinsky's "manner" that enabled the choreographer to echo it so well in dance. Although rooted in the classical tradition, both the score and the choreography broke from that heritage to lead art in a new direction that was labeled neoclassic. Stravinsky himself stated that the success of *Apollo* (the title the composer preferred over *Apollon Musagète*) "must be attributed to the dancing of Serge Lifar and to the beauty of Balanchine's choreography." This work was the beginning of perhaps the most inspired artistic collaboration in the history of modern ballet.

THE BALLET

A prelude introduces briefly stated themes of subtle grandeur, the last theme identifying Apollo, the new god about to be born. The curtain rises. Revealed in a shaft of light atop a barren crag in Delos sits Leto, in the pains of childbirth. Pulled down by a last contraction, she begins to swirl her head, her matted hair lashing wildly, in spasmodic circles. With a throbbing accent of the strings, Apollo, son of Zeus, is born. Wrapped in swaddling clothes, he hops forward helplessly. Two handmaidens scurry to help the infant god, who with a silent cry falls into their waiting arms. They circle around him, unwinding the cloth, but before they finish, he spins free and begins to step about awkwardly.

To a more emphatic recapitulation of Apollo's theme, the two maidens approach. Supported under the arms, one maiden advances on *pointe* with elegant extensions of her legs while in a suspended sitting position. She bears a gift that will become the god's symbol —a lute. Standing behind Apollo, the maidens reach over his head, hold the instrument before him, and pluck the strings instructively. Apollo then plucks its strings, tentatively at first but soon with confidence. The scene goes black.

In radiant light, we next see Apollo in a short white tunic, alone in his new realm. In half profile he stands firmly on one leg while the other, with bent knee, is crossed in front of him, poised on *demi-pointe*. One arm is held in a gracious curve above his head, while the other grasps the neck of the lute, its body braced on his hip. His free arm circles down across the strings of the instrument. The lute's music, heard as a solo violin, accelerates in time with the sweeping circles of Apollo's arm. In reverent, overlapping gestures, he places the instrument on the ground before he dances alone; then he takes it up again for further inspiration. He holds the lute in front of him and slowly revolves in *attitude*, as if drawn by the divine power of music.

In silence, three Muses *bourrée* toward Apollo and bow respectfully. Surrounding the god, who holds his lute aloft, they bend low in *arabesque penchée*, one on either side of him and one behind, their extended legs framing him like a nimbus of stylized light rays. To a lyrical theme, Apollo then stands before the Muses and, with an extended arm, urges them toward him one at a time in *relevés arabesques*. Separating one Muse from the others, he gently supports her as she kneels to the floor. Then, with powerful arms, he holds the other two as they also slowly kneel. After the single Muse dances around her sisters, all three stand in a line, one behind the other, with arms held rounded above their heads. As Apollo circles behind them in broad leaps, they bend their torsos in rhythm with the music.

Apollo then promenades each Muse in turn, then leads them in procession, as they rise and fall on *pointe*. After another aureole-like pose, they place their bodies in tight proximity, hands supporting each other's head, and shuffle backward on their heels, like a moving musical staff. The Muses dance together for Apollo as the musical passage concludes. Apollo next presents each Muse with the symbol of her artistic domain: a tablet for Calliope, Muse of Lyric Poetry; a mask for Polyhymnia, Muse of Mime; and a lyre for Terpsichore, Muse of Dance and Song. Holding their gifts, the Muses hop twice sidewards and Apollo sits.

Calliope comes forward first, clutching her tablet to her breast. She then places it on the ground and performs a dance based on the rhythms of Alexandrine meter. Her body contracts intensely as she rises on one *pointe* and thrusts her arm forward, opening her mouth with silent emotion. She prances about lightly, then returns to her former emoting and scribbles on her hand as if composing a lyric verse. Calliope goes to Apollo to show what she has written, but the god turns his head in disapproval and she departs.

A jolting burst of music announces the arrival of Polyhymnia. With her finger lifted to her lips to suggest her silent art, she gallops with esprit through her dance. So carried away is she by her exuberance that her lips part, breaking the law of her art. Her hands fly to her mouth in a desperate attempt to retract her error, but realizing it is too late, she runs off dejectedly.

With lyre in hand, Terpsichore next appears. Lifting it aloft, she moves as if her body were an extension of the instrument. Hers is the most daringly inventive dance of all, at once bold and restrained, marked by control, clarity, and dignity. Her perfection meets with Apollo's unqualified approval, and he commends her before she leaves the stage.

In solitary majesty, Apollo then rises on *demi-pointe*, with arms and flattened palms pushed heavenward. He jumps with perfect leg beats, landing on one bent knee with both arms outstretched behind him. Then, in an elegant bending position, he holds one arm close behind him and one reaching to heaven and alternately opens and closes his fists like miniature sunbursts. His dance continues flawlessly and culminates in a reiteration of his initial movements. Then, he reclines on the ground and Terpsichore reenters and touches her forefinger to his, completing a tableau reminiscent of Michelangelo's *Creation of Adam*.

A theme of sweet ecstasy introduces a *pas de deux* in which the god and the Muse dance with equal perfection. At one point, they kneel facing each other and Apollo rests his head childlike upon Terpsichore's cradling palms. Then, as he turns from her, she rests the full length of her body on his back in an image suggesting swimmers or angels in flight. Rising, Apollo arches his back and Terpsichore curves seamlessly within the arch.

To a sudden rush of strings, Calliope and Polyhymnia return to join Apollo and Terpsichore in a coda of unbounded vigor. Later, in thrilling unison, everyone begins a syncopated *galop* during which Apollo is pulled forward by the joyously unbridled Muses, evoking the image of Apollo the Sun God and his

Mikhail Baryshnikov and Heather Watts in Apollo. *New York City Ballet*

horses. Forming a bower of interlocked arms, the four travel in small shuffling steps, weaving under and over each other as they go. The three Muses then face their god, clap their hands, and hold out their palms for him to rest his head upon.

Four ascending calls from Olympus are heard, and the Muses sink to their knees. Their still-offered hands become a gesture of obeisance rather than support. Sitting on the ground and resting backwards on their arms, they each lift one leg to touch the down-turned palm of Apollo, who stands behind them with outstretched arm. Forming a corona with his arms, the god lifts them sequentially to their feet. As if mesmerized by the voice of Zeus, they begin the march to Olympus. With Apollo in the lead, they reach the summit of a promontory; all are bathed in a radiant light. Below, Leto returns to see her son fulfilling his immortal destiny and swoons into the arms of her handmaidens after bidding him farewell.

Karin von Aroldingen, Ib Andersen, Kyra Nichols, and Suzanne Farrell in Apollo. *New York City Ballet*

THE PRODIGAL SON

1929 ◆ *Music by Sergei Prokofiev* ◆ *Choreography by George Balanchine*

Among the contemporary composers Diaghilev engaged to score his ballets in the 1920s were Stravinsky (first and foremost), Nicholas Nabokov, Erik Satie, Darius Milhaud, Francis Poulenc, Vittorio Rieti, Henri Sauguet, Vladimir Dukelsky (later Vernon Duke), and Sergei Prokofiev. In 1915, Prokofiev had written the music for *Chout*, a ballet which Diaghilev did not produce until 1921 and which then met with little success. In 1927, he wrote the score for *Le Pas d'Acier*, a ballet dealing with contemporary Soviet life, with choreography by Léonide Massine.

Although Diaghilev wanted to commission another ballet from Prokofiev, this time he wanted the work to be far less controversial—ideally a suite of dances with a connecting theme of a certain universality. After much discussion among the impresario and his advisers, Boris Kochno, Diaghilev's secretary and librettist for the Ballets Russes, suggested a ballet based on the parable of the Prodigal Son from the Gospel of St. Luke. The idea was received with enthusiasm, and Diaghilev immediately sought out Henri Matisse for the ballet's decor. When Matisse declined, Kochno once again saved the day by suggesting the painter Georges Rouault, who accepted and immediately joined the company in Monte Carlo. Rouault's failure to produce one design or even a sketch tried Diaghilev's patience, until he finally threatened to send the designer back to Paris. Faced with this alternative, Rouault set to work and in one night created the outlines of his masterful decor.

On the other hand, George Balanchine created his rendering of the story without presenting any problem whatsoever. After the classical purity of *Apollo*, the inventive structure and sparse but profound drama of *Prodigal Son* demonstrated that Diaghilev's belief in Balanchine was well founded. The title role offered Serge Lifar another vehicle to display his special talents, and, as the Siren, the elegant Felia Doubrovska imbued her role with a mysterious sensuality that has become legendary. At its Paris premiere on May 21, 1929, *The Prodigal Son* (*Le Fils Prodigue*) was an instant success for all concerned.

Diaghilev's Paris season ended on a triumphant note and was followed by equally successful engagements in Berlin, London, and Vichy, where, on August 4, the Ballets Russes danced its last performance before its summer holiday. Two weeks later, on August 19, 1929, Serge Diaghilev was dead, and with him ended

twenty years of the most innovative, visionary artistic creativity the ballet had ever known. While *Prodigal Son* was a last glorious tribute to Diaghilev's vision, for Balanchine it was only the beginning of what he would accomplish for the ensuing fifty years, and more.

THE BALLET

After a brief, spirited opening theme, the curtain rises on a nomadic dwelling in an ancient biblical setting. It is morning and outside the patriarch's tent two youths are busying themselves in preparation for a journey. A third youth soon emerges from the tent with his two sisters. Greeting his friends joyfully, the youth commences a dance filled with unbounded energy. His leaps toward the four corners of the stage reveal that he is possessed of restless yearnings and expectations.

His two sisters watch with a certain apprehension. Just as their brother completes his dance, they are joined by their father, a figure of intimidating solemnity. When he calls his three children to him, his daughters go willingly, his son with reluctance. They sit in a small circle at their father's feet, and he joins their hands, invoking God's blessing. The youth turns away, but his father reaches for his head and gently but firmly pulls it back into an attitude of submission. But the son will not be restrained—he willfully breaks from the circle to repeat his dance of freedom. As his two friends gather their chattel and rush off, he follows them over a fence with a last defiant leap and a calling gesture. With stoic resignation, the patriarch watches the departure of his son and then summons his two saddened daughters back into the tent.

A throbbing, sensual theme opens the second scene, which reveals a sumptuously prepared banquet table inside an open tent. Onto the scene come a group of hideous pagan revelers. With their splayed, turned-out legs bent at the knees and their arms alternately linking and unlinking around one another's waist, these bald creatures march in single file with simple-minded glee, giving the appearance of a bizarre, humanoid millipede. They rush to the fence still onstage from Scene 1 and carry it over to the banquet table; turning it over, they transform it into another table. They frolic with repulsive lewdness until the Prodigal and his friends come upon them. The Prodigal and his companions, after sharing some wine with the revelers, are

a scarlet bodice, the headdress of a priestess, and a long, billowing crimson cape. She floats on *pointe* as if in a trance and begins a suggestive dance, drawing her cape through her legs and around her hips. Falling into a backbend, she walks on her hands and toes, then kneels forward to draw the cape in large folds over her body. The fascinated Prodigal approaches the enticingly covered figure and tears the cape from her. The two perform a sinuous dance of seduction, which concludes with the Prodigal helplessly entwined with the Siren. The revelers now pull the lovers apart and force more wine on the Prodigal. They lift him and the Siren aloft, holding their bodies close together, and lower them upside down, clinging together like some ripe, exotic fruit.

The Prodigal senses danger and attempts to flee. As he runs over the fence-table, the menacing revelers tilt it upward and he slides into their captivity. Pushed against the upended table, the vanquished Prodigal is robbed of his garments. After his captors leave, the heartless Siren tears an amulet from his throat and furtively rushes off. In a passage of great poignancy, the stripped Prodigal blindly crawls away as the stage grows dark.

In a brief interlude, the wicked revelers return with their booty. They turn the fence-table over and climb into it. With the Siren poised before them like a figurehead, they hold her cape open like a sail to form an eerie seafaring tableau. Again the stage grows dark.

Scene 3 opens with a musical passage of desperate melancholy. The Prodigal, battered and bloody, in a tattered woolen garment, crawls weakly homeward on his knees with the aid of a rough-hewn staff. He finally reaches the familiar gate to his home, but falls in a faint before he can open it. Soon the Prodigal's sisters emerge from the tent and gently lead their brother home. The father comes out and sees the crushed body of his son, but does not give vent to his emotions. At the sight of his father's proud figure before him, the kneeling Prodigal turns away in shame. But then, with overwhelming need and repentance, he drags himself, prostrate, to his father's feet. Clinging pitifully to the patriarch's robes, the son pulls himself upright with great effort. He embraces the neck of his father, who lifts

drawn into a weirdly spirited dance, culminating with the Prodigal atop the fence-table.

A voluptuous melody introduces a majestic woman dressed in

him like an infant in his cradling arms. In a last forgiving gesture, the patriarch covers his son protectively with his cape as he turns to carry him into the tent.

Above: Karin von Aroldingen as the Siren in The Prodigal Son. *New York City Ballet*
Opposite: Mikhail Baryshnikov as the Prodigal Son. New York City Ballet

THE GREEN TABLE

1932 ◆ *Music by Frederic (Fritz) Cohen* ◆ *Choreography by Kurt Jooss*

As a new Germany rose from the ashes of World War I, a radical form of dance expression was being espoused there by the innovative teacher and theorist Rudolf von Laban and his three most prominent disciples, Mary Wigman, Harald Kreutzberg, and Kurt Jooss. This form of dance rejected classical ballet's artificial technical structure and composition in favor of a systematized approach to movement as plastic rhythm on its own terms. An elaboration of the principles of anatomical expression and gesture conceived by François Delsarte in the mid-nineteenth century, Von Laban's teachings attempted to enable the dancer to control his or her body so that any part of it could be tensed with an awareness of what that movement or gesture would convey to the observer. It was Kurt Jooss who applied Von Laban's theories to great theatrical effect.

Jooss first studied with Von Laban at Mannheim's National Theater in 1921 and soon became the teacher's assistant and principal dancer. In 1924, he formed a small dance company, the Neue Tanzbühne, with the composer and conductor Fritz Cohen, the dancers Sigurd Leeder and Aino Siimola, and the designer Hein Heckroth. With a repertoire consisting of his own works, Jooss toured Germany for two years, and for the rest of the decade formed and directed other dance groups. When Rolf de Maré, co-founder of Les Archives Internationales de la Danse, announced an international choreographic competition to be held in Paris in 1932, Jooss conceived for it a medieval Dance of Death in modern terms. He did not have to look far for his inspiration, for Germany was still suffering the aftermath of war as well as vainly struggling to combat the rise of Nazism. His work, known as *The Green Table*, won first prize.

The triumphant reception of *The Green Table* led to the formation of the Ballets Jooss, which made a successful world tour for the next year. Because of his distaste for the Nazi regime, Jooss would not return to Germany until well after World War II. Throughout those years in exile, his chief centers of activity were in England and the United States. Although Jooss, who died in 1979, choreographed a number of distinctive and socially relevant ballets (such as *The Big City, A Ball in Old Vienna,* and *Pavane*) and took part in reviving ballet schools and companies in postwar Germany, it is *The Green Table* that endures as his greatest tribute to the power of expression in dance. Its shocking indictment of war has never been surpassed.

THE BALLET

A harsh, percussive introduction by the piano (the sole instrument for which the score was composed) foreshadows the ballet's grim conclusion, but then the curtain rises to a tango of cabaret intimacy. Around a rectangular green table, twelve masked diplomats in morning coats and spats move like marionettes in cordial, conferential gestures. Divided into two "teams," these sinister diplomats lean on their elbows, chatter among themselves, bend low over the table, and are urged to rally to the "cause" by a chairman. The leader of the left side of the table comes up with a point, and he emphasizes it by lifting his foot to the table. He is applauded by his side, but the other side begins to bicker. Pounding their fists and bracing themselves against the table to thrust their feet into the air, the men are about to come to blows. Courtesy prevails, however, and the diplomatic ritual continues. Finally, with no solution to the increasing tension, the diplomats take pistols from their vests, bow to each other, and fire into the air. The scene goes black.

Next we see, alone on stage, the grotesque, skeletal figure of Death attired in the helmet and breastplate of Mars, the god of war. To a hypnotic, baleful, and percussive march, Death conjures up war. With legs spread open and turned out, he stomps rhythmically, rises on one leg, arching his back with upraised arm in a gesture of triumph, draws back, lunges forward, leaps, spins, pounds his heels, thus defining his limitless territory.

In a broad circle of leaps, the Flagbearer enters, carrying his banner with pride and dignity. Two more soldiers join him, and then a third leaps in. The rallying march becomes more insistent as the soldiers practice shooting and march in formation. A fourth soldier enters with his fiancée, who in a brief, tender *pas de deux* tries to keep him with her, but he too joins the ranks. A fifth man, accompanied by two women, his mother and sister perhaps, is drawn to the martial call despite the pleas of the women. The Profiteer, a sleazy character in bowler hat and white gloves, comes on the scene. The soldiers march in a circle as the three women follow with stylized gestures of anguish. The Profiteer bows to Death, his master, and then leans lasciviously over the sorrowing fiancée, who lies prone on the ground.

The battle commences as the soldiers crisscross the stage in mounting confusion. The sides are ill-defined, but it matters very little—one by one, the soldiers die and the only victor is

Death, who dances a slow march. The Profiteer moves amid the carnage with sinister glee, sweeping over the bodies to gather loot. The scene goes dark.

Accompanied by a musical theme of lamentation, seven women form a tableau of grief. The Mother dances a despairing solo during which her daughter tries vainly to comfort her. With the approach of Death, all withdraw in fear except the Mother, who answers his summons with a dazed obedience. Death and the Mother dance a macabre minuet, until she finds the ultimate comfort of being lifted into Death's arms. Left alone, the weeping daughter is accosted by the Profiteer.

A dynamic theme is heard as the Partisan Woman, with waving scarf, bounds onto the scene for a solo of strength, conviction, and revenge. When the marching soldiers return, the Partisan hides herself. Stealthily pursuing one of the soldiers, she throws her scarf over him and he dies. But then Death enters and the Partisan freezes. Three soldiers form a firing squad and the woman is drawn backward by Death; as he turns his back, Death becomes a wall against which she dies.

The Flagbearer, banner in hand, crouches and rocks back and forth, unaware that Death is mimicking him from behind. Death rises and takes hold of the flag and, with the soldier, waves the banner in slow arcs. They begin a dirgelike march and are joined by the Partisan Woman, the Mother, the fiancée, and the soldiers. With Death and the Flagbearer at their center, the dazed figures march in a circle, and finally fall, one by one, to the ground. Triumphantly, Death holds the flag upside down.

One last soldier dances valiantly to a reprise of a patriotic theme, but Death lifts the flag and the soldier soon weakens. The others rise on half-toe, their arms bent upward in a gesture of surrender, and the soldier falls into line with them as they resume their somnambulistic death march. The Profiteer scampers after them, but crouches in fear when he sees Death. To the pounding music of Death's incantation, the Profiteer struggles to escape, but not even he is spared the throes of death. Death stands victorious as he repeats his initial stomping march of doom. The scene goes black.

Pistol shots are heard and the lights come up once again on the conference room. To a reprise of the tango, the diplomats reenact their cynical charade. In a final, ironically comic pose, they freeze in a tableau depicting a stalemate.

Above: Robert Thomas as the Standard Bearer and Christian Holder as Death. The Joffrey Ballet
Overleaf: The Diplomats in The Green Table. *The Joffrey Ballet*

SERENADE

1934 ◆ Music by Peter Ilyich Tchaikovsky ◆ Choreography by George Balanchine

For the next few years after Diaghilev's death in 1929, George Balanchine led a rather peripatetic existence, which included—after a serious illness—staging balletic interludes for the popular Cochran Revue in London; serving briefly as ballet master for the Royal Danish Ballet in Copenhagen; and creating new works for the Nemchinova Ballet in Paris, the resurrected Ballets Russes de Monte Carlo of René Blum and Colonel W. de Basil, and his own Les Ballets 1933. Although Les Ballets 1933 enjoyed a certain *succès d'estime*, the company foundered because of financial difficulties. But it did last long enough to be seen in its London season by Lincoln Kirstein, a wealthy young American esthete who had come to Europe to find a ballet master in whose hands he could place the task of establishing a strictly American ballet style and tradition. Balanchine, whose goals seemed closely linked to Kirstein's, accepted his offer with alacrity, saying that he would be thrilled to work in a country that had produced a woman as beautiful as Ginger Rogers!

On October 18, 1933, George Balanchine arrived in New York City and soon after—on January 1, 1934—the doors opened on the School of American Ballet, the first step in establishing the foundation of the new American ballet. In March of the same year, Balanchine began work on his first ballet created in America. From day to day he choreographed segments of this new work on as many of the students (mostly amateurs) available to him at any given time, and sometimes he even incorporated the dancer's errors into the choreographic structure. Thus, in this rather haphazard manner, he created *Serenade*, to Tchaikovsky's Serenade in C Major for String Orchestra, and three months later, on June 9, 1934, it was first performed by students of the School of American Ballet at the estate of Felix M. Warburg, in White Plains, N.Y. That performance passed with scant notice, but the work survived in various repertoires until, on October 18, 1948—fifteen years to the day after Balanchine's arrival in America—*Serenade* was performed during the first season of the New York City Ballet.

Serenade has endured so long as a signature piece of the New York City Ballet because, like most of Balanchine's greatest

Above: The Dance Theatre of Harlem in Serenade

works, it remains true to a central artistic concept of the company: the ballet itself is the "star." Rather than depending on the personality or virtuosity of any one particular dancer, *Serenade* requires technical strength, tensile energy, and fluid lyricism of its ensemble as well as its principals. Indeed, as the critic Edwin Denby so eloquently put it, "*Serenade*, in its dream-like speed and poignancy, uses the ensemble less to corroborate the principals than to weave their fragments of adolescent romance into the unwearied rush of immortal space."

THE BALLET

The noble phrases of Tchaikovsky's opening theme are heard before the curtain rises to reveal one of the most breathtaking opening tableaus ever seen on the ballet stage. Bathed in romantic blue light, more than a score of young women in billowing blue tulle skirts and simple bodices stand in crossing diagonal lines. Holding their right arms upward with out-turned palms, they seem to be shielding their eyes from the glow of a celestial light.

Like a sudden intake of breath, the melody changes and with it the dancers move into full-bodied action. As the music swells, they respond in intricate swirling patterns and combinations of leaps, turns, and arm configurations. The first theme suddenly returns and the dancers resume their opening tableau; another woman, as if lost, enters among them. Moving into the pattern, she too raises her right arm with out-turned palm. Then, a man, walking with solemn dignity, approaches her. He stands behind her, she rises on *pointe*, and the other women turn and walk slowly from the scene.

To the strains of the next movement, a silken waltz filled with rapturous hesitations, the couple dance and are soon joined by the other women. At the waltz's whispering denouement, all depart except for five women who, to the last three notes of the waltz, sit together on the ground.

As the third movement (the fourth in Tchaikovsky's original score) begins, each of these women offers her right hand to the one on her left, and her left hand to the one on her right. With arms thus entwined, they rise from the ground and briefly walk together on *pointe*. Soon a lively Russian melody breaks forth, and the five dancers are joined by the others, among them the waltzing couple. All dance with unbridled gaiety to this sweeping, insistent melody. Near the end of the dance, the opening theme is broadly reiterated. The dancers step slowly backward and, as the theme accelerates, hop swiftly in arabesque to either direction. Then, as if blown by a sudden wind, they all *sauté* from the scene to leave one woman fallen on the ground, her head buried in her arms.

The fallen figure is alone only momentarily, for, to the opening of a poignant elegy, a man and a woman enter. The man walks slowly toward the woman on the ground. Directly behind him, with one arm crossed over his chest and the other covering his eyes, his companion seems to guide him. The prone woman rises slightly, resting on one elbow, and looks up at them. The man kneels beside her as his companion rises on *pointe* in arabesque; the man grasps his companion's standing leg and rotates her in place. All three then dance a *pas de trois* in which the man is torn by his devotion to both women. The dejected woman drops to the ground again, with the man once more kneeling beside her and his companion behind them. As if in a trance, he rises and blocks the body of his guide, but her arms, in deliberate, stylized movements, finally clutch his breast and move up to cover his eyes. The two visitors resume their journey.

A small group of women enters, and prominent among them is one with a certain maternal authority. The prone woman rises and rushes about the stage, as if frightened. She runs through the colonnade formed by the other dancers and presses herself desperately to the maternal figure's breast. Three men enter and, as if answering some far-off call, the woman allows herself to be lifted, standing, into the air. To the abating strains of the elegy, they form a cortege, followed by the other women and the maternal figure. The solemn group moves into a diagonal shaft of light, and the woman held aloft arches backward swooningly as the curtain falls.

Kay Mazzo and Lauren Hauser in Serenade. *New York City Ballet*

JARDIN AUX LILAS

1936 ◆ Music by Ernest Chausson ◆ Choreography by Antony Tudor

In 1928, a London-born acting student named Antony Tudor enrolled in ballet classes with Marie Rambert. Rambert, who had been Nijinsky's assistant in the creation of *Le Sacre du Printemps*, was impressed with the enthusiasm of the nineteen-year-old latecomer to the ballet. In little more than a year, she engaged him as her secretary and made him a member of her small dance company, the Ballet Club (later called Ballet Rambert), where another young Britisher, Frederick Ashton, was already emerging as the company's chief choreographer.

As early as 1931, Rambert let Tudor try his own hand at choreography, and, drawing upon his theatrical background, he produced his first ballet, entitled *Cross-Garter'd*, followed by such notable works as *Lysistrata*, *Adam and Eve*, and *The Descent of Hebe*. In all these works, Tudor's choreographic style drew deeply upon the eloquence of pantomimic gesture and the narrative structure of drama rather than upon the conventional idioms of balletic expression.

In 1936 the scenic designer Hugh Stevenson suggested a subject for a new ballet to Tudor. Its theme of unrequited love was set in an Edwardian context in which the protagonists repress their desires and bend to the restrictive middle-class mores of their era. For this intimate tragedy of the emotions, Tudor needed the perfect musical setting to create the desired aura, which had to be as hauntingly delicate as the scent of lilacs in a garden on a summer evening. (Indeed, the ballet would be called *Jardin aux Lilas*, or *Lilac Garden*.) Tudor eventually found the music he needed in Ernest Chausson's exquisite *Poème* for violin and orchestra, composed in 1896. Tudor's work proved to be a great success for Ballet Rambert, and Rambert herself considered it a perfect *ballet psychologique*, the dance equivalent of Stendhal's *roman psychologique*.

In 1939 Tudor was invited, together with Hugh Laing, the chief male interpreter of his ballets, to come to America and participate in the inception of Ballet Theatre. For that com-

Erik Bruhn as the Man She Must Marry and Gelsey Kirkland as Caroline. American Ballet Theatre

pany's first season, in January, 1940, Tudor restaged three of his British works; the first to be seen on an American stage was *Jardin aux Lilas*. The ballet won instant acclaim for the choreographer as well as for Ballet Theatre, and it became clear that the destinies of the two would be linked for years to come.

Jardin aux Lilas is a ballet that relies less on virtuosic dancing than on the ability to capture the subtlety and nuance of dramatic gesture and, furthermore, to be carried by the music's phrasing rather than by its meter. Tudor's singular genius for portraying the psychological moment is most evident in this work, matched only by his even more anguished *Dark Elegies* and *Pillar of Fire*. In all his ballets, Tudor imbues every movement, gesture, look, and stance with emotional significance, posing a difficult challenge for dancers. Only when performed with intelligence and depth of feeling does a Tudor ballet come to singular and memorable life.

THE BALLET

The curtain rises on a garden redolent with the perfume of lilacs. Standing in the evening shadows is a young woman, Caroline, the Bride-to-Be, wearing a white lace evening gown. At her side is a dignified older man in formal Edwardian attire, The Man She Must Marry. The couple seem worlds apart.

A handsome young man in uniform then enters the garden. By her yearning gaze toward him, Caroline reveals that he is Her Lover, but with a subtle gesture she indicates to him that he must leave. Arm in arm, Caroline and her fiancé walk stiffly from the garden, with Caroline glancing over her shoulder.

An aristocratic woman dressed in brilliant blue now enters the garden alone. She looks about her, clearly searching for someone. A group of guests come into the garden, Caroline among them. Moments later, the lover reappears. The two, momentarily left alone, move backward toward each other. Caroline swoons against her lover and, turning to face each other, they dance a brief, passionate *pas de deux* fraught with apprehension. The ardent lover kisses Caroline's hand just as the woman in blue appears in the shadows to observe them. Caroline quickly withdraws her hand and courteously introduces the two. A polite *pas de trois* ensues. Two male guests enter. Caroline and her lover leave as the woman in blue is escorted away by the new arrivals.

Caroline then performs a solo that reveals her private anguish over entering a marriage of convenience. Deeply troubled, she feigns composure when guests pass through the garden. Alone once more, she expresses her anguish by desperate spins and turns. At the last of these, she is caught in the arms of her lover, who rapturously lifts her high in the air, then gently returns her to the ground, where they both kneel together briefly. Caroline suddenly rises to run off, once more followed by her young officer.

Caroline's fiancé walks into the garden to join the dancing guests and the imperious woman in blue. Upon seeing Caroline's husband-to-be, the woman in blue rushes into his arms and their dance makes it clear that she is An Episode in His Past. Their dance is passionate yet guarded, for the man must remain above suspicion. Caroline and her lover now join the older couple in a constrained *pas de quatre*. For a moment, all the guests perform a formal dance, then everyone departs, leaving Caroline and her lover to dance out their poignant dilemma.

There now follows a series of entrances and exits which, with ever-increasing psychological depth, denote the loves, regrets, repressions, and deceptions of each of the protagonists in a socially correct ambience. This seamless flow of encounters and partings builds to a gestural denouement in which all the characters freeze into a symbolic tableau of various tense yet revealing poses. As this moment remains suspended in time, Caroline alone begins to move among the stilled characters. She subtly enacts her private tragedy, then returns to take her place with the others, clearly unable to alter her fate.

The guests begin to move, and the four leading characters unite for a grave and stately walk forward — Caroline on the arm of her fiancé, the woman in blue on the arm of Caroline's lover — their turbulent, repressed emotions registering on their faces and in their restrained movements. Then, as the music reaches its own denouement, the guests make their farewells. The Man She Must Marry brings Caroline her cape and places it on her shoulders. She takes his arm and, without looking back, the two walk slowly away. The woman in blue takes the arms of two male guests and, with an air of resignation, also departs. Caroline's lover is left alone, facing desolately into the lilac garden.

Overleaf, left: Lise Houlton and Kevin McKenzie in Jardin aux Lilas. *American Ballet Theatre*
Overleaf, right: Denise Jackson in Les Patineurs. *The Joffrey Ballet*

LES PATINEURS

1937 ◆ *Music by Giacomo Meyerbeer, arranged by Constant Lambert* ◆ *Choreography by Frederick Ashton*

Among the many young people to whom the great Anna Pavlova brought the beauty of ballet and the inspiration to dance was Frederick Ashton, who saw her perform in Lima, Peru, in 1917. (Of British parentage, Ashton grew up in South America.) He found his way to London, where, throughout the 1920s, he studied ballet with Massine, Rambert, and Nijinska. Ashton began to choreograph almost as soon as he learned to dance and in 1926 created his first major work, *A Tragedy of Fashion*. By 1930, he was engaged by Rambert to choreograph for the Camargo Society, England's attempt to replace Diaghilev's Ballets Russes and to establish a foundation for British ballet. Among the works Ashton created for the short-lived society were *Pomona* (1930) and *Façade* (1931).

When Marie Rambert formed her own company, called the Ballet Club, in 1930, Ashton emerged as its first choreographer (to be followed, after his departure, by Antony Tudor). But the "starvation wages" he received from the Ballet Club prompted him to accept the invitation of Ninette de Valois in 1933 to choreograph for the newly founded Vic-Wells Ballet. Even more than Rambert, De Valois would be the guiding force in establishing a British national ballet, which became a real possibility through Ashton's emerging choreographic genius.

Almost from the beginning, Ashton demonstrated his unique choreographic style in works such as *Les Rendez-vous* (1933), *Le Baiser de la Fée* (1935), and *Apparitions* (1936). In *Apparitions*, Ashton first collaborated directly with the brilliant composer-arranger Constant Lambert and employed the talents of the young Robert Helpmann and Margot Fonteyn. With this extraordinary quartet of artists, the future of British ballet was assured.

In 1935, a ballet based on the Hogarth lithographic series *The Rake's Progress* was intended as a choreographic project for Ashton, while De Valois was to create a ballet to Lambert's arrangement of incidental music from Meyerbeer operas. Eventually, the two choreographers came to exchange their respective projects. With *Les Patineurs*, Ashton demonstrated not only the ever-growing sophistication and wit of his choreographic style, but also the high level of technical virtuosity the British ballet had already achieved.

Les Patineurs was an instant success at its premiere at the Sadler's Wells Theatre on February 16, 1937, and has been retained ever since in the repertoires of many ballet companies. Upon the choreographer's own admission, it is not the kind of narrative ballet for which he has received so much acclaim but is rather more of a "ballet *divertissement*." Even so, the work bears Ashton's unmistakable stamp: insouciant charm, wit, and a pronounced yet subtle technical éclat.

THE BALLET

A jolly theme in pronounced three-quarter time provides a brief overture and is recapitulated with a merry swirl as the curtain rises on a moonlit winter scene, a skating pond in the middle of a forest clearing. Onto the pond come four young couples, arms linked, gliding in the characteristic movements of ice skaters. Circling the pond, the girls glissade and pirouette on the outside, while the men leap together into the center. The couples reform, link arms, then skate off.

To a jaunty *galop*, two very determined young ladies, attempting to master their art, enter. With concentrated effort, they prance on *pointe*, arms swinging back and forth in rhythm with their legs. They slip back twice, but catch themselves before falling, and finally prance off. The four couples return with intensified speed, and one couple, faltering, falls to the icy surface. After they pick themselves up, the girl delicately dusts off her young escort's coattails and they skate off with a charming hauteur.

To a giggling trumpet staccato, a solitary Boy in Blue (in some versions, in green) glides onto the pond. He leaps in *entrechat*, points his feet, and pirouettes to one knee. He then dances a solo of dazzling virtuosity, replete with *cabrioles*, *sautés*, *sissonnes*, *ronds de jambe en l'air*, *tours jetés*, and double *tours en passé en l'air*. In concluding his demonstration of technical perfection and self-assurance, he spins to one knee, then to the other, and rises from the ground in arabesque before departing.

A romantic theme accompanies the entrance of a loving couple dressed completely in glistening white. They float in a circle as he lifts her rapturously and she falls into his arms. The young woman pirouettes, is supported and turned in arabesque by her partner, and is lifted into an upside-down split on her partner's hip. Trusting to the support of her escort, she then sits on one bent leg on *demi-pointe* and is spun by him dizzyingly. Finally, swooning back into her partner's arms, she is carried off.

The eight young revelers return in their familiar circle and break into crisscrossing lines. Another pair of ladies join the skaters, dance in their midst, join hands, and leap off. The four couples continue dancing and are joined by the couple in white, who float in turn around each of the couples in a figure-eight pattern. The Boy in Blue enters with flying leaps. The couple in white again execute their upside-down split and skate away. The skating continues as the Boy in Blue makes a circle of *coupés jetés*, spins, then, with small flicking leg movements (*pas de papillon*), leaps off.

To a rambunctious mazurka, the Boy in Blue and two girls next perform a *pas de trois*. This is followed by the entrance of two other ladies, who rise on *pointe*, turn, momentarily fall, get up, dance some more, then primly glide off.

The infectious spirit of the winter revelry does not abate. There is more lively "skating" until the entire group forms a charming tableau suggesting a sleigh, in which the girl in white is carried aloft on the shoulders of two young men. In tandem, two girls reiterate their sustained rising on *pointe*, then leap off. Fast upon this, the entire group in single file, heads cocked to one side, prance on their toes, with arms swinging emphatically.

Snow begins to fall, and to mounting exhilarating music, the skaters begin to leap back and forth and then to rush, one by one, from the pond. At the climax the four solo girls spin across the pond to a whirling *perpetuum mobile*. They leap off, leaving the pond to the Boy in Blue, who continues to spin madly in pirouettes *à la seconde* as the curtain falls once, then rises and falls again.

Cynthia Anderson and Patricia Miller in Les Patineurs. *The Joffrey Ballet*

FRANKIE AND JOHNNY

1938 ◆ *Music by Jerome Moross* ◆ *Choreography by Ruth Page and Bentley Stone*

The spell of Anna Pavlova touched young people in America as well as those, like Frederick Ashton, abroad. Ruth Page first saw the legendary ballerina perform in Indianapolis in 1915, and, in just a few years, she appeared with Pavlova's company on its second tour of South America. Returning to New York, Page studied with Adolph Bolm who, after her triumphant debut in the title role of his ballet *The Birthday of the Infanta*, named her *première danseuse* of his Ballet Intime and, later, of his experimental company, Chicago Allied Arts. During the 1920s, Page studied with Enrico Cecchetti, appeared on Broadway, danced for a lightning-fast time with Diaghilev's Ballets Russes in Monte Carlo (the only American female dancer ever to have performed with that company), and embarked on a world tour. But her first love was choreography and, like Ashton, she made dances almost as soon as she learned to dance.

In her own words, Page was never "married to the classical ballet," and in the mid-twenties and early thirties she began to choreograph ballets based on American themes to music she commissioned from American composers. The earliest of these was a duet entitled *The Flapper and the Quarterback* (1926), with music by the American composer Clarence Loomis. In 1933, she daringly produced the first American all-black ballet, based on a West Indian legend called *La Guiablesse*, at the Chicago Opera. A year later, she created the first ballet to be produced with a commissioned score from the young Aaron Copland, a courtroom ballet entitled *Hear Ye! Hear Ye!* But Page was not through with her shocking innovations, for in 1938, in collaboration with Bentley Stone, her dance partner and co-director of the Chicago WPA Theatre Project, she created a ballet based on the low-down ballad "Frankie and Johnny," with a score by yet another brilliant young American composer, Jerome Moross.

Frankie and Johnny was a sell-out smash in Chicago when it premiered on June 19, 1938. Several years later, however, when Sergei Denham's Ballet Russe de Monte Carlo produced the ballet, its raucous theme and ribald characters—including pimps, prostitutes, and lechers—were too much for the city fathers, and the work had to be "cleaned up" before the curtain was allowed to go up. In 1950, *Frankie and Johnny* was included in the repertoire of Page and Stone's own company, Les Ballets Américains, the first American company to visit postwar Paris. Despite an even more vociferous *scandale* among conservative Parisian audiences, the company, and *Frankie and Johnny*, remained firmly entrenched at the Théâtre des Champs-Elysées for a month, playing to sold-out houses.

Page herself has called *Frankie and Johnny* a purposely "crude, wicked serio-comedy." It is Americana painted in the broadest strokes, with two-dimensional characterizations expanded to larger-than-life proportions. Borrowing unabashedly from every style of American dance, the choreographers presented a fleeting cross section of the American ethos. Perhaps only a few dancers have understood the almost intangible balance of seriousness and parody with which Page and Stone danced the title roles in the original production. Recent revivals of the ballet indicate, however, that contemporary American dance companies, as part of their search for the roots of Americana, are attempting to recapture the original vitality and period authenticity of this seminal work.

THE BALLET

A percussive introduction of the familiar tune "Frankie and Johnny" serves as the overture. The curtain rises on a street scene in an unsavory quarter of a Midwestern city in the early 1920s. At one end of the street is a two-story tenement house with a bannistered flight of stairs leading to the second floor. There is a saloon next door, and on the street corner a lamppost. Reclining languorously on the tenement's stairs is Johnny, wearing a "snazzy" ragtime outfit. Sitting at the windows are Frankie, on the first floor, and Nelly Bly, on the second, both with obviously come-hither expressions on their faces.

Down the street walk three Salvation Army ladies, here called Saving Susies, who in a dirgelike tempo beat their drum and tambourines and sing the opening line of the ballad. The street swings into action to a ragtime tune, "The Bawdy House Stomp." Men from various walks of life swagger toward the house, and after they visit the ladies in their rooms, they pay Johnny his "fee." The activity continues relentlessly until suddenly the street clears, leaving Johnny alone.

Frankie comes from her room into the street, sits on the bannister, and allows Johnny to take off her cape. They begin a *pas de deux* of sinuous and suggestive reclining, lifting, and embracing. The dance concludes with Frankie back on the

Suzanne Smith, Gregory Begley, and Cynthia Ann Roses in Frankie and Johnny. *Chicago Opera Ballet*

bannister and Johnny replacing her cape. She then returns to her room for the next "shift."

The front of the saloon rises to reveal a bartender serving men and their lady companions. Johnny dances cockily into the street to join in the jazzy dancing. Nelly Bly scurries down the stairs and struts into the street. She flirts with Johnny and they immediately begin a suggestive duet. Frankie reemerges from the house on the way to the saloon "to buy her a large glass of beer" and asks "Has my lovinest man been here?" With beer mug in hand, she joins the dancers in their ragtime bacchanal, unaware that hidden in the group are Johnny and Nelly Bly, who soon rush up the stairs into Nelly's room.

With sleazy, vulgar gestures, the bartender dances into the street and makes overtures to Frankie. To a low-down blues theme of hypnotic insistence, Frankie, with a tolerant air of amusement, dances around the bartender, never once letting him touch her. Angry and frustrated, the bartender gleefully tells Frankie of Johnny's deception. Working herself into a frenzy, Frankie spins, kicks, rolls on the ground, and crawls up the stairs like a desperate animal. She bangs on Nelly's door, then hides as she sees Johnny and Nelly lift the window shade to peer out. With determination, Frankie runs to her room and quickly returns wielding a gun. She finds a ladder, climbs to the second-floor window, and crawls through it. Johnny and Nelly rush out of the house and, despite Nelly's pleas and attempts to

shield Johnny, Frankie takes aim and shoots him mercilessly.

Mortally wounded, Johnny rolls down the bannister, lands on the ground with his feet in the air, and then somersaults weakly into the street. The instantly remorseful Frankie rushes to his aid, but Johnny dies.

A dirge begins as a group of tap-dancing men carry in an empty coffin on their shoulders. The grieving Frankie straddles her dead lover, closes his eyes, and embraces his feet. Women wearing black scarves and men carrying black wreaths gather on stage. The women mourn with comically stylized operatic gestures. As the monotone repetition of the music builds, Frankie grabs the black shroud that covers Johnny and tries to hang herself with it from the lamppost. She is saved from suicide by Nelly, who has descended the stairs with a large wreath of lilies framing her face. With sisterly commiseration, the two embrace and watch as the men pick up Johnny's stiffened body. The women help them place the body in the coffin, Frankie lovingly lowering Johnny's feet and Nelly his torso.

The "Frankie and Johnny" tune swirls operatically. Nelly takes a policeman upstairs as Frankie stretches her body over the lid of Johnny's coffin. Then, sitting up, she pitiably holds the wreath before her as the Saving Susies sing, "This story just goes to show you that you can't trust any man." Standing behind the coffin, they clink their beer mugs and take a deep swallow as the curtain falls.

Bentley Stone and Ruth Page in the original production of Frankie and Johnny, *1938*

BILLY THE KID

1938 ◆ *Music by Aaron Copland* ◆ *Choreography by Eugene Loring*

Ballet Caravan, a company established to create and present new works as a showcase for American dancers, choreographers, artists, and composers, gave its first performance in July, 1936, at Bennington College, Vermont. Among the ballets presented that first season was *Harlequin for President*, a satirical work choreographed to music by Domenico Scarlatti by a young member of the American Ballet, Eugene Loring. Loring, who was born in Milwaukee, had come to New York a short time before to study at the School of American Ballet, and had danced at Lewisohn Stadium with a company formed by Michel Fokine. His background had been in acting: although he had been featured in Balanchine's works for the American Ballet,

his approach to dance was not rooted in the classical idiom.

After Loring's next ballet, *Yankee Clipper* (1937), Ballet Caravan began to seek a wider audience and was engaged for a tour of the United States. In October, 1938, in Chicago, the company presented another Loring ballet, *Billy the Kid*, in which the choreographer conceived a panoramic view of the heritage of the American West. *Billy* was the greatest success Ballet Caravan would have; within a matter of four years, it was considered a classic. When it was taken into the repertoire of the newly formed Ballet Theatre in December, 1940, the work was given a permanent home as the company's signature piece.

Loring's "free-form movement" in *Billy the Kid*, relying so

Joseph Clark as Billy and Keith Kimmel as Alias. Ballet West

little on classical ballet technique, is the work's greatest achievement. Because the dynamics of the ballet's movement seem more closely allied to the esthetic of American modern dance, it can be argued that *Billy the Kid* had little effect on balletic style per se. Still, it is a landmark composition, perhaps the masterpiece of Americana ballets, providing one of the greatest virtuoso dramatic roles for the dancer portraying Billy. Many of its interpreters have garnered acclaim, starting with Loring himself and continuing through the decades with the performances of John Kriza, Scott Douglas, Michael Smuin, Terry Orr, Daniel Levans, Eliot Feld, Dennis Wayne, Kirk Peterson, Warren Conover, and Joseph Clark.

THE BALLET

A shaft of reddish-gold light illuminates the figure of a man, who through a series of stylized gestures suggests a pioneer opening up the West. Soon others join him: pioneers, cowboys, prospectors, Mexicans, and frontier women. The moving tableau mounts in contrapuntal harmony, like an ode to the American West; then, with the gesture of a gun firing, the stage suddenly goes black. The lights come up on a sunny street in a bustling frontier town. After Pat Garrett and a group of cowboys enter and mingle with the townsfolk, a woman in tasteful, Eastern-style dress appears with her young son, Billy, who gazes in wonder at the colorful characters around him. As they depart, four girls tease Alias, a sinister and haughty figure.

To a tender melody, Billy returns to dance with his mother, who playfully chucks him under the chin. Then a fight breaks out between Alias and another cowboy. Alias pulls a gun to shoot the cowboy, but hits Billy's mother instead. Stunned, Billy looks first at his dead mother and then at the villain. Pulling out a knife, Billy stabs Alias in the back, and then rushes off.

Time has passed, and Billy returns as a young man, now a feared outlaw. In a solo that tells us something of what he has become, Billy performs a set sequence of stylized movements expressing pride, anger, and a life of hunting and being hunted. A soft interlude that brings back the past to Billy is quickly suppressed as he repeats his vengeful dance. Alias returns, in the guise of a land agent. Billy first stalks him, then, spinning in pirouettes and thrust by his anger into a double *tour en l'air*, he lands with his gun drawn and shoots Alias in the back. Billy

callously kicks the corpse and repeats his initial dance of revenge until the scene goes black.

The next episode takes place in the glow of a campfire. Sheriff Pat Garrett is playing cards with Billy. It soon becomes apparent that Billy cannot refrain from cheating even his friend. After an argument, Garrett gallops off, with a smirking Billy flicking his hat in ironic farewell. Billy returns to his cohorts at the fireside; suddenly, they hear shots. A gun battle begins, and soon only Billy is left, surrounded by his pursuers. Attempting to escape, he trips over one of the corpses, and Pat Garrett and his deputy, Alias, capture him. In a last defiant gesture, Billy snatches Alias's gun and shoots him in the back.

Thinking that the lawlessness has ended, the townsfolk and cowboys celebrate in a lighthearted dance. Only a beautiful Mexican girl in a glittering violet dress seems to be distressed. She is Billy's sweetheart, and she finally leaves sadly.

The next scene takes place in the jail. Alias, now Billy's jailer, seems more concerned with their card game than with keeping a watchful eye on his prisoner. By a ruse, Billy snatches his gun and cold-bloodedly shoots him.

A whispering, lonely theme opens the next scene, in which the escaped Billy rides alone looking for a hideout. Alias, disguised as a frontier guide, leads him to a secluded refuge and then stalks away. Temporarily secure, the exhausted Billy takes off his chaps, hat, and guns and begins to play solitaire. A vision of his sweetheart comes to him, and they dance a tender *pas de deux*. Billy's abstracted manner indicates that she is never fully real to him, perhaps only an echo of the love he still feels for his mother. Billy lies down to sleep as his vision fades from view.

Alias furtively leads Pat Garrett to Billy's hideout. Billy awakens suddenly, and the outlaw and his former friend circle each other in the darkness. Billy shouts, "¿Quién es?" ("Who is it?"), but hears no response. Chuckling to himself, he starts to light a cigarette. Garrett sees the flame, leaps spinning into the air, takes aim, and shoots Billy. The outlaw's body arches backward with a spasmodic jerk, and he sinks slowly to the ground in death. A group of Mexican women mourn their beloved outlaw as the scene goes black.

In the golden shaft of light, the procession of pioneers resumes, freed by the elimination of lawless outcasts like Billy. In the final moments of the ballet, they kneel and arch backward in a gesture of homage to their nation's destiny.

Terry Orr and Marianna Tcherkassky in Billy the Kid. *American Ballet Theatre*

RODEO

1942 ◆ *Music by Aaron Copland* ◆ *Choreography by Agnes de Mille*

When Antony Tudor created his *Judgment of Paris* in 1938, the role of Venus was taken by an American dancer-choreographer, Agnes de Mille. De Mille was no stranger to England, for she had studied with Marie Rambert and performed there on and off for the better part of a decade. But her own origins were far from London. Born in New York City, she graduated cum laude from the University of California. While there, she no doubt benefited from the fact that she was the daughter of William C. de Mille, brother of Cecil B., the legendary Hollywood director, and had studied with Theodore Koslov, a noted Russian dancer who had come to teach and perform in Hollywood. Gifted with a quick and retentive intelligence, De Mille synthesized Koslov's ballet training with her own observations of the American dance scene and soon embarked on a fledgling career of solo dance recitals.

During stays in England and the Continent, she formed her connections with Rambert's company, appeared in British musical productions, and choreographed the 1933 London production of *Nymph Errant*. When she returned to the United States to join the brand-new Ballet Theatre, her first work for that company's premiere season was *Black Ritual*, an all-black ballet which proved a noble failure. But her next work, *Three Virgins and a Devil* (1941), was a smashing comic success that established De Mille as a choreographer.

Philip Jerry, Tom Fowler, Jerel Hilding, and Gregory Huffman in Rodeo. *The Joffrey Ballet*

The following year, De Mille created for Sergei Denham's Ballet Russe de Monte Carlo, a company of international dancers, a ballet unmitigatedly reflective of her American roots. *Rodeo, or, The Courting at Burnt Ranch* starred the British Frederic Franklin, the Slavic Casimir Kokitch, and De Mille herself. At its triumphant premiere at the Metropolitan Opera House in New York on October 16, 1942, *Rodeo* received twenty-two curtain calls. De Mille went on to choreograph the Broadway musical *Oklahoma!* (1943), an expanded variation on the Americana themes portrayed in *Rodeo*.

Rodeo is certainly not as profound a portrait of the American West as *Billy the Kid*, nor is it as unabashedly bold as *Frankie and Johnny*. Indeed, its pantomimic representations of Western gestures and its use of American tap dancing echo elements of the two earlier ballets. Furthermore, its theme of a woman whose primary goal is to "find her man," and who sacrifices her individuality to do so, provides ample cause for feminist displeasure. However, De Mille's creation remains craftsmanlike and original and also enjoys the added advantage of Copland's magnificent score. Given the proper performance, it offers a fresh and vivid view of the American spirit.

THE BALLET

A syncopated, brassy tune, bursting with the rousing spirit of the American West, precedes the rise of the curtain on a Western tableau. Against a background of an open, sun-drenched prairie, a group of cowboys are standing around a corral, waiting for the weekly rodeo to begin. One of the figures moves and, surprisingly, it is a young girl dressed like her companions—only her pigtails protruding from under her stetson set her apart.

The Champion Roper enters, energetically twirling an imaginary lasso. The Cowgirl's attempts to join the men are turned back by their hard stares. Left alone, she mimes riding a horse; moments later, when the cowboys return and strut around, she mimics their movements.

The Ranch Owner's Daughter and three of her girl friends now enter the corral to watch the rodeo. Their demure and flirtatious demeanor contrasts sharply with that of the tomboyish Cowgirl. The Champion Roper shows off for the young

ladies, as do the Head Wrangler and the rest of the cowboys. The Cowgirl thrusts herself awkwardly into the group, and to the amusement of one and all, stumbles and falls to the ground.

The Head Wrangler ignores the Cowgirl's desperate attempts to attract him and flirts instead with the Ranch Owner's Daughter. As the men continue their rodeo feats, the Cowgirl frantically tries to emulate them, becoming more and more of a nuisance. Finally, the Head Wrangler tells her to leave, which she does, but not without making a fuss. As the rodeo comes to an end, the men start to leave with the girls; the Cowgirl returns just in time to see the Head Wrangler in pursuit of the Ranch Owner's Daughter. She dejectedly dances out her anguish. Oblivious to the Cowgirl, the Champion Roper enters and, snapping his fingers, happily tap-shuffles across the corral. The Cowgirl, in tears, throws herself to the ground.

A drop curtain of brilliant blue painted with galloping horses comes down on the scene and serves as background for an interlude in which, without musical accompaniment, four couples perform a lively square dance to their own hand-clapping and the shouts of a caller.

The drop rises to reveal a patio with the ranch house in the rear. It is time for the Saturday night dance. Seated on a bench to one side of the house is the lonely Cowgirl, who watches forlornly as the cowboys dance with the young women. The Champion Roper and the Head Wrangler emerge from the ranch house to urge the Cowgirl to join the dance, but the Ranch Owner's Daughter soon calls them away. Alone again, the Cowgirl once more falls to the ground in tears.

The Ranch Owner's Daughter, the Head Wrangler, and three couples then run out of the house for a dance. The Cowgirl joins the ladies in the group for a moment, but is soon left without a partner. She waltzes awkwardly with an imaginary partner, landing at the side of the Champion Roper, who leans dreamily on her shoulder, as if she were a fence post. The Cowgirl begins to cry, and the sympathetic Champion Roper offers to teach her to dance. Clumsily she follows him in a waltz until the Head Wrangler and the Ranch Owner's Daughter waltz by gracefully. At the sight of their harmonious rapport, the Cowgirl struts off with determination. All the couples come from the house to perform a slow waltz of intricate patterns.

A loud burst of music heralds the beginning of the evening's

Overleaf: Gregory Huffman and members of the Joffrey Ballet in Rodeo

highpoint, the hoedown. The music comes to an abrupt halt, however, as the Cowgirl returns in a garish red dress and awkward black boots. Amazed at how girlish and even pretty she looks, the Head Wrangler approaches her with sudden interest, but the Champion Roper stops him. The Cowgirl and the Roper dance romantically until the hoedown resumes in full force with much foot-stomping and skirt-shaking.

In the midst of this joyous reeling, the Head Wrangler and the Champion Roper both compete for the Cowgirl. The Roper lures her toward him by executing a subtly seductive tap-travel. The Cowgirl also taps, but still gazes dreamily into the face of the Head Wrangler. Not to be outdone, the Champion Roper performs a virtuosic tap solo, which draws the Cowgirl away from the Wrangler. She kneels to admire his fancy footwork, as does everyone else.

At the conclusion of the tap dance, the Ranch Owner's Daughter asserts herself, but the tables have turned and the two men are more concerned with winning the Cowgirl's attentions. Finally, when the Champion Roper plants a fervent kiss on the Cowgirl's lips, she realizes that he has been her man all along. Everyone launches into the riotous conclusion of the hoedown as the curtain falls.

Russell Sultzbach as the Champion Roper and Beatriz Rodriguez as the Cowgirl. The Joffrey Ballet

FANCY FREE

1944 ◆ *Music by Leonard Bernstein* ◆ *Choreography by Jerome Robbins*

Among the members of Ballet Theatre's corps de ballet in its premiere season in 1940 was a young New York City–born dancer, Jerome Robbins. Robbins had come to Ballet Theatre with a background of richly varied dance studies and performances in such Broadway musicals as *Great Lady*, *Stars in Your Eyes*, and George Balanchine's *Keep Off the Grass*. At Ballet Theatre, he immediately established himself as a soloist of unique presence and talent in ballets like De Mille's *Three Virgins and a Devil*, Lichine's *Helen of Troy*, Fokine's *Bluebeard* and *Petrouchka*, and Tudor's *Romeo and Juliet*. But Robbins's interest in the dance went beyond performing. In the early

forties, he made his first attempts at choreography at Camp Tamiment in the Catskills, but these fledgling works were never seen on the New York stage. However, early in 1944, the directors of Ballet Theatre commissioned Robbins to create a small ballet.

Robbins wanted a distinctly American theme, probably because Ballet Theatre's repertoire at the time was overburdened with works in the Russian classical style and because patriotism was running high in wartime America. Leonard Bernstein, who had recently become an overnight sensation as a last-minute replacement for the ailing New York Philharmonic

Fernando Bujones in Fancy Free. *American Ballet Theatre*

conductor, Bruno Walter, was engaged for the score; Oliver Smith, whose decor for De Mille's *Rodeo* contributed in no small measure to its success, was to design the ballet. Despite much enthusiasm about Robbin's scenario for the commonplace theme of sailors on one-night shore leave in New York City, the creation of the ballet was not without its problems, most of which were logistic. Bernstein was in great demand for conducting assignments throughout America, Robbins was on tour with Ballet Theatre, and Smith was in Mexico. It was only through the use of long-distance telephone, letters, cables, and tapes that the ballet was completed.

At its premiere at the Metropolitan Opera House in New York on April 18, 1944, *Fancy Free* was an unqualified triumph. Ballet Theatre's New York season was extended two weeks to allow twelve additional performances. Instantly acclaimed an American classic, the work assured Robbins's place as a major American choreographic talent. Within the year, Robbins, Bernstein, and Smith had created, with songwriters Betty Comden and Adolph Green, a smash-hit musical comedy, *On the Town*, based on *Fancy Free*. A pattern was thus established: for many years, Robbins's career would be divided between the ballet stage and the American musical comedy theater.

In *Fancy Free*, Robbins created a perfectly structured ballet in which story, music, characterization, gesture, and dance idioms are melded to form a totally satisfying portrait of American life. Incorporating colloquial, off-the-street behavior, authentic 1940s dance styles, and classical ballet steps, he captured the atmosphere of a particular period with poignant sensitivity, while also retaining a timeless esthetic composition. *Fancy Free* remains as infectiously audacious today as in 1944 and provides a singular opportunity for unforgettable performances by the dancers undertaking the three male roles. Indeed, the original cast, including Robbins himself as the rhumba-dancing sailor, Harold Lang, and John Kriza, is remembered fondly to this day.

THE BALLET

A jukebox is heard playing a soulful Billie Holiday song as the curtain rises on a New York side street during World War II. There is the framework of a bar and its interior, a lamppost on the corner, and, in the background, a suggestion of skyscrapers with crisscrossing patterns of lights. A bartender, lazily turning

Fancy Free, *New York City Ballet: opposite, Jean-Pierre Frohlich; above, Peter Martins, Bart Cook, and Jean-Pierre Frohlich*

the pages of a newspaper, stands behind the bar. To a burst of percussive swing from the orchestra, three sailors spin, in cartwheels, onto the scene.

The gobs, in summer whites, are overflowing with pent-up energy. They leap into the air and strut about, playfully tripping and kicking one another. Obviously looking for action, they amble into the bar, order three beers, toast their fellowship, and take deep swigs from their mugs. Two sailors outwit the third for payment, and then they all swagger out. Standing under the lamppost, they each take a stick of gum and compete to see who can throw his wrapper the farthest.

The music suddenly becomes a jazzy siren song as, from the street behind the bar, a young woman appears in a flouncy yellow skirt, tight black jacket and black pumps. Seeing their first potential conquest, the buddies begin to primp and show off, but to no avail. One of the sailors grabs the girl's red shoulder bag and imitates her mincing walk. The girl stamps her feet in protest, but only succeeds in making the boys more teasing. She finally retrieves her purse and struts off with two of the sailors in determined pursuit.

The remaining sailor is left alone for only a moment before the arrival of another young woman, who wears a simple office dress and seems softer than the other girl. Overflowing with happiness at his good fortune, the sailor approaches the girl and starts fast-talking her. After the stage goes black briefly, we see the sailor and the girl seated on the barstools. He concludes a tale of his wartime bravery and then asks her to dance. To a sultry blues, their duet becomes increasingly sensual, yet never loses a certain innocence. At its peak, the sailor lifts the girl high above him, and as he slowly lets her down she touches his lips with her finger.

The two other sailors then fly back onto the scene with the first girl, who now flirtatiously enjoys their company. The third sailor tries unsuccessfully to escape with his girl, but the two girls catch sight of each other and reveal, with giggles, that they are friends. The group goes to the table, and, after a little melee over seats, the three sailors drag the girls onto the dance floor. When another contest for the girls' attention ensues, the girls suggest a competition in which they will be the judges.

The contest begins. The first sailor dances a solo of virtuosic bravado, beginning with quick double *tours en l'air* landing in a split, followed by somersaults, high leg extensions, kicks, thigh-slapping, and whirling *chaîné* turns. In his enthusiasm, he bounds on top of the bar and jumps off, leaping high into the air and touching his toes. He ends with an abrupt sustained extension of one leg to the side, his hands clasped over his head in a triumphant prizefight gesture.

Next, the shy sailor begins his solo to a quiet waltz, swinging one leg and then the other. His movements are lyrical executions of turns, extensions, and jumps marked by a characteristic romantic swaying. He finishes his dance in a slow slide to the floor at the feet of the second girl. The third sailor's dance is an unabashedly sexy version of a rhumba. With the tight Latin pride of a matador, he seductively wiggles his hips, snaps his fingers, and claps his hands. He sinuously slides one leg to the floor and flutters his hand as if to cool off this "hot" gesture. Banging out the rhumba rhythm on the barstool, the bar, and even on his chest, he finishes with a flourish.

The ladies' choice is not an easy one. The impatient sailors break into another fight, this time in earnest. They push the girls around, even knocking one of them to the floor, then fly over the bar. The incensed girls walk out in a huff. Suddenly the sailors are aware they are alone. They run out into the street, but the ladies are nowhere in sight. The boys mime an "Aw, shucks!" and are immediately smitten with the aches and pains of their fisticuffs. Leaning chummily against each other, they go back to the bar to repeat their friendship toast, then go outside again for another gum wrapper competition.

As a low-down piano blues plays, a third girl, clearly more available than the previous two, slinks in suggestively and pauses to place a finger coyly to her cheek. The buddies press tightly against each other and tilt to and fro, at a steep angle, as they watch this vision. One sailor breaks from the group, but his buddies pull him back, reminding him of what happened last time. The three begin walking away with a great show of casualness as the girl disappears beyond the bar. There is a brief pause. Then suddenly, one by one, the boys race frantically after her, holding down their hats and skidding on one leg.

APPALACHIAN SPRING

1944 ◆ Music by Aaron Copland ◆ Choreography by Martha Graham

Perhaps because they were pioneers themselves, the creators of American modern dance, especially those of the "second generation," began to explore through their dance the roots and nature of the American sensibility. As early as 1931, Doris Humphrey created a seminal work based on an American religious sect, the Shakers. Throughout the thirties, she and her partner-collaborator, Charles Weidman, continued to explore American themes. Martha Graham, who had escaped from the overriding pseudo-orientalism of the Denishawn Company even earlier than Humphrey and Weidman, had been deeply committed to finding her own style of dance expression since 1926. In 1935, she created a solo work entitled *Frontier*, which expressed the thoughts of a woman facing the prospect of a pioneer existence.

Graham had employed Aaron Copland's Variations for Piano for a dance she called *Dithyramb* in 1931, and for more than a decade since then, she and Copland had intended to create a

work together. In the early forties, the Elizabeth Sprague Coolidge Foundation asked Graham to choreograph three new works for its festival at the Library of Congress and also commissioned a Copland score for one of these works. Graham, who had continued her investigation of Americana in dances such as *American Document, Letter to the World*, and *Salem Shore*, not surprisingly presented the composer with a scenario for still another piece of Americana. The resulting work, premiered in Washington in 1944, was entitled *Appalachian Spring* (from the title of a Hart Crane poem) and possessed a score that would prove to be one of Copland's most beloved.

The ballet itself was both a culmination of all the Graham works that preceded it and a turning point in the development of the Graham genre. The work marked her furthest departure from the investigation of the "interior landscape" which had most prominently characterized her earlier works (and to which she would return in her later mythic ballets). The characters in

Martha Graham in the original production of her Appalachian Spring

Appalachian Spring possess perhaps the most fully realized identities, independent of the inner world of the heroine's mind, of any portrayed in Graham works.

In the simple context of a frontier wedding, Graham makes her most positive statement of the triumph of the human spirit. Her economical use of movement, gesture, and stance and her blending of balletic steps with her characteristic contractions and releases resulted in a ballet that is accessible to the broadest public, even those unfamiliar with modern dance idioms. For this reason, *Appalachian Spring* may well outlast most of the other Graham works and is already the piece that the public most closely associates with her company (which is the only one performing it today).

THE BALLET

The curtain rises in silence on a dark landscape, given definition by Isamu Noguchi's spare structural outline of a farmhouse and, opposite it, the suggestion of a fence. A subdued, hymnlike melody begins and with it a muted light, like the dawn of a new day, illuminates the scene. In a solemn procession, the ballet's characters enter: the stern Preacher; the stately, warmly human Pioneer Woman; the Husbandman, followed by his demure Bride; and, last, four female Followers of the Preacher. As the Husbandman passes by the house, he touches its wall with equal feelings of awe and aspiration; he then goes to the fence and looks out at the frontier. The Pioneer Woman sits on a rocking chair and the Bride on the porch steps.

To a joyous exclamation of string arpeggios, the four Followers begin a dance, marked by hops, sudden balances, and clapping of their cupped hands, which is representative of their energetic spirit and religious zeal. The Pioneer Woman joins them in the dance, which ends in a kneeling, praying gesture. After the Pioneer Woman dances a solo of maternal assurance, she sits by the house with the Bride.

Next, the Husbandman dances a solo in which he conveys his hope for the future with bravado turns, handstands, hopping, galloping, and near-balletic leaps. Going to his bride, he urges her to dance with him. Their duet is filled with tender innocence, but also reveals their inner strength. The Preacher next descends from his crude "pulpit," where he has remained aloof throughout the preceding action. His religious fervor lifts him

into the air and brings him to his knees. His four adoring Followers join him in an intricate dance that carries them to the point of near frenzy. But the mania subsides when the Pioneer Woman moves among them urging spiritual temperance.

As the Preacher and Followers withdraw, the Pioneer Woman sits beside the Bride, who seems to have been lost in her own thoughts. The Bride now dances a soliloquy suggesting the dreams of a young woman embarking on a new life. She moves to her husband, and back to the Pioneer Woman, who mimes the cradling of a baby, which the Bride briefly takes from her and then returns to the older woman.

The Preacher comes forward and the Followers dance around him while the young couple embrace and then gaze at the landscape as if looking toward their shared destiny. The Preacher walks with the Pioneer Woman as the Husbandman approaches. He shakes the Preacher's hand, and the Preacher in turn grants his benediction to the young couple, who then break into a kind of square dance, interspersed with solos of private joy. At the conclusion of the dance, the Preacher, who has once more returned to his pulpit, is urged by his Followers to dance. He hands them his hat, which they hold aloft, and breaks into a solo of terrifyingly bizarre religious frenzy. Once again, the Pioneer Woman restores calm by kneeling in prayer.

The Husbandman makes another solo dance statement while the Pioneer Woman sits by the Bride. A merry group dance follows, observed by the Husbandman, who has joined his wife. Now, as if suddenly aware that her future would bring not only joy but tribulation as well, the Bride dances another solo representative of her fears. But in the end, she sits briefly on the rocker to compose herself, and the reassuring Husbandman takes her to him. They dance together in mutual trust.

The Followers and the Pioneer Woman then whirl into an ecstatic dance of celebration. Encouraged by the happy support of the community, the Husbandman embraces the Bride, assuring her that they will endure the hardships as well as the times of peaceful security. The Pioneer Woman leads a procession from the scene: first the Followers and then the Preacher move offstage after her. In a tableau of the hope of a young couple facing an unknown future together, the Bride sits once again on the rocker and the Husbandman stands firmly behind her with his hand resting on her shoulder, as the curtain falls.

Takako Asakawa and Tim Wengard in Appalachian Spring. *The Martha Graham Dance Company, as seen on WNET/13's "Dance in America"*

SYMPHONIC VARIATIONS

1946 ◆ *Music by César Franck* ◆ *Choreography by Frederick Ashton*

During World War II, Frederick Ashton, who had been chief choreographer of the Sadler's Wells Ballet, served in the RAF. Like many others fearful for the future, he sought spiritual solace—in the works of Saint Theresa of Avila and Saint John of the Cross and in music, particularly Franck's Symphonic Variations for Piano and Orchestra, a work of strong religiosity.

When, in 1946, for its first postwar season, Sadler's Wells asked Ashton for a new ballet, the choreographer saw an opportunity to use Franck's composition and also to convey in dance his immersion in mysticism. At first, Ashton devised an elaborate scenario involving the concept of Divine Love conveyed through the natural cycle of the seasons, but he soon realized that ballet in England was becoming entirely too literary and that his new work would have to dispense with such allusions and decorative embellishments.

Throughout the rehearsal period of *Symphonic Variations*, Ashton revised his concept and redefined the choreography, altering it from the original idea of a large group work to an abstract ballet for three men and three women. When Michael Somes, the ballet's *premier danseur*, sustained an injury, the premiere of the new work was postponed for five weeks; during that time, Ashton revised and pared down his choreography even more. The result was a work of such sublime purity that it is considered by many critics to be a masterpiece of classicism equaled only by Fokine's *Les Sylphides* and Balanchine's *Apollo*.

Ashton is hailed as the choreographer who has most brilliantly preserved the essence of the nineteenth-century Romantic narrative ballet tradition, rendered in unique twentieth-century terms. However, in *Symphonic Variations*, he undeniably revealed that beneath his craft in story-telling lay a profound understanding and love of ballet classicism coupled with an ability to portray it abstractly with pristine simplicity and lyrical technical virtuosity. *Symphonic Variations* demonstrated several important realities of postwar British ballet: that two choreographic directions—the narrative and the abstract—were firmly entrenched in the repertoire of the Sadler's Wells Ballet (later the Royal Ballet); that they flowed with equal inspiration from the genius of the same man, Frederick Ashton; and that British ballet dancers, epitomized by Margot Fonteyn, could perform both these styles with inimitable perfection.

THE BALLET

The curtain rises to reveal a backdrop of luminous pastel green and yellow crisscrossed with curving, slanted black lines. Before it six dancers stand motionless. The three women face front in a straight line, each with her right leg crossed slightly bent and resting on *pointe* in front of the standing leg. Their left arms cross close in front of their chests parallel to the floor, while their right arms curve over their heads, which incline with downcast eyes to the side. Three men stand with their backs to the women in a parallel line behind them. The men also have their legs crossed like the women's, but their arms rest gently at their sides.

The music begins its statement of pronounced but subdued grandeur while the dancers remain still. As the piano solo enters with its reflective melody, the women begin to move. They stop and hold another pose as the orchestra picks up the piano's melody. One of the male dancers turns and begins to dance with the women in configurations of pure classicism, reminiscent but not imitative of movements in Balanchine's *Apollo*. The man pauses, and the women dance around him until he partners each of them individually.

The other men join the first, taking up the position of the women at the ballet's opening, while the women remain still. As the variations on the opening theme progress, these two men take the part of the orchestra, while the first echoes the piano solo. The women now join the men; two women perform a duet which becomes a *pas de trois* as one of the men joins in. Next, as five of the dancers remain still, the principal male performs a solo of quiet virtuosity. In the next variation, the ballerina is accompanied by the three men, who dance in harmony behind her. The high point is reached in the *pas de deux* of the principal *danseur* and the ballerina, who move with exquisite spiritual tenderness, the ballerina literally floating with the support of her partner in fluttering *bourrées*.

There is a brief pause before the piano begins to trill delicately in tremulous expectation, soon to be released in lyrical orchestral cascades. The dancers flow together in rapidly mounting virtuosic combinations until, in the music's last magisterial measures, they return to their original tableau of poetic contemplation.

Opposite: Moira Shearer, Margot Fonteyn, Michael Somes, and Pamela May in the original production of
Symphonic Variations. *Sadler's Wells Ballet*
Overleaf: Merle Park in Symphonic Variations. *The Royal Ballet*

THEME AND VARIATIONS

1947 ◆ Music by Peter Ilyich Tchaikovsky ◆ Choreography by George Balanchine

In the late 1940s, Ballet Theatre's resident choreographers were under constant pressure to produce new works to satisfy the demands of an ever-increasing public and growing number of stars. Thus, when the company's directors sought a new ballet to showcase the extraordinary gifts of prima ballerina Alicia Alonso and her partner, *premier danseur* Igor Youskevitch, they had to look outside the company. They approached George Balanchine with the idea of a ballet set to the last movement of Tchaikovsky's Suite no. 3 in G Major, "Tema con Variazioni." Responding with an immediate and confident "Yes," Balanchine set to work and in a total of thirty-nine hours' rehearsal time created the nineteen-minute *Theme and Variations*, presenting the two stars with a dazzling vehicle and Ballet Theatre with one of the greatest gems in its repertoire.

Although Balanchine had paid due homage to Petipa and the nineteenth-century classical ballet tradition of Imperial Russia in his earlier *Ballet Imperial* (1941), he distilled the essence of this tribute in *Theme and Variations*. Its ballerina role is one of the most demanding ever created in an abstract classical ballet, the *danseur* must almost equally be a technical virtuoso, and each member of the corps de ballet is as integral a part of the work as its principals. The clarity of the work most probably derives from the impeccably refined score by Tchaikovsky—next to Stravinsky, Balanchine's most fertile source of inspiration. So fond was the choreographer of the entire Suite no. 3, that more than twenty years later he created a ballet employing its first three movements, to which he appended *Theme and Variations*. If that work, *Tchaikovsky Suite No. 3*, has been interpreted as a choreographic essay on Balanchine's view of women, then by extension, *Theme and Variations* may be seen as a paean to the classical ballerina, embodying the maxim most commonly attributed to Balanchine, "Ballet is woman."

THE BALLET

After a brief, triumphant overture, the curtain rises on a stage ablaze with light; fourteen dancers stand in two symmetrical formations at oblique angles to each other. Each group is composed of four female corps de ballet dancers and two female soloists; the ballerina heads the left formation, and the *danseur* the right.

To the stately opening theme, the first of twelve dance variations, the ballerina moves with simple but perfectly executed *pointes tendues* and classical *ports de bras*. She concludes her opening combination, and the *danseur* responds in exact imitation. They repeat their movements singly and then together, and bow courteously to each other before leaving the stage in opposite directions.

The corps de ballet and soloists move forward on the next variation to perform delicate yet deliberate prancing steps on *pointe*, echoing in movement the music of the low pizzicato cellos. The third variation, of dizzying momentum, is performed by the ballerina with the corps de ballet behind her. With a virtuosity that seems to explode spontaneously without preparation, she spins in *soutenus*, pirouettes, and flying *gargouillades* which carry her across the stage in a vision that is at once a blur of bravado movement and a highly articulated statement of technical precision.

A restrained recapitulation of the theme in the fourth variation accompanies the corps de ballet and soloists as they perform the graciously complex interweaving configurations which have become a hallmark of Balanchine's choreography.

The *danseur* now enters down the center space vacated by the corps to perform the fifth variation, a theme of noble expansiveness. To its opening measures, he leaps softly from one foot to the other with legs in overlapping extensions to the front, punctuated by whispering beats in the air. When the melody changes to a richly rephrased statement of the theme, he twice leaps *en tournant*, opening his arms toward the audience in a gesture of courtly embrace. The sixth variation, a continuation of the fifth, is a robust statement in which the *danseur* whirls in a series of pirouettes before a reprise of the music and gestures of the preceding variation.

The seventh variation, a fugue, is danced in cascading canon by the corps de ballet and soloists. The *danseur* returns for the eighth variation, in which he crosses the stage in flying *sautés* with double *ronds de jambe en l'air*. Then, at center stage, he performs an incredibly difficult series of alternating double *tours en l'air* and double pirouettes.

The corps de ballet then *bourrées* into a single line with a space in the center, which is taken by the ballerina for the opening of the ninth variation. To its plaintive measures, she is supported by the corps while she executes a series of fluid

pas de chat en tournant, and whirling *chaîné* turns that finish in a triumphant classical pose.

Just at that moment, a poignant interjection by the solo violin introduces the eleventh variation as the *danseur* enters. Although he and the ballerina move toward each other with the aristocratic courtesy typical of the nineteenth-century classical *pas de deux*, the adagio they perform is clearly Balanchine's twentieth-century rendering of that form. Supporting the ballerina under her arms, the *danseur* assists her in the delicately hesitant opening measures in a series of *sissonnes fermées*, front, back, and to the side. They dance together in positions of elegant articulation, separate briefly for individually executed combinations, then rejoin to repeat the opening lifts.

To one of those unforgettable Tchaikovskian resolutions, the ballerina, supported by her partner with one hand, rises on *pointe* to execute a slow *développé à la seconde*, which she sustains while the *danseur* changes his support from one hand to the other. As the music mounts, there follows a series of partnered combinations which peak as the ballerina is promenaded in *grands ronds de jambe* into arabesque again and again and finally finishes, as the melody seems to drift away, in a last perfect arabesque.

A sudden fanfare sounds and as the ballerina and *danseur* rush off, the corps de ballet and soloists, now joined by male partners, enter for the twelfth variation. They perform an extended polonaise which comprises a series of group variations of magisterial brilliance. The dancers are led by the principals in a grand cortege in which the men polonaise in stately measure while the women twirl in *chaîné* turns at their side. There is a restatement of the rapturous adagio for the ballerina and *danseur*, followed by exuberant variations for all the men and for all the women.

In the exhilarating conclusion—one that only Balanchine could have composed—all the dancers join together in kaleidoscopic configurations of shifting and swirling patterns that reflect the crashing crescendos of the music. After a brief restatement of the polonaise, the music begins its last resounding rise and fall; the men leap in double *tours en l'air*, the women pirouette, and then the entire ensemble freezes in a tableau of *révérence* to the ballerina, who is lifted aloft on her partner's shoulder.

développés to the front, side, and back into an *arabesque penchée*; the corps, with joined hands, *bourrées* in latticelike formations through one another's arms. At the music's quietest moment, the ballerina's attendants release her and float on *pointe* from the stage.

For the supremely virtuosic tenth variation, the ballerina, perfectly echoing the mounting acceleration of the music, at first prances with stabbing thrusts of her *pointes* and then moves into a rapid succession of arm and leg positions in constantly shifting directions. She concludes with swift pirouettes, flying

Above: Peter Martins in Theme and Variations. *New York City Ballet*
Opposite: Gelsey Kirkland in American Ballet Theatre's production of Theme and Variations

ORPHEUS

1948 ◆ *Music by Igor Stravinsky* ◆ *Choreography by George Balanchine*

For the 1948 season of Ballet Society, his recently established and still financially troubled ballet company, George Balanchine commissioned Igor Stravinsky to write a score for a new ballet based on the Orpheus legend. Balanchine had tackled this theme once before in his controversial 1936 treatment of Gluck's *Orfeo ed Euridice* for the Metropolitan Opera. This time, unfettered by conventional taste, Balanchine set to work with Stravinsky on the score for *Orpheus*, while Lincoln Kirstein commissioned the innovative sculptor, Isamu Noguchi, to design the sets and costumes, which, in their ultimate organic abstractionism, bore no trace of ancient Greece.

The collaborative effort on this work was perhaps the closest in the history of contemporary ballet. Stravinsky, who had steeped himself in the music of Monteverdi's *Orfeo*, would request from Balanchine the length of each dance sequence down to the last second; however, the spare, muted lyricism of his final score bore no hint of this almost mechanically exact process. For his part, Balanchine created a ballet of lean gestural poetry devoid of the sharp neoclassic definition of most of his earlier work. Noguchi, master of spare yet evocative theatrical design, provided *Orpheus* with sets and costumes which in their powerful and bizarre immediacy provided the perfect setting for the work's mysterious music and fluid, fantastic choreography.

Orpheus was first presented in April, 1948, at New York's City Center, a municipally supported theater. During one of its first performances, Morton Baum, a member of the City Center finance committee who had no previous knowledge of ballet, literally wandered into the theater. So smitten was Baum with *Orpheus* that he went to the City Center board and convinced them to take on Ballet Society as their resident company. Renamed the New York City Ballet, the company opened its first season at the City Center on October 11, 1948, with a program of three Balanchine masterpieces: *Concerto Barocco*, *Symphony in C*, and *Orpheus*. The future of one of the greatest ballet companies in history was thus assured.

Besides its historical importance to the New York City Ballet, *Orpheus* demonstrated that Balanchine was not only a master of neoclassicism but also an ingenious interpreter of lyric classical poetry in dance. A work entirely devoid of conventional ballet technique, *Orpheus* displays the most subtly refined construction, requiring of its dancers a sensitive grasp of poetic

dramatic interpretation. From the outset, it marked the New York City Ballet as a company that would enjoy a repertoire of the widest range because of Balanchine's unique artistry. It also hinted of even greater Balanchine-Stravinsky collaborations in works that would continue to stun the ballet world.

THE BALLET

Muted harp and strings provide a brief, haunting prelude before the curtain rises to reveal the lone figure of Orpheus, standing at the grave of Eurydice, his back to the audience in a posture eloquently expressive of grief. Against the calf of his leg rests his lyre, the instrument of his divinely inspired song. In the distance are three large white rocks.

One at a time, three of Orpheus's friends enter the scene. One carries a golden mask, the second a bow, the third an object that resembles a woman's wig. Approaching the grieving Orpheus, they plant the bow upright into the earth, place the wig on the tip of the bow, and set the mask down on the ground before it. The effect is that of a symbol of Eurydice, the dead wife for whom Orpheus mourns. The friends gently place their hands on Orpheus's shoulder in a brief gesture of solace, and then depart.

Orpheus moves with a sigh, blindly reaching backward for his lyre. Plucking its strings forlornly, he performs a dance of anguish around the symbol of Eurydice. He concludes his soliloquy by prostrating himself before the bow, but still lifts one arm to pluck the instrument, which he has leaned against it.

From behind one of the rocks leaps a satyr, accompanied by four nature spirits. They dance to console Orpheus, but he remains grief-stricken and they depart. Once again, Orpheus picks up his lyre, bends deeply over it, and resumes his dance of mourning; at its conclusion, he hangs the instrument on the bow and from a distance plucks the air.

From a far corner of the landscape appears the Dark Angel, messenger of the gods. His deliberate sideward movements and the thin black tube that encircles his head and torso give him a menacing aspect. This somber figure dances around Orpheus with large, sinuous contracting movements. The Dark Angel then covers Orpheus's face with the golden mask and insists that Orpheus is to remain thus blinded until his journey is over.

Orpheus, *New York City Ballet: opposite,* Mikhail Baryshnikov and Kay Mazzo; *overleaf,* Adam Lüders
and Peter Martins

Taking up the lyre and reaching through it, he takes hold of Orpheus's hand to lead him on his journey to Hades in search of Eurydice.

As Orpheus follows the Dark Angel with hesitant, lunging steps, a billowing white curtain wafts to the ground behind them. That the two are descending deeper and deeper is indicated by the slow ascent of the luminous rocks.

The curtain then rises on Hades, a surreal vision framed by gigantic, protruding, riblike structures suspended in space. Dominating the open area is a mound around which stand the faceless figures of the Lost Souls, bending under the burden of the huge rocks they must carry. This eerie domain is guarded by Furies, their bodies covered with tentacles. Orpheus and the Dark Angel stand motionless, their hands still joined, as the Furies fling themselves into a dance of frenzied kicks, hops, spins, and stiletto prancing.

The Dark Angel now urges Orpheus to play his magical lyre. Together they pass through an intricate interlinking of arms, never letting go of each other. Orpheus falters a few times and falls weakly against his guide, but each time, with the Angel's help, Orpheus stands upright and dances with renewed vigor. Throughout his struggle, Orpheus continues to play the lyre and gradually soothes even the Furies and Lost Souls of Hades. As he finishes, the mound revolves to reveal the figure of Pluto, god of the underworld, and, in his grasp, Eurydice.

Eurydice reaches out in beckoning gestures to Orpheus, but Pluto moves forward threateningly as the leader of the Furies escorts the sightless Orpheus to Eurydice. Softened by the divine song of Orpheus, Pluto joins the hands of the reunited lovers; at that very instant, a tear of brilliant blue rends the sky, dropping into Hades like an omen from Heaven. Pluto will grant Orpheus's request to free Eurydice, but she will regain life only if Orpheus refrains from gazing upon her face until they return to Earth. For a short way, the Dark Angel, holding Orpheus's lyre aloft, leads the couple on their return journey, then disappears.

Now that they are alone together, Eurydice attempts to attract Orpheus and gain comfort from him. She rests her head on his shoulder, leans against his back, touches his face and embraces him. But Orpheus resists and will not look at her. Still yearning for his gaze, she wraps her body around his and swoons over his leg. Again and again, in this *pas de deux* of passionate desperation, Eurydice circles Orpheus and entwines herself around him, but he stoically keeps his pledge. Finally, Orpheus gives in to temptation, rips the mask from his face, and looks into the eyes of his beloved. At that moment, she sinks lifeless to the ground and is drawn from his frantically clinging arms into the billowing void. Orpheus, once more bereft, falls to the ground.

A fanfare sounds, and Orpheus, rising to his feet, sees that he is again on Earth. This landscape is different from the first, for in the distance is a large green knoll. Suddenly his lyre appears in the distant darkness. Orpheus rushes to it for consolation, but the instrument disappears as he tries to reach for it. The sky now bursts into a flaming blood red, and a terrifying Bacchante, with long, streaming hair, appears. Her movements are ruthless and staccato, punctuated with crouches and kicks. She calls forth her sister Bacchantes, who surround the horrified Orpheus. Still clinging to his mask, he struggles to escape.

The Bacchantes drag Orpheus to the ground, where their leader whisks the mask from his hand and flings it away. Finally, they push the helpless Orpheus back against the knoll; they tear his body limb from limb and scatter it out of sight and then victoriously prance away.

As the sky transmutes into a celestial blue, there appears the divine presence of Apollo, holding up a larger version of the mask of Orpheus. Kneeling, he plucks lovingly at the mask as if it were a lyre, and we hear the music of Orpheus floating heavenward. Apollo stands again, moves about the stage as if offering the symbol of Orpheus's music to the world, and finally places the mask at the base of the knoll. As he does so, the lyre of Orpheus, entwined in laurel leaves, rises from the knoll. Apollo steps back to hail it in a classical pose of homage, as the curtain falls.

CINDERELLA

1948 ◆ *Music by Sergei Prokofiev* ◆ *Choreography by Frederick Ashton*

For those choreographers who enjoy creating narrative ballets with an aura of fantasy, the fairy tales of the seventeenth-century French poet Charles Perrault are a rich source of inspiration. As his *Sleeping Beauty* served Petipa and Tchaikovsky, so did his *Cinderella* provide an equally ideal subject. In 1893, the first Russian ballet treatment of the fairy tale, with a score by Boris Schell and choreography by Ivanov, Cecchetti, and presumably Petipa, furnished the vehicle for the Maryinsky debut of the great Italian ballerina, Pierina Legnani. For the next fifty years, various choreographers, including Ruth Page (1931), Andrée Howard (1935), and Fokine (1938), created their own versions, but none to enduring effect. In Russia, in 1945, Sergei Prokofiev composed a score for a full-length ballet based on *Cinderella* (called *Zolushka* in Russian) which was staged by two companies: the Bolshoi Ballet (1945; choreography by Rostislav Zakharov) and the Kirov Ballet (1946; choreography by Konstantin Sergeyev).

Prokofiev's wistful score reached England, and Frederick Ashton, who had thought of choreographing *Cinderella* since 1939, set to work in the fall of 1948. Drawing upon the story's elements of fortuitous love as well as its comic pantomime, he created, in six weeks, England's first full-length ballet in the nineteenth-century narrative style. Ashton saw his ideal Cinderella in Margot Fonteyn, but when the ballerina sustained an injury, the title role went instead to the ravishing young Moira Shearer. At the last moment, he created the role of the second Ugly Stepsister for himself, *en travesti.*

At the ballet's premiere by the Sadler's Wells Ballet on December 23, 1948, Ashton's performance turned out to be an unexpected triumph—"the sort of accident," as Edwin Denby put it, "that happens to geniuses." Although the ballet was deemed flawed, it was enormously popular, with equal honors given to Shearer, Robert Helpmann (as the first Ugly Stepsister), and Pamela May (as the Fairy Godmother). But it was Ashton's performance that made *Cinderella* the unforgettable theatrical experience that it was, and later performances without him and the great mime Helpmann never seemed quite as compelling.

Coming at a time when Ashton's works had been losing critical favor, *Cinderella* proved that his choreographic powers remained unimpaired. Though it owed much to Petipa in its format and structure, the ballet was still, in its fluidity, inventiveness, comedic farce, and alluring grace, a work that was most definitely British. *Cinderella* captured the hearts of young and old, and its survival in the repertoire of the Royal Ballet is a testament to its timeless, enduring charm.

THE BALLET

The Act I curtain rises on the interior of the house of Cinderella's father. Kneeling beside the large fireplace is the hapless Cinderella, dressed in tattered clothes and a housemaid's kerchief. Across the room sit Cinderella's father and her two Ugly Stepsisters, who are sewing a scarf. At first the music expresses Cinderella's pathetic condition, but soon its mounting whirl of expectation indicates that the hideous stepsisters are preparing for an exciting evening.

The sisters squabble over the scarf, and their stepfather tries to calm them but leaves when he is ignored. The scarf is torn in two, and the sisters depart, battling all the way. Cinderella then dances alone with her broom, her movements expressing her longing for happiness. As she lights a candle and holds it up to the portrait of her dead mother, her father returns and tries to console her, but the dictatorial sisters soon come back.

Unexpectedly, a hunchbacked old woman in rags wanders into the room. Although the stepsisters resent the hag's presence, Cinderella kindly offers her a morsel of bread. The first stepsister starts to intimidate the beggar, but is strangely smitten with a toothache. The hag looks at Cinderella gratefully, then suddenly disappears. Next, a group of tradesmen enter to prepare the Ugly Stepsisters for the evening's ball. The ridiculous pair preen foolishly as they are decked out in their new finery, and the dancing master hypocritically praises their ridiculous gavotte. In a last whirlwind of excitement the primping stepsisters hurry off to their waiting coach.

The ignored Cinderella gazes forlornly into the fire, dreaming of the ball. All at once, to a spinning magical theme, the tattered hag reappears and her rags fly off to reveal a radiant fairy in a diaphanous gown, Cinderella's Fairy Godmother. She tells the astonished young girl that her dream has come true—she, too, will attend the ball. Four fairy attendants, representing the seasons, dance a group of variations before helping to prepare Cinderella for her adventure. Then the Fairy Godmother trans-

Overleaf: Anthony Dowell, Antoinette Sibley, and Frederick Ashton (far right) in Ashton's Cinderella. *The Royal Ballet*

forms a pumpkin into Cinderella's coach and dresses the girl in a gossamer gown of white and gold, a glittering crown, and a billowing cape. She warns Cinderella to return from the ball before the stroke of midnight, when this magical transformation will end. Surrounded by the fairies and a constellation of stars, Cinderella mounts the carriage that will take her to the ball as the curtain falls.

Act II takes place at the ball in the resplendent palace garden. Cinderella's stepsisters arrive with their stepfather, who is mortified by their outlandish appearance and behavior. The two sisters demonstrate their "brilliant" dance technique: the addled younger sister pathetically forgets everything she has learned; the rambunctious efforts of the smug elder sister present a laughable spectacle.

Prince Charming and his friends now enter the garden. After the friends perform a *pas de quatre*, a magical theme sounds. A coach draws up to the garden gate and out steps Cinderella, who dazzles the entire assembly with her radiance. No one, including the Ugly Stepsisters, knows the identity of this mysterious beauty. Prince Charming, struck by her loveliness, invites Cinderella to walk in the garden. After a masked dance and the prince's solo, Cinderella dances alone with a glittering, joyful assurance. The stepsisters, meanwhile, chatter jealously about this stranger who has won the prince's attention.

Cinderella and Prince Charming then perform a romantic and tender *pas de deux* in which the girl dances as if she were royally born. As a symbol of his new love, the prince gives Cinderella an orange, the most valuable gift of nature in the kingdom. (He also presents two oranges to the Ugly Stepsisters, who are atwitter with glee but soon quarrel over whose orange is the larger.)

As Cinderella and Prince Charming fervently lead the assembly in a grand waltz, the resounding chimes of the clock strike midnight. The startled Cinderella deserts the prince without explanation and flees through the crowd of guests, losing a slipper as she runs. At the garden gate, her splendid attire vanishes, and she is once again in her tattered dress. As the bewildered prince and guests look on, the music swells in a recapitulation of the lovers' duet.

Act III is set in the home of Cinderella's father. Cinderella, again in her drab work clothes, thinks that the ball and Prince Charming were only a dream until she finds a dancing slipper concealed in her apron. Then she dances happily with her broom, this time reliving her wondrous adventure. When the tired, aching stepsisters return from the ball, they are not too weary to taunt Cinderella, telling her how Prince Charming had eyes only for them. A group of women then enter with the news that Prince Charming is searching for the mysterious girl who disappeared from the ball, and the sisters throw themselves into a paroxysm of activity to primp for his arrival. Prince Charming, the Court Jester, and attendants enter, and the prince declares that the lady whose foot fits the shoe in his hand will become his wife. With absurd assurance, the sisters accept the challenge and the prince stands by courteously, watching the outrageous spectacle that ensues.

In attempting to help one of her stepsisters pull the shoe off, Cinderella bends down and the other shoe falls from her apron. Prince Charming then asks Cinderella to try on the slipper he has brought and she obeys despite her stepsisters' frantic efforts to stop her. Of course, the shoe fits, and the prince joyously announces he has found his bride. The Fairy Godmother reappears, and with a wave of her magic wand transforms the scene into an enchanted garden.

The four fairies and the prince's friends return to dance in the garden, and as the constellation of stars frames the scene, Cinderella and Prince Charming perform a *pas de deux* of mutual adoration. With the Fairy Godmother and her entourage paying homage, Cinderella and her prince board a magical boat. As the music swells then fades glitteringly away, the boat carries them into a life of "happily ever after."

Galina and Valery Panov in his version of Cinderella. *The Berlin Ballet*

THE MOOR'S PAVANE

1949 ◆ *Music by Henry Purcell, arranged by Simon Sadoff* ◆ *Choreography by José Limón*

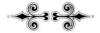

In 1930, a twenty-four-year-old Mexican of Olympian stature and beauty arrived at the New York studio of modern dance pioneers Doris Humphrey and Charles Weidman. José Limón was a former art student at the University of California at Los Angeles who had come to the city to pursue a career in painting—until he saw his first dance concert, given by the fledgling Humphrey-Weidman Company. So impressed and moved was he by the expressiveness of their movements that he became their student. Within a few years, Limón developed into a dancer of powerful yet poetic impact and became, after Weidman, the most important male dancer in the company. Like all members of the group, Limón was encouraged to choreograph, and his first efforts, promising but unfocused, were performed as early as 1932 by an offshoot of the parent company called the Little Group.

After being enlisted to produce army entertainments in World War II, Limón returned to New York to find the Humphrey-Weidman Company disbanded and almost immediately made plans to form his own company with his mentor Humphrey as resident choreographer and artistic advisor. Up to this point, Limón's choreographic output had been relatively sparse, but with Humphrey's continuing encouragement his creative drive became more insistent. Years later, he was to say, "I try to compose works that are involved with man's basic tragedy and the grandeur of his spirit... to probe the human entity for the powerful, often crude beauty of the gesture that speaks of man's humanity." In view of this statement, it is not surprising that Limón went to Shakespeare as the source for the first work that would herald him as a major voice in American modern dance.

For the 1949 season of the American Dance Festival at Connecticut College, New London, Limón planned a work based on Shakespeare's *Othello*. Rather than a detailed retelling of the tragedy, it would be a distillation of the play's dramatic themes—particularly jealousy—performed by four dancers in a courtly pavane, whose formality disintegrates under the destructive forces of envy and intrigue. Its score would utilize several pieces by Henry Purcell, among them the incidental music to *Abdelazer, or The Moor's Revenge* (1695), in an arrangement by Simon Sadoff. With Limón as the Moor, Betty Jones as Desdemona, Lucas Hoving as Iago, and Pauline Koner as Emi-

lia, *The Moor's Pavane* was an unmitigated triumph at its premiere and confirmed Limón as the masterful heir to the Humphrey-Weidman tradition.

Although rooted in the modern dance tradition, the work evinces the simple but grand expression of human passion that is one of the constants of the ballet stage. Each role is choreographically portrayed with equal dramatic dimension, and therefore each poses a challenge for the artistically mature dancer. *The Moor's Pavane* has found its way into the repertoires of many ballet companies and is still being performed by members of the José Limón Company (which survived the choreographer's death in 1972). Although many critics have stated that the original cast has never been surpassed in their ensemble interpretation, some of the greatest dramatic dancers have been drawn to the challenge of this work, notably, Rudolf Nureyev, Ivan Nagy, Sallie Wilson, Toni Lander, Bruce Marks, Gary Chryst, Christian Holder, Erik Bruhn, Louis Falco, and Cynthia Gregory.

THE BALLET

To a stately Purcell theme, the curtain rises to reveal four figures in Elizabethan costumes of rich color and texture. They are two couples, the Moor (Othello), the Moor's Wife (Desdemona), His Friend (Iago), and His Friend's Wife (Emilia), who stand facing each other in a formal square. Each bends backward, away from the others, and then they move apart. As the women bow graciously to each other, the two men meet in the center and then separate with a slight push of their palms. Returning to his wife, the Moor presents her with a handkerchief, which she accepts with sweet innocence, as the other couple looks on.

After a brief sequence of passing encounters, Iago places his clawlike hands on the Moor's shoulders and furtively whispers in his ear. As Othello listens, spellbound, to the words of his friend, his head turns sharply in the direction of Desdemona. Moments later, Desdemona comes to her husband and, softened by her presence, the Moor dances briefly with her, but they are interrupted by Iago. Then, in a telling, sensual duet, Iago and Emilia reveal that they are involved in a more worldly and complex relationship than the Moor and his wife. Although Emilia struggles with her husband, he obviously dominates her.

The couples come together again to repeat the steps of the

Christian Holder and Denise Jackson in The Moor's Pavane. *The Joffrey Ballet*

opening pavane, now executed with a larger, forced cordiality. During the dance, Emilia takes the handkerchief from Desdemona, toys with it, then returns it to her. Later, the Moor's wife drops the handkerchief and Emilia snatches it up from the ground. The ladies then move into the background while the men engage in a heated exchange. Iago continues his torrent of falsehoods, and the enraged, wounded Moor finally strikes out at the informer. After this torturous encounter, the men return to their wives. Emilia shows her husband the purloined handkerchief, and he instantly takes it away from her. To the Moor's horror, Iago triumphantly produces the handkerchief as proof of his accusations.

The Moor goes to his wife and at first treats her lovingly, but soon his jealous frenzy overpowers him and he grasps her roughly. As her husband's anger turns to rage, the terrified Desdemona tries vainly to escape. With thrashing arms, the Moor proceeds to murder as the other couple walks ceremoniously forward, concealing the deed. Iago and Emilia move apart and the Moor is revealed gazing in disbelief at what he has done. Iago and Emilia point accusingly at one another, each blaming the other for the tragedy. In an attempt to silence the voice of truth, Iago moves to strangle his wife, but the Moor prevents this by grasping each of them by the wrist and forcing them to look into the face of his dead wife. As the Moor prostrates himself over Desdemona's body, Iago and Emilia *plié* deeply, as if pushed down by the burden of their crime. Each reaches out one arm despairingly, Iago in cowardly disavowal of his guilt, Emilia in anguish over her unknowing treachery.

AFTERNOON OF A FAUN

1953 ◆ *Music by Claude Debussy* ◆ *Choreography by Jerome Robbins*

One day in the early 1950s, in a studio of the School of American Ballet in New York, a young boy stood against the ballet *barre* in a shaft of sunlight and began to stretch his body in a sensuous, almost animalistic way. And choreographer Jerome Robbins, observing this unconscious moment of feline grace, found his inspiration for *Afternoon of a Faun*. (The boy, incidentally, was the young Edward Villella.)

Since his triumph with *Fancy Free* in 1944, Robbins had had a string of successes on the ballet stage and on Broadway. Between 1944 and 1948, he created the ballets *Interplay* and *Facsimile* and choreographed the musicals *On the Town*, *High Button Shoes*, *Miss Liberty*, *Billion Dollar Baby*, and *Look, Ma, I'm Dancin'!* After joining the year-old New York City Ballet as dancer, choreographer, and associate artistic director in 1949, he created *The Guests*, *Age of Anxiety*, *The Cage*, *The Pied Piper*, *Jones Beach* (with George Balanchine), and *Ballade*. Thus, within ten years of his first ballet, Robbins became the most prolific and successful native-born choreographer America had ever known.

In *Afternoon of a Faun*, Nijinsky's original mythical treatment of adolescent erotic self-awakening is translated into the cool yet equally sensuous self-involvement of the contemporary ballet dancer. Robbins was no doubt abetted by Debussy's sublime score: serving as the impetus for every fluid choreographic movement, it raises the mundane fact of a dancer's unavoidable narcissism to a contemporary poetic myth. From its first cast, Francisco Moncion and Tanaquil LeClercq, to such couples as Jacques d'Amboise and Allegra Kent, Edward Villella and Patricia McBride, Helgi Tomasson and Kay Mazzo, Peter Martins and Suzanne Farrell, and Anthony Dowell and Antoinette Sibley, *Faun* has offered its interpreters the opportunity to create performances that glow with each dancer's distinctive radiance.

THE BALLET

The curtain rises in silence to reveal the seemingly suspended outline of a ballet studio: three walls and the ceiling are made of diaphanous white silk; the fourth wall, the one separating the stage from the audience, is an invisible mirror.

Lying on his back on the floor, close to the "mirror," is a young man asleep. His torso is bare and he wears black tights, white socks, and ballet slippers. The sinuous opening line of Debussy's

haunting tone poem begins, and the boy stirs into wakefulness. Arching his back languidly, he stretches one leg straight up into the air, perpendicular to the floor. He sits up and gazes intently into the imaginary mirror. His eyes never turning from the mirror, he stands, contracts catlike over his extended leg, somersaults onto the floor, stretches full-length on his stomach, and contentedly falls asleep again.

To a whirring, mysterious musical phrase, a young woman in a practice tunic enters from beyond the studio. Her long hair flows loosely over her shoulders. Reaching the opening that suggests a door in the back wall, she steps through it. From the moment she enters the room, her eyes are fixed on her own image in the mirror. She goes to the *barre* and begins to *plié*. At that moment, the boy, aware that he is not alone, awakens.

The boy steps behind the girl at the *barre*, takes hold of her as she extends her leg, and lifts her into the air seamlessly, as if she were floating away from the *barre*. Now, the eyes of both dancers are fixed on their own images in the mirror. The girl stands with

Opposite and above: Peter Martins and Allegra Kent in Afternoon of a Faun. *New York City Ballet*

one leg bent and resting on *pointe*, gazing admiringly at herself; the boy goes to her and touches her hair. He then supports her in formal balletic positions, but with a sudden surge in the music, she turns over his arm onto his shoulder and poises there with arms over her head. Her legs undulate delicately back and forth as he walks with her.

After the boy releases the girl, they go to opposite sides of the studio and, still watching themselves in the mirror, slide toward each other in slow lunges. When they reunite, the boy raises his arms in a *couronne* framing the girl's head. The girl slowly raises her arms through the boy's encircled arms, and her body magically follows the course of her arms until she is extended full-length in midair, supported only by the circle of the boy's arms.

At this moment, the music reaches its peak of tender ecstasy. Then, in an almost imperceptible transition, the girl's body folds liquidly from its extended position and her partner lowers her, gently kneeling, to the floor. The girl remains kneeling, gazing into the mirror, but it seems at this instant that she might be drawn from her self-adoration to a full awareness of him. Already drawn to the girl, the boy kneels on one knee beside her, gently leans in her direction, and kisses her softly on the cheek. While the girl's hand lifts, as if of its own accord, to her cheek, the boy returns to admire himself. The girl turns from her own image to look directly at the boy, but seeing him again transfixed by the mirror, she too gazes back into it. Without taking her hand from her cheek, she rises, walks backward through the door, as if in a trance, and departs. The boy remains gazing in the mirror and soon resumes his stretching, seemingly unaffected by this revery. With one final lift of his torso from the floor, he rests his head on his folded arms and returns to sleep.

Afternoon of a Faun, *New York City Ballet: opposite, Ib Andersen and Patricia McBride; above,*
Francisco Moncion and Allegra Kent

THE CONCERT

1956 ◆ *Music by Frédéric Chopin* ◆ *Choreography by Jerome Robbins*

"One of the pleasures of attending a concert," Jerome Robbins has written, "is the freedom to lose oneself in listening to the music.... The patterns and paths of these reveries are influenced by the music itself, or its program notes, or by the personal dreams, problems, and fantasies of the listener."

In 1956, Robbins embodied these notions in his ballet *The Concert* and created what is undeniably the funniest ballet of all time. This accomplishment is even greater than it sounds, because dance history has shown that it is next to impossible to choreograph a truly and consistently funny ballet. To be sure, there are amusing ballets, such as the classic *La Fille Mal Gardée* and *Coppélia* and, in modern times, Massine's *Three-Cornered Hat* and Tudor's *Gala Performance*, but the "comic" elements of these works arise primarily from the farcical nature of their stories, rather than from the comedy inherent in their movement. Indeed, ballet, by definition, requires a seriously disciplined technique and strict adherence to form, which allow little opportunity for the distortion necessary to produce humorous theater. In *The Concert*, Robbins revealed that his understanding of the nature of ballet was so profound that he could, without the aid of a story per se, hilariously distort technique, form, gesture, and situation.

The Concert's comedic force derives in large part from its ironic use of Chopin's music. While some have considered this device blasphemous, Robbins himself has stated that his intention "was to denude certain pieces of their banal titles — 'Butterfly,' 'Raindrop,' etc. —perhaps restoring them to their purity by destroying the fabricated interpretations." And, in fact, the choreographer displays only the most reverential treatment of Chopin's music in his masterpiece *Dances at a Gathering* (1969) and in *In the Night* (1970) and *Other Dances* (1976).

After the ballet's highly successful premiere by the New York City Ballet, Robbins revived it in 1958 for his own Ballets: U.S.A. at the first annual Festival of Two Worlds in Spoleto, Italy. Two episodes were eliminated, and Saul Steinberg's decor replaced the original one; in this form it was revived again by the New York City Ballet in 1971 (the production described here).

THE BALLET

To an orchestral rendition of Chopin's *Polonaise Militaire*, the curtain rises on a scrim with a caricature of a concert hall filled with people. This rises to reveal a stage empty except for a grand piano at one side. The pianist takes his seat and then proceeds to dust off the piano keys with his handkerchief, raising a cloud of dust at the far end of the keyboard. Irritated, he stares the laughing audience into silence. He begins to play with utmost depth of feeling Chopin's Berceuse op. 57.

An onstage audience then begins to gather, all with folding chairs to sit on. First comes a timid, bookish gentleman dressed in a shapeless unitard of powder blue; he is followed by two chattering girl friends in straw hats with ridiculous flowers, who finally settle down after some fussing. Next, a girl with a wide-brimmed, floppy hat and long, flowing hair rushes to the piano, opens her arms wide to embrace it, and rests her head against it. A determined young woman of serious musical persuasion stomps in, sits with a thud, and with large, gathering gestures urges the music to pour forth.

Then, a henpecked, cigar-chewing husband enters with his domineering wife, who immediately begins to scold him for reading the newspaper. A shy boy wearing glasses then tiptoes

Opposite: Francisco Moncion in The Concert. *New York City Ballet*
Above: Lynn Seymour and Graham Fletcher. The Royal Ballet

147

in; frightened by an unfriendly look from the wife, he sits apart from the group. An usher leads in a latecomer, and a passage of hilarious confusion over seating arrangements ensues.

As everyone settles down, fantasy overtakes them. Led by the floppy-hatted girl, they all *bourrée* ridiculously around the stage, carrying their folded chairs. They float from the scene, leaving only the girl in the floppy hat and the shy boy.

To Chopin's stormy Prelude op. 28 no. 18, this mismatched pair perform a ludicrously frantic duet in which the girl flings herself around the stage and into her partner's arms, in obvious parody of the classical *pas de deux*. Next, to the frenzied Prelude op. 28 no. 16, a group of men rush about the stage like Keystone Cops, carrying girls in various stiff postures. After they place the immobile girls in a clump, they dash off as the girls assume a balletic tableau.

To the Waltz in E Minor (here known as the "Mistake" Waltz), the very serious girls perform an undulating waltz in which they desperately attempt to dance in unison, but never succeed. There is always an arm out of place, a leg misdirected, a head turned incorrectly, or a girl totally out of place. The boys return, frantically grab the girls up, fold them into small "packages," and carry them off.

The Prelude op. 28 no. 7, eternally associated with Fokine's *Les Sylphides*, is parodied next in three treatments. First, the floppy-hatted girl, the meek gentleman, and the usher mime a vignette involving a woman selecting a hat and the comic outcome of her choice. Then, the henpecked husband acts out his murderous fantasies toward his wife, as the Prelude is reiterated. Finally, to an orchestral version of the Prelude, two men carry on two women wearing feathered hats. Their *pas de quatre*, obviously parodying Balanchinean configurations, quickly dissolves into a convoluted tangle of legs, arms, and bodies.

To the robust Mazurka in G Major, the husband and a group of men perform a raucous version of that Polish dance. The floppy-hatted girl joins them, but the revelry is squelched at its height by the arrival of the ever-domineering wife. The mood changes in the Prelude op. 28 no. 4. Various groupings of dancers enter with black umbrellas. After a vastly amusing interchange built around the opening and closing of the umbrellas, a single umbrella floats up into the air, carrying with it the girl with the floppy hat. She reaches out her palm to feel for raindrops; feeling none, she closes the umbrella and slowly drifts down. The crowd disperses.

Next, the badgered husband returns alone wearing wildly

Above: Merle Park and Michael Coleman in The Concert. *The Royal Ballet*
Below: Bart Cook. New York City Ballet

decorated butterfly wings and antennae. To Chopin's Ballade op. 47 no. 3, he begins a frolicsome dance, all the while holding his cigar clenched firmly between his teeth. He gambols about delightedly with the floppy-hatted girl, also clad in butterfly wings. With melodramatic anguish, the "wronged" wife appears and calls forth squadrons of butterflies to defend her. Amid much frantic fluttering and flapping of wings, chaos ensues.

The pianist, now at the end of his rope, begins to chase the lunatic mob with an enormous butterfly net. As the scrim is lowered, the principal characters rush in front of it with their folding chairs, sit down, cross their legs, and smile as if nothing had happened.

Christine Redpath, Steven Caras, and Sara Leland. New York City Ballet

AGON

1957 ◆ *Music by Igor Stravinsky* ◆ *Choreography by George Balanchine*

The Balanchine-Stravinsky *Apollo* of 1928 had heralded the beginning of the neoclassic era in dance; their *Orpheus* of 1948 was a profound essay in plastic classical poetry. As the New York City Ballet developed into a company of unique international importance during its first decade, it seemed right that a third ballet be created for the company to complete a trilogy inspired by ancient Greece, and in 1953, Lincoln Kirstein commissioned the music from Stravinsky. *Agon*, the Greek word for contest, would be the new work's title and, as it turned out, its only Greek element.

From seventeenth-century manuals of French court dances, Stravinsky garnered an idea for a suite of twelve variations for twelve dancers. The composer was also influenced by Anton Webern's twelve-tone music, and his finished score would be a terse reflection of the atonal style.

Between late 1953 and the spring of 1957, Stravinsky worked intermittently on the score —all the while in close consultation with Balanchine. Because they felt atonal music would be somewhat inaccessible to the general public, it was decided that the ballet would last no more than twenty minutes. Within this time restriction, the entire work was divided into three sections, the twelve dances were broken down into precise time spans, and the number of dancers employed in each section was decided. Ironically enough, Balanchine knew everything about the ballet's structure long before he knew how the music would sound. When he received the completed score, Balanchine realized that Stravinsky had written music of such dense metrical construction, rich contrapuntal rhythms, and evolving asymmetrical harmonies, that nothing like it had ever been heard before. Excited by the prospect of complementing this grand innovation, Balanchine set to work on the central *pas de deux*. That one dance took Balanchine, as he admitted himself, longer to create than anything he had ever done —two weeks.

Agon is an abstract, plotless work in which the dancers appear in simple black and white practice clothes. Its dazzling display of relentless tension and energy is made the more startling by complex and inventive technical demands. Yet despite all its density and intellectual rigor, the ballet is almost antiseptic in its lean economy of gesture, conveying compelling psychological intonations, wit, drama, and even sensuality. *Agon* requires from its dancers the accuracy of an IBM computer, and although

also performed by the Stuttgart Ballet, London's Royal Ballet, the Dance Theatre of Harlem, and the Paris Opera Ballet, the work belongs to the dancers of the New York City Ballet, for it confirms them as the supreme instruments of Balanchine's vision and the inimitable interpreters of Stravinsky's music.

THE BALLET

The curtain rises on a stage devoid of decor but suffused with glaring light. At the rear of the stage stand four men in a horizontal line, their backs to the audience. As a blaring, staccato trumpet fanfare sounds, the men turn to face the audience. With emphatically swaying arms and swaggering steps, they advance diagonally across the stage. In contrapuntal sequence, they perform a *pas de quatre* punctuated by backward thrusts of one leg into the air while the other rests on the heel of a flexed foot. The dance is replete with musical echoes of contemporary tension, contrasted with references to Renaissance instrumentation. The *pas de quatre* ends on a resounding plucked note.

Eight women enter for the double *pas de quatre* and keep pace with the relentlessly nervous atonality of the music, which seems to impel their bodies to and fro in patterns of jabbing legs, angular leaps, and snapping fingers. The four men join the women for the triple *pas de quatre*, an enlarged variation on the previous theme.

The stage clears but for three dancers, two women and one man, who are to perform the first *pas de trois*. To another fanfare, accompanied by drum rolls, the dancers swagger forward in unison for the subdued introduction. The two women leave and the man dances a *sarabande*, which begins and ends with a bent-legged leap into the air and a jab of one leg forward as he comes downstage. The women return for a duet, a *gaillarde* in which the dancers' courtly execution mirrors the Renaissance tonality of the music. The coda is a witty trio which exhibits a similar correspondence between the dancers' fluid, slinky movements and the quirky antiphony of the music. The trio ends with a return to unison in which each dancer suddenly strikes a courtly bow with torso bent over an extended leg.

Another fanfare introduces the second *pas de trois*, this time performed by two men and one woman. The two men dance a *branle simple*, taking the parts of two trumpets. They spin in

Victor Castelli and Tracy Bennett in Agon. *New York City Ballet*

rapid canon, with legs extended first back and then front and bodies jutting in zigzagging patterns. The dance concludes on an abrupt note when the men freeze with linked arms in an asymmetrical yet classical pose. The men step to either side of the stage as the woman enters. Clapping their hands to the irregular rhythm of castanets, they accompany the woman as she performs a sinuous dance featuring undulating arm movements. The coda, for all three, is characterized by tense determination. One man promenades the woman on *pointe* while holding her by both hands as the other man passes beneath their arms; this pattern is then repeated with the men exchanging places. Later, the woman stands in *piqué arabesque* as the men each hold one of her arms. Releasing her arms, they rush to exchange places while she rests suspended on *pointe*. The dance concludes as the woman is thrown into the air and then caught in the arms of one man, while the other kneels facing them.

To another fanfare, the leading couple enter to perform the central *pas de deux*. To a mysterious, meandering adagio for strings, undercut by an edge of repressed tension, the dancers move through barely tangible transitions from one bizarre configuration to another. At one point, the man lies on his back on the floor, and holding one hand of the woman, who is in deep *arabesque penchée*, he promenades her by rapidly propelling himself in a semicircle with traveling movements of his feet. After each dances a brief solo variation, the *pas de deux* concludes as the man kneels with one leg under the woman's bent leg, extended forward on *pointe*, and their bodies slump over each other, intertwined in a posture suggesting grief.

Suddenly the dancers of the first two *pas de trois* return, and there is a *danse des quatre duos* which soon increases to a *danse des quatre trios* in which the four men and eight women move in intricately shifting patterns that in their momentum and precision rival the mechanisms of a machine. An elaboration of the opening fanfare has returned; in its fading measures the eight women leap off and the men repeat their initial swaggering march, only in reverse. Reaching the back of the stage, they form two groups as each man thrusts one arm forward toward the man facing him. Then, to the last abrupt note of the music, they all execute the same arm gesture in one direction to strike a stunning tableau.

Agon, New York City Ballet. Men: Kipling Houston, Tracy Bennett, Peter Martins, and Bart Cook; women in foreground: Suzanne Farrell, Renée Estopinal, and Merrill Ashley

STARS AND STRIPES

1958 ◆ *Music by John Philip Sousa, arranged by Hershy Kay* ◆ *Choreography by George Balanchine*

Within two months of the premiere of Balanchine's astonishingly innovative and daringly cerebral *Agon* in late 1957, the choreographer created *Stars and Stripes* for the New York City Ballet, a work that was about as far from *Agon* as one could get.

Though he was born in Imperial Russia and created his early works in Europe, Balanchine became Americanized almost as soon as he stepped on American soil in 1933. Within seven years, he had become an American citizen, and although his first loyalty was to New York, the city which had given him his artistic fulfillment, his devotion to the United States embraced the whole nation. For Balanchine, no music so typified the spirit that had fired his imagination as the rousing patriotic marches of John Philip Sousa. He had long wanted to create dances to them and eventually commissioned arrangements from Hershy Kay, an American composer-arranger who had brilliantly and wittily orchestrated *Cakewalk* and *Western Symphony* for the New York City Ballet.

Balanchine dedicated *Stars and Stripes* to New York's beloved mayor, Fiorello H. La Guardia, a man who to many embodied the American spirit. (Not so incidentally, it was also under this feisty little man's administration that the city government underwrote the support of the City Ballet.)

Asked to explain exactly what this ballet was about, the always enigmatic yet pointedly direct Balanchine replied, "The United States." And, in fact, *Stars and Stripes* does reveal a keen insight into the American popular sensibility. While certain critics questioned the ballet's somewhat outrageous flamboyance, bordering on *kitsch*, they could not deny its stunning choreographic complexity. The corps de ballet here needs absolute precision and as much technical virtuosity as is demanded by any corps role in a full-length classical ballet. *Stars and Stripes* is a soul-stirring masterpiece of virtuosic ensemble choreography, shot through with knowing wit and affection for both the American spirit and the classical ballet tradition.

THE BALLET

A lushly orchestrated martial tune, "Corcoran Cadets," opens the ballet as the curtain rises on a brightly lit stage revealing the First Campaign: a regiment of twelve girls in admittedly garish but delightfully patriotic tutus and hats. Standing in front of them is their leader. Almost immediately, their all-encompassing smiles lead into exuberant dancing and infectious prancing on *pointe* in kaleidoscopic patterns. To a charming tinkling pizzicato interlude, the leader twirls a majorette's baton and marches with insouciance —the image of the all-American girl. The girls then parade in more military patterns before their leader returns, flying repeatedly in high split *jetés*, in time with the crashing cymbals. As the girls assume a diagonal formation, their captain takes hold of her heel with one hand, stretches her leg to the side, high above her head, and travels in rising and falling *relevés*; her troop admiringly salutes her. Their finale is a show-biz parade concluding with the troop's marching toward the audience in alternating turned-in *passés* and high kicks to the side. As the girls march off, their leader flies after them in a sequence of splits *à la seconde*, finishing at the last moment with a high *jeté* into the wings.

The Second Campaign is danced to Sousa's jaunty "Rifle Regiment" by a group of female cadets and their leader. Their jolly marching and intricate patterns have a more broadly sweeping character, partly because these girls are taller than those in the first group. The comic high point comes when the leader, with bugle held to her lips, executes some fancy time-step footwork, which she concludes with wittily determined stamping of her feet. An exhilarating drum roll changes the pace as the entire group covers the stage in flying *coupés jetés* and the leader executes a circuit of *piqué* turns. For its bounding conclusion, the regiment circles in alternating forward *balancés* and high-kicking *emboités* which carry them offstage.

An accelerating dialogue of drum rolls brings on the Third Campaign —the male cadets of the "Thunder and Gladiator" regiment. With military swagger they take their opening positions, then sweep into intricate patterns of *sautés*, beats, *tours en l'air*, and converging *jetés*, all the while led by their cocky leader, who infiltrates their ranks with his own virtuosic tricks. As their dance reaches its climax, the men crisscross the stage in *grands jetés*, passing each other in midair. To the last pounding drum rolls, they punctuate their marching in place with a series of double *tours en l'air*, concluding with a final good-natured salute to the audience.

A triumphant military fanfare introduces the two commanders of all the campaigns: the "Liberty Bell" ballerina and "El Capitan" *danseur*. Though infused with an ingratiating sense of

Merrill Ashley in Stars and Stripes. *New York City Ballet*

154

fun, the duet they perform rivals any of the great classic *pas de deux*. Its coda is a thrilling recapitulation of their effortless virtuosity and lovable wit and, at its conclusion, El Capitan lifts Liberty Bell high above him in a *grand jeté* and carries her off as she gives a last happy salute.

Not surprisingly, the ballet ends with Sousa's immortal "Stars and Stripes Forever." The first two regiments enter one at a time, escorted by the men of the Third Campaign. The Corcoran Cadets come on in sweeping zigzag *sautés* and the Rifle Regiment girls march pertly on *pointe*. El Capitan carries on Liberty Bell as she executes whistling leg beats. Patriotic fervor overtakes everyone, and as the regiments parade, the leading couple stand at opposite sides of the stage to review them. For the heart-pounding climax, the entire legion assembles at the rear of the stage and advances forward as the backdrop rises to reveal an immense replica of the American flag. The regiments, with Liberty Bell lifted to the shoulder of El Capitan, form a victoriously patriotic tableau as the curtain falls.

Above: Members of the New York City Ballet in Stars and Stripes
Opposite: Jacques d'Amboise in Stars and Stripes. *New York City Ballet*

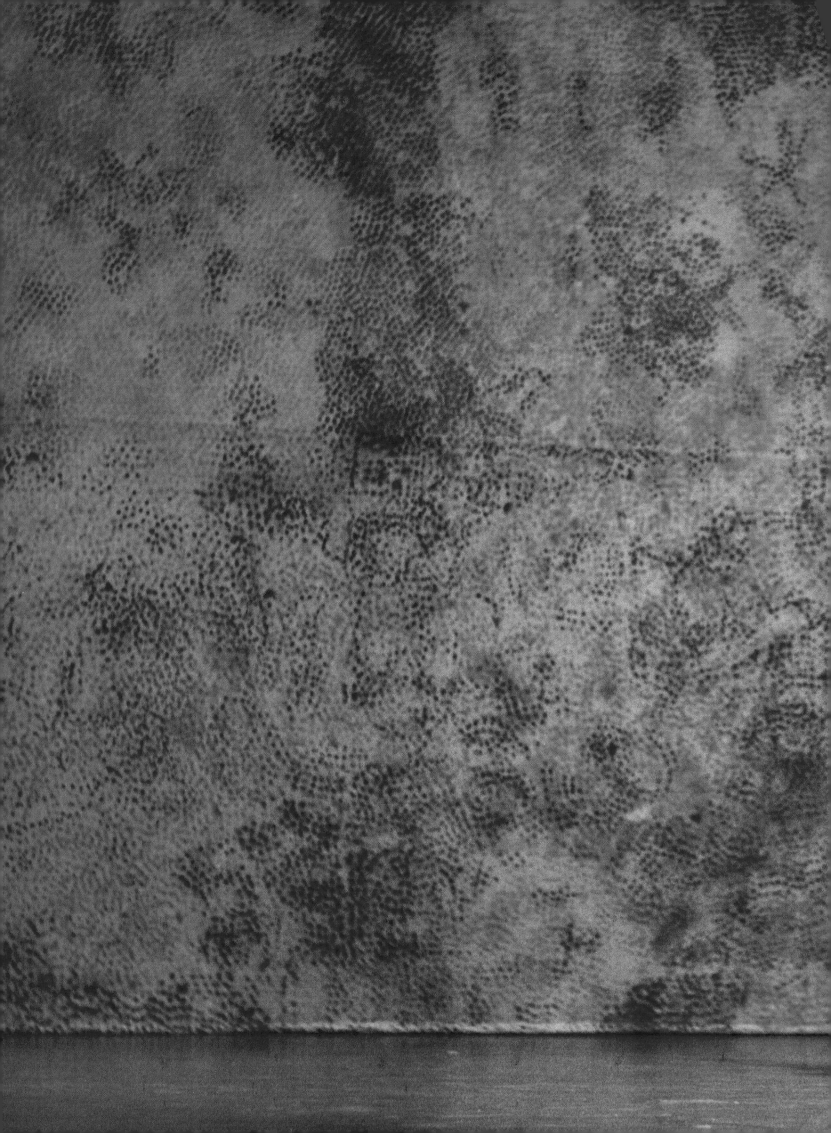

SUMMERSPACE

1958 ◆ Music by Morton Feldman ◆ Choreography by Merce Cunningham

Unlike Doris Humphrey and Charles Weidman, her creative peers in modern dance, Martha Graham used no men in her company until the late 1930s. Erick Hawkins, who had danced with the American Ballet and Ballet Caravan, came to Graham as a guest artist in 1938 and stayed with her company as its principal dancer until 1951. Shortly after Hawkins's arrival, Merce Cunningham, a young man from Centralia, Washington, enrolled in the Bennington College Summer School of the Dance at Mills College, Oakland, California, where Graham was artist-in-residence. Noting Cunningham's spry, lithe, and impish quality, the choreographer saw him as a welcome addition to her company.

Cunningham joined Graham's company in the fall of 1939, and for the next several years created such major roles in its repertoire as the Preacher in *Appalachian Spring*, the Acrobat in *Every Soul Is a Circus*, March in *Letter to the World*, and the Christ Figure in *El Penitente*. Almost from the beginning, he also made explorations into the field of choreography. In 1945, he left Graham to choreograph and to teach a modern dance class at the School of American Ballet. Two years later, Ballet Society, the precursor of the New York City Ballet, commissioned a work from him. This ballet, entitled *The Seasons*, passed with little *réclame*, but a mutual respect was established between Cunningham and Lincoln Kirstein, co-founder with Balanchine of Ballet Society.

In 1952, Cunningham formed his own company, which gave its first season that year at the off-Broadway Theater de Lys in New York City. Between 1952 and 1958, the choreographer created a score of works which made it clear that he was a unique voice in American modern dance. *Suite by Chance, Septet, Suite for Five, The Changeling*, and *Antic Meet* were among the many dances exhibiting Cunningham's esthetic, which was based primarily on the ordered sequence of isolated dance movements determined by chance.

In 1958, for the annual summer session of the American Dance Festival at Connecticut College in New London, Cunningham created a work entitled *Summerspace* which further explored his preoccupation with the random movements of ·dancers in space. From the outset, Cunningham had employed the talents of outstanding avant-garde artists and composers to accompany his works, though not necessarily to be integral

elements of the choreography itself. In *Summerspace*, however, the pointillist decor of Robert Rauschenberg, the graph-score music of Morton Feldman, and Cunningham's chance choreography melded into a serendipitously unified piece of a certain sylvan haziness.

Sensitively rendered by Cunningham's own dancers at its premiere on August 17, 1958, *Summerspace* had an effect that was almost translucently romantic. Since this quality seemed not incompatible with the movements of ballet dancers, Cunningham was invited in 1966 to stage the work for the New York City Ballet. Although the dancers of the company acquitted themselves nobly, their basic upward-directed lightness, abetted by *pointe* shoes, worked against the fleet but essentially "floor-grounded" Cunningham style. The City Ballet performances of *Summerspace* were well received, but it was clear that the work did not belong in the repertoire of a classical ballet company, even this most contemporary one, and it was soon dropped. *Summerspace* has been staged for other ballet companies, including the Cullberg Ballet in Sweden and the Boston Ballet, but its richest portrayal continues to be by Cunningham's own dancers, who perform it with consummate understanding, refinement, and clarity.

THE BALLET

"Dancing to me is movement," Cunningham has said. "People moving in time and space. It has nothing to do with romanticism, sentimentality, or love, but with *activity*. Dancing is an enlargement of energy... it must be done fully and completely and clearly so that it takes on its own life.... Movement should be able to exist by itself."

In *Summerspace* these precepts are carried out by six dancers, four women and two men in costumes painted with tiny dots of color, who move against a coolly shimmering pointillist backdrop. It is a continuum of whirling, leaping, sliding, running, walking, hopping, and prancing performed by the dancers with no clear relationship to one another and only an occasional interaction. Cunningham said that the work's flow of random movement should "carry one through a space, and not only into it, like the passage of birds stopping for moments on the ground and then going on, or automobiles more relentlessly throbbing along turnpikes and under and over cloverleaves."

Preceding pages: Merce Cunningham in Summerspace. *Merce Cunningham Dance Company*

REVELATIONS

1960 ◆ *Music: Afro-American spirituals* ◆ *Choreography by Alvin Ailey*

By the late 1950s, American ballet and modern dance had most definitely come into their own, but they had featured regrettably few black dancers. Although blacks had been very much in evidence on the American variety and musical comedy stages and in films, they were nearly always cast as tap dancing virtuosos. Two fleeting attempts at black ballet, Ruth Page's *La Guiablesse* (1933) and Agnes de Mille's *Black Ritual* (1940), both failed to survive. In the forties, black dancer-choreographers,

including Pearl Primus, Katherine Dunham, and Talley Beatty, gained a certain prominence, but most of their successful work was characterized by strong ethnic strains, African in the case of Primus, Caribbean for Dunham.

At the same time, in California, the school and company of choreographer Lester Horton became a breeding ground for exceptionally gifted and arresting dancers, most of whom were black. Among the most notable of these were Carmen de

Donna Wood and members of the Alvin Ailey American Dance Theater in Revelations

161

Lavallade, Janet Collins, James Truitte, and Alvin Ailey. As a teenager, Ailey had come to California from his native Texas, and while attending the University of California he began dance studies with Horton. He became a member of Horton's company and soon one of its leading soloists. Following Horton's untimely death in 1953, Ailey remained with the company as choreographer and concurrently made his Broadway debut as a featured dancer, with De Lavallade, in the musical *House of Flowers* (1954).

Gradually, Ailey established his separate identity as a dancer-choreographer and soon after his first New York recital in 1957, he formed his own company, the Alvin Ailey American Dance Theater. With his 1958 work *Blues Suite*, Ailey was clearly recognized as the major voice of the American black in dance. Less than two years later, there was universal acclaim for Ailey's *Revelations*, a brilliant evocation of the black experience, tracing its evolution from the oppression of slavery through exultation in freedom to a final triumph of the spirit. For more than two decades, the vibrant character of the piece has remained intact, and it is undeniably the signature piece of the company.

From its original conception as almost a chamber work, *Revelations* has been revised and expanded to a dance that is nothing short of spectacular. Over the years, the number of dancers in the work has increased and a chorus of singers has sometimes accompanied them. Judith Jamison's flamboyant performance as the umbrella-carrying woman made her a star, and the soul-stirring, introspective solo "I Want to Be Ready" has been a triumphant vehicle for the men who have performed it, from its originator, Truitte, to recent interpreters Dudley Williams, Clive Thompson, and Kelvin Rotardier. The thrilling conclusion to "Rocka My Soul in the Bosom of Abraham" has brought audiences cheering to their feet throughout the world. In *Revelations* Ailey has created an ecstatic celebration of humanity as seen in the indomitable black sensibility.

THE BALLET

Revelations is a ballet in three parts. The first section, Pilgrim of Sorrow, portrays the faith of American blacks under the burden of oppression. The curtain rises on a stage empty but for a broad shaft of warm light pouring over a huddled group of dancers who are bent forward with heads down and arms extended in wide arcs to the side. To the traditional song "I Been Buked," the dancers move in forceful gestures of spiritual need and appeal. They stretch their arms heavenward with wide-open hands or reach out in supplication with one arm while soothing their burden-heavy backs with the other. Throughout this opening dance, the weight of earthly travail is evident in the dancers' deeply bent legs, bowed heads, and curving torsos.

Two women and a man next perform a dance for deliverance to "Daniel," which is followed by a *pas de deux* of moving consolation to "Fix Me, Jesus." At its conclusion, the woman stands on the extended thigh of the man, who has been her spiritual guide, and reaches out as he leans back, holding her by one arm.

The mood of the piece brightens when the lights come up for the second section, Take Me to the Water, a theatrical rendering of the cleansing ritual of Baptism. For the processional, dancers clad in costumes of bright white are led onstage by a man carrying a pole decorated with streamers of white cloth. Among the dancers parading with revivalist spirit is a vivacious woman with an enormous white umbrella, who oversees the young man and woman who are to be baptized. To "Wading in the Water," all three dance among two large, billowing cloths, one of white, one of blue, which fill the stage and represent the purifying waters. The exuberant mood of the ceremony becomes solemn once more for the solo "I Want to Be Ready," in which the contractions and spasms of the man's body express his anguished repentance for his sins.

Exuberance gives way to exultation in the last section, Move, Members, Move. The first dance, to "Sinner Man," is for three men who race relentlessly around the stage in a frenzied attempt to shake loose the burden of their sins. Next a group of women enter wearing long dresses and broad-brimmed hats and carrying fans. To "The Day Is Past and Gone," they evoke a comic but personable society of black women who gather at the end of the day to gossip and chatter. Equally impressive and bursting with energy, the men, with crisp shirts and brightly colored vests, join the women. Together, in a rousing finale to "Rocka My Soul in the Bosom of Abraham," they fill the stage with jubilantly strutting bravura dancing.

Judith Jamison in Revelations. *Alvin Ailey American Dance Theater*

MARGUERITE AND ARMAND

1963 ◆ *Music by Franz Liszt, orchestrated by Humphrey Searle and later Gordon Jacob* ◆ *Choreography by Frederick Ashton*

Frederick Ashton had created roles for Margot Fonteyn since 1935, and it would not be an exaggeration to suggest that his early works, rather than her roles in the classics, were responsible for Fonteyn's emergence as England's prima ballerina. As they entered the second decade of their association, it seemed to some that Ashton had become dependent on Fonteyn's interpretations for the success of his ballets. And so, in the mid-1950s and early 1960s, the choreographer began to branch out by creating works for other ballerinas and other companies. With the great success of *La Fille Mal Gardée* in 1960 and *The Two Pigeons* in 1961, Ashton's powers were confirmed as independent of Fonteyn's artistry. (The preceding years had also proved that the ballerina's own stature was secure without an endless stream of masterpieces to sustain it.)

When Ashton began to consider a subject for a new vehicle for his favorite ballerina, he was torn between the two tragic heroines Manon Lescaut and Marguerite Gautier, but finally settled on the latter. Finding an appropriate score for the ballet also proved difficult until he quite by accident heard a radio performance of Liszt's Piano Sonata in B Minor and instantly knew he had found the perfect music.

Perhaps the most important element in the evolution of Ashton's new ballet was the burst of electrifying energy brought to the Royal Ballet by the presence of the Russian dancer Rudolf Nureyev. Only a year before, Nureyev had soared to world fame following his spectacular defection from the Kirov Ballet at Le Bourget Airport in Paris. It seemed natural that the brilliant, passionate Nureyev should dance with Fonteyn, the ballerina in

Marguerite and Armand, *The Royal Ballet:*
opposite, Margot Fonteyn and Michael Somes; above, Margot Fonteyn, Rudolf Nureyev, and Leslie Edwards

the glow of her artistic maturity, and, on February 21, 1962, when the two first performed in *Giselle*, it was clear that a history-making partnership had been born. Aware of the extraordinary magnetism between these two artists, Ashton cast Nureyev as Armand to Fonteyn's Marguerite.

Though not a critical triumph upon its premiere, *Marguerite and Armand* was nevertheless a sweeping portrait of tragic romantic passion and proved the vehicle through which the partnership of Fonteyn and Nureyev captured the hearts of an adoring public. Ashton's choreography and Cecil Beaton's minimal but richly evocative decor perfectly reflected the accompanying program note, which, rather than detailing the saga by Dumas fils, states: "In the last stages of her fatal illness, The Lady of the Camellias re-lives some incidents of her tragic life."

Originally designed to suit an artist in her technically waning years, the ballet in fact enabled Fonteyn to reveal not only the continuing depth and power of her dramatic gifts but also a revitalized technical mastery. As a symbol of the beginning of an inimitable partnership, *Marguerite and Armand* has rightly never been performed by any other dancers; it is fortunately preserved on film to remind later generations of the special magic of Fonteyn and Nureyev.

THE BALLET

As she lies dying of consumption, the delirious Marguerite Gautier sees her life pass before her. Her lover, Armand, comes rushing onto the scene and reveals his grief in an impassioned solo. As Marguerite reaches out for him, a billowing curtain falls and the scene returns to happier days. Marguerite is now seen on the same chaise longue in a dazzling scarlet gown decorated with white camellias, which also adorn her hair. She is surrounded by male admirers, among them her current patron, the Duke. The vibrantly handsome Armand enters and Marguerite is instantly drawn to him. Armand approaches her and kisses her hand; alone, they dance together. When the Duke returns and sees Marguerite in Armand's embrace, he angrily demands that Marguerite leave with him. Before departing, she tosses one of her camellias to Armand.

The second scene takes place in Marguerite's country home, where the lovers dance with unbridled rapture, as if they will never lose their perfect happiness. After Armand leaves, Marguerite sits quietly musing until suddenly a disturbing figure enters. It is Armand's father, who by his bearing suggests the stiff conventionality that will disrupt the lovers' idyll. Marguerite listens incredulously as the man demands that she clear his son's reputation by abandoning him. She frantically begs the stern parent to relent, and he does feel a brief moment of pity when she falls exhausted onto the couch. But as Marguerite regains her composure, he renews his demands before leaving.

Armand returns and notices that Marguerite avoids his eyes. However, her passion soon overrides her anguish and she dances in tragic desperation with him. At the conclusion of their *pas de deux*, Marguerite sits at Armand's knee. For a moment, she rests her body on his, but then she unexpectedly recoils from him and runs off, to Armand's bewilderment.

In the next scene, Marguerite has returned to the Duke. Although arrayed in diamonds and a stunning black gown, she is clearly in poor health. Fired by his passion and still not understanding the reasons for Marguerite's betrayal, Armand enters the salon. He goes to Marguerite, tears the diamond necklace from her throat, and throws it to the ground. Mortified, Marguerite attempts to escape, but he restrains her and, in a shocking gesture, flings a handful of money in her face before leaving. Marguerite is completely disconsolate; when Armand's father appears and sees the tragic result of his self-righteousness, she refuses the comfort of the now-contrite old man.

Marguerite is near death in the last scene. Armand's father has remained at her side, but she is beyond temporal help. Her delirium is filled with visions of Armand, and finally her lover does rush in, his black cape swirling about him. Taking Marguerite rapturously into his arms, he kisses her and lifts her high above him. She reaches out in one last ecstatic expression of their union and then dies. Armand slowly lowers her to the ground, and then clutching her lifeless hand, he brings his other hand to his brow in a gesture of heartrending agony. Armand's father turns away remorsefully as Marguerite's hand drops from Armand's grasp.

Margot Fonteyn as Marguerite. The Royal Ballet

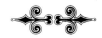

THE DREAM

1964 ◆ *Music by Felix Mendelssohn, arranged by John Lanchbery* ◆ *Choreography by Frederick Ashton*

For the four-hundredth anniversary of the birth of William Shakespeare in 1964, Britain's Royal Ballet intended to mount special performances of ballets based on his works, including a revival of Robert Helpmann's *Hamlet*, a new work by Kenneth MacMillan based on Shakespearean love lyrics, and a new ballet by Frederick Ashton inspired by *A Midsummer Night's Dream*. Ashton's ballet, called *The Dream*, was created in a relatively short time, for the choreographer condensed and simplified the complexities of Shakespeare's pastoral revery. He eliminated the roles of the Duke of Athens and the Queen of the Amazons and reduced the importance of the four confused and bewitched lovers and of the "rude mechanicals." The emphasis was thus placed on the quarreling rulers of fairyland, Titania and Oberon, and the mischievous sprite, Puck.

Having recently created *Marguerite and Armand* for Fonteyn and Nureyev, Ashton turned for his Titania to a rising young soloist in the Royal Ballet, Antoinette Sibley, and for his Oberon to a young man, Anthony Dowell, who had only recently begun to perform solo roles in the company. At first, Sibley and Dowell did not realize they had been cast in the principal roles, thinking instead that they were to dance two of the four mortal lovers.

No doubt influenced by his familiarity with Tyrone Guthrie's 1937 Old Vic production of the play, Ashton set his ballet in a Victorian milieu. The action was dominated by the feuding of Titania and Oberon, and in Sibley and Dowell the choreographer found elements that were at once fey, aggressive, romantic, and sensual. Always a master of characterization in an almost music-hall comedy style, Ashton created a brilliant *pointe* solo for Bottom when he is transformed into an ass. Henry Bardon's setting and David Walker's costumes were of a truly shimmering, sylvan quality, perfectly evoking the transparency of a dream. The ballet met with mixed success upon its premiere, but when it was first performed by the Royal Ballet in the United States in 1965, it was a triumph and began the rise to stardom of Sibley and Dowell, whose transcendent partnership was to approach the greatness of Fonteyn and Nureyev's.

There has been a continuing debate as to the relative merits of the two major balletic treatments of Shakespeare's comedy — Ashton's work and George Balanchine's *A Midsummer Night's Dream*, premiered in 1962 by the New York City Ballet. Cer-

tainly, Balanchine's follows the play more strictly and is closer to Shakespeare's poetry in its concern with the philosophical ideal of love. On the other hand, Ashton, by concentrating on the actual interchange of conflict-ridden love, makes of his *Dream* a more theatrically human work. Strictly speaking, there is no lengthy reconciliation of Titania and Oberon in Shakespeare, but by enlarging that reunion, Ashton encapsulates, in a supernatural context, all the mortal confusions of love. Additionally, the two radiant leading roles in the Ashton work clearly demonstrate the strength of Ashton's creation of a masterful, poignant work of ballet theater.

THE BALLET

As the curtain rises, Oberon, the king of the fairies, stalks among the trees of a wooded glade at evening. He is awaiting the arrival of his queen, Titania, with whom he is heatedly arguing over the possession of a changeling Indian boy. Oberon sends his impish servant Puck to seek out a certain flower whose magical juice will, when applied to a person's eyes, make that person fall in love with the first creature he or she espies. Unknowingly crossing the path of the scheming king of the fairies, two happy mortals, Hermia and Lysander, come into the forest to share their love in solitude. They are followed by another couple — Demetrius, who is in love with Hermia, and Helena, who is desperately in love with Demetrius. Oberon decides to resolve this hopeless conflict by applying some of the flower's juice to Demetrius's eyes so that he will fall in love with Helena. Upon his return, Puck is sent to find Demetrius, who has wandered off with the other three mortals.

Titania and her retinue of fairies in gowns of gossamer tulle then enter and dance in patterns reminiscent of classical forms. As the others leave, the weary fairy queen remains behind to sleep in her bower. The ever-watchful Oberon drops the magic liquor onto Titania's eyelids and withdraws to await the outcome.

Next, the rustic buffoon, Bottom, who has been transformed into an ass by the naughty Puck, wanders into the glade. He performs a ridiculous but endearing dance, prancing on his toes, and awakens Titania, who instantly falls passionately in love with him. Dancing with the absurd Bottom as if he were a divine creature, she calls her fairy attendants to honor him. As the

Larry Grenier as Bottom in The Dream. *The Joffrey Ballet*

168

ecstatic Titania leads Bottom away to show him her kingdom, the four mortal lovers return.

Puck has incorrectly followed Oberon's instructions: he has applied the potion to Lysander's eyes rather than to those of Demetrius, and Lysander now loves Helena. The ensuing comic interchange makes the lovers look more foolish than ever. Coming across this scene of ludicrous mishap, Oberon angrily calls Puck and directs him to conjure up a thick fog. In the haze, the confused lovers are separated and returned to their proper affections. Oberon then releases Titania from her spell, and she sees with horror her misguided affection for Bottom. For his part, Bottom is returned to his mortal state and goes off befuddled.

At the ballet's conclusion, Titania and Oberon perform a *pas de deux* of exquisite symmetry and sublime tenderness. In their reconciliation, the fairy king and queen reveal an ardor, an understanding, and a respect that transcends mortal definition and is somehow linked to the most profound laws of Nature.

Anthony Dowell as Oberon in The Dream. *The Royal Ballet*

ROMEO AND JULIET

1965 ◆ *Music by Sergei Prokofiev* ◆ *Choreography by Kenneth MacMillan*

William Shakespeare's *Romeo and Juliet* has been an inspiration to choreographers and composers from the earliest days of ballet. Although the first treatment for which there is a permanent record was choreographed in 1811, by Vincenzo Galeotti for the Royal Danish Ballet, the most notable productions have come in the twentieth century and have utilized Sergei Prokofiev's 1938 score for a full-length version. The most influential of these premiered on January 11, 1940, when the Kirov Ballet mounted Leonid Lavrovsky's three-act *Romeo and Juliet*, with Konstantin Sergeyev and the incomparable Galina Ulanova in the title roles. Perhaps for the first time in ballet under Soviet rule, a work went beyond the precepts of Socialist Realism to the heart of human tragedy. It was with this production that the Bolshoi Ballet made its stunning debut in the West at Covent Garden, London, in 1956, and in which the performance of Ulanova was a special revelation.

Inspired by Lavrovsky's version, several Western choreographers began to try their hand at Prokofiev's *Romeo and Juliet*. John Cranko's 1958 production was staged for La Scala in Milan and triumphantly remounted for his own Stuttgart Ballet in

Mikhail Baryshnikov and Merle Park in Kenneth MacMillan's Romeo and Juliet. *The Royal Ballet*

171

1962, providing ballerina Marcia Haydée with her first major starring vehicle. Curiously enough, London's Royal Ballet did not stage its own *Romeo and Juliet* until the mid-1960s, when a new full-length production was announced with choreography by Kenneth MacMillan.

Like Cranko, MacMillan had served his choreographic apprenticeship with Sadler's Wells Theatre Ballet. Since 1956, he had created works for the Royal Ballet, among the most notable being *The Invitation* (1960) and *The Rite of Spring* (1962). *Romeo and Juliet* was to be MacMillan's first three-act ballet, and he had selected the bright young stars of the Royal Ballet, Lynn Seymour and Christopher Gable, to dance the title roles. But Gable was incapacitated before the ballet's premiere, and the first performance, on February 9, 1965, starred Margot Fonteyn and Rudolf Nureyev, whose partnership was already reaching legendary heights. Yet the strength of MacMillan's *Romeo and Juliet* did not depend solely on the magic of Fonteyn and Nureyev, for the ballet has attained the status of a modern classic and has remained one of the most beloved and distinguished works in the Royal Ballet's repertoire.

Romeo and Juliet is charged with passion, theatrical spectacle, rollicking humor, and breathtaking solos and dances for small groups and ensembles —all working to convey the grandeur and emotion of Shakespeare's tragedy. The work has provided audiences with unforgettable memories of such partnerships as Fonteyn and Nureyev, Seymour and Gable, Antoinette Sibley and Anthony Dowell, and more recently, with Dowell, Natalia Makarova and Gelsey Kirkland.

THE BALLET

The curtain rises on the empty marketplace in Verona. Romeo, a member of the House of Montague, is unsuccessfully pursuing the haughty aristocrat Rosaline, who belongs to a rival family, the Capulets. Moments after she escapes, Romeo is joined by his friends Mercutio and Benvolio, and the marketplace springs to life.

Romeo joins his friends in baiting Tybalt, a stern nephew of the House of Capulet, and the square is suddenly filled with feuding Montagues and Capulets. Some on both sides are mortally wounded, but the chaos abruptly ceases with the entrance of the Duke of Verona. The duke angrily curses both houses and orders all the men to lay down their swords. Although Lord

Montague and Lord Capulet pretend to reconcile, their kinsmen form a tableau of restrained antagonism.

Scene 2 takes place in Juliet's bedroom in the Capulets' palace. To a giddy scherzando in the music, the young Juliet, carrying a doll, rushes into the room with youthful enthusiasm and wakes her sleeping nurse. Lord and Lady Capulet soon enter with the handsome nobleman Paris, whom they intend Juliet to wed. The frightened girl runs to her nurse for protection and Paris soon leaves with her parents. When the wise nurse reminds Juliet that she is no longer a child, by gently placing her hands on Juliet's breasts, the girl sadly lets her doll drop.

In Scene 3, an elegant procession of aristocrats approaches the gates of the Capulet palace to be admitted as guests to a ball. Among them are the uninvited Romeo, Mercutio, and Benvolio disguised in masks and long capes. The friends perform a brilliant *pas de trois* before they rush through the palace gates. As the lights come up on Scene 4, the ball guests are performing a stately court dance. Then, while Juliet and Paris dance, Romeo and the girl catch sight of each other. They are instantly smitten.

When Juliet plays the mandolin to accompany her friends' dance, Romeo joins the girls and circles around Juliet, finishing in front of her on his knee. Juliet then dances a solo of delicate *piqués arabesques*, turns, and sailing *sautés*, at one point moving directly into Romeo's arms. Paris intervenes and Juliet runs shyly away.

Mercutio and Benvolio then perform rollicking and droll solos, all the while watched suspiciously by Tybalt. After the ballroom empties, Juliet returns alone and suddenly Romeo appears. She rushes into his arms and he effortlessly lifts her aloft as she swoons backward in rapture. In the midst of their dance, Tybalt enters and orders Romeo to leave. Romeo bows once more to his newfound love and then departs.

Scene 5 reveals the balcony to Juliet's bedroom later that night. Filled with thoughts of Romeo, Juliet lifts one arm heavenward. As if in answer to her prayers, Romeo rushes into the courtyard. She runs to him, and their rapture bursts into an impassioned duet filled with soaring lifts and melting swoons. They kiss passionately before Juliet returns to the balustrade. She reaches out a yearning arm to her lover as the curtain falls.

Act II opens in the bustling Verona marketplace. Juliet's nurse rushes into the square with a letter for Romeo. After much

Boris Akimov as Mercutio in Yuri Grigorovich's version of Romeo and Juliet. *The Bolshoi Ballet*

teasing by Mercutio and Benvolio, she finally finds him, and the young man is overjoyed to read Juliet's plea that they must meet to be married. Scene 2 takes place in Friar Laurence's cell, where the pious monk unites the lovers as the nurse stands by, weeping with a joy tinged with apprehension.

The action returns to the marketplace. Tybalt tries to provoke Romeo into a fight, but the young man, filled with a compassion born from his union with Juliet, refuses. Amazed over Romeo's sudden lack of spirit, Mercutio accepts Tybalt's challenge in his place. A duel ensues, and when Romeo clutches his friend in an attempt to restrain him, Tybalt stabs Mercutio in the back. Although at first pretending that his wound is minor, Mercutio finally sinks dying to the ground, cursing both the Capulets and Romeo. The agonized Romeo slays Tybalt and then rushes away as Lady Capulet kneels in grief at the side of her murdered kinsman.

Act III opens in Juliet's bedchamber. It is early morning, and Romeo, in bed beside his young bride, kisses her. They rise and dance a rapturous *pas de deux* shot through with the sad knowledge that they must part. After Romeo leaves, Juliet returns to the bed and feigns sleep. When Lord and Lady Capulet enter with Paris, Juliet, filled with love and concern for Romeo, cannot even pretend to accept his attentions. The distraught parents leave with Paris, and in desperation Juliet flees to the

cell of Friar Laurence. The monk offers Juliet a strange potion which, when drunk, will give her all the appearances of death, though she will be merely asleep. The terrified girl accepts only because it will enable her to join Romeo.

Later, in Juliet's bedchamber, the young woman promises to wed Paris. Then, torn between her fear and her longing for Romeo, she drinks the potion. Morning comes, and Juliet's nurse and friends arrive with flowers and her wedding dress. As Lord Capulet gently shakes his daughter, he finds to his horror that the girl appears to be dead.

In the final scene, Juliet lies on a bier in the Capulet family crypt. As her grieving family and the clergy depart, Paris remains behind to mourn Juliet. Romeo, disguised as one of the monks, confronts Paris and kills him. He lifts Juliet's body from the bier and dances with the lifeless girl one last time. Though inanimate, her body responds harmoniously to his tender lifts and caresses. Resting her back onto the bier, Romeo drinks poison and dies.

At that moment, Juliet revives and is terrified at first by her dismal surroundings. Her relief that the potion has worked soon gives way to shock as she sees Romeo's dead body. Overcome by the hopelessness of her fate, Juliet takes his dagger, still wet with Paris's blood, and plunges it into her heart. She lives only long enough to lay herself tenderly across Romeo's body.

Gerd Larsen as the Nurse and Antoinette Sibley as Juliet. The Royal Ballet

Boris Akimov as Mercutio. The Bolshoi Ballet

EUGENE ONEGIN

1965 ◆ *Music by Peter Ilyich Tchaikovsky, arranged and orchestrated by Kurt-Heinz Stolze* ◆ *Choreography by John Cranko*

Except for a brief period in the 1760s when Jean-Georges Noverre, the great French choreographer and dance theorist, was ballet master at the court of the Grand Duke of Württemberg, the city of Stuttgart had held a minor position in the ballet world. In 1961, as a young choreographer named John Cranko was invited to become the director of the Stuttgart Ballet, that situation was about to change.

Cranko, born in Rustenburg, South Africa, had his early ballet training there, but at nineteen went to England to study at the Sadler's Wells Ballet School. Almost immediately he began to choreograph ballets for Sadler's Wells Theatre Ballet, and by 1951, with his *Pineapple Poll* and *Harlequin in April*, he was acknowledged as a major voice in British choreography. In 1957, he created the first full-length all-English ballet, *The Prince of the Pagodas*, for the Royal Ballet. During the fifties, Cranko also choreographed for other companies and produced a musical revue, *Cranks*, a smashing success that proved his theatrical ken went beyond the boundaries of the ballet stage.

With the invitation from Stuttgart, however, Cranko had for the first time an entire ballet company and government subsidy at his disposal. Freed to explore and refine his artistic goals of dramatic veracity and choreographic integrity, Cranko poured forth a stream of work: restagings of his own earlier ballets such as *The Lady and the Fool*, *Antigone*, and *Romeo and Juliet*; his versions of classics such as *The Sleeping Beauty*, *Coppélia*, and *Swan Lake*; and new works, including *Scènes de Ballet*, *The Seasons*, *Daphnis and Chloe*, and *Jeu de Cartes*. Featured in these works were dancers who might rightly be considered as much Cranko's creations as were his ballets—Marcia Haydée, Richard Cragun, Egon Madsen, and Birgit Keil.

In 1965, Cranko planned a new full-length work based on Alexander Pushkin's masterpiece, *Eugene Onegin*. A free-verse novel, *Onegin* was not a work of epic proportion but rather an episodic analysis of individual character and romantic love. Its subtle, evasive themes would be daunting to most choreographers, but to Cranko they were an inspiration. For the ballet's score, Cranko asked the German composer-arranger Kurt-Heinz Stolze to find suitable compositions by Tchaikovsky (barring selections from his opera inspired by the same novel).

At its premiere in Stuttgart on April 13, 1965, and later, when the company made its United States debut in 1969 at the Metropolitan Opera House in New York, *Eugene Onegin* was a triumphant success. Cranko proved that, in the middle of the twentieth century, a choreographer could create a narrative dramatic ballet comparable to the nineteenth-century classics. With nothing short of genius, he blended the dramatic impact of stillness with that of movement, seamlessly interweaving both with soaring *pas de deux* and finely constructed ensemble dances. Ballerina Haydée attained stardom with her powerful yet poignant characterization of Tatiana.

THE BALLET

The Act I curtain rises on the vernal garden of Madame Larina, a member of the provincial aristocracy of early nineteenth-century Russia. Seated at a table in a corner of the garden are Madame Larina, her daughter Olga, and a nurse. At a far end of the garden, lying on the ground and lost in the pages of a romantic novel is Tatiana, Madame Larina's older daughter. Tatiana, whose birthday party is approaching, has little interest in the happy preparations of Olga and the nurse. She is finally drawn away from her book when several of her girl friends enter the garden. Their vivacious dancing is suddenly disturbed by the sound of distant gunshots.

Olga's fiancé, Lensky, a handsome and dashing young poet, arrives and tells the ladies that he has been hunting with a friend from St. Petersburg, Eugene Onegin. The friend appears and Tatiana's romantic fantasies are instantly aroused by the sight of this stranger dressed severely in black. She becomes girlishly animated, but Onegin seems as bored with her as with everything else around her.

Scene 2 takes place in Tatiana's bedroom. She is sitting at her writing desk composing a letter. From the intensity with which she fills a page, then tears it up and begins again, it is clear she is writing a love letter to Onegin. Settling on a last version, Tatiana asks her nurse to deliver it to Onegin, and, at the nurse's urging, attempts to sleep. Through the mirror comes a vision of Onegin, and Tatiana dances with it ecstatically.

Act II opens with Tatiana's birthday celebration. The guests are all aflutter with two romances in their midst—Olga and Lensky, already affianced, and Tatiana and Onegin. But Onegin, who has come to the party only at Lensky's urging, thinks the proceedings tiresome. He yawns and finds it difficult not to

snub the other guests, whom he finds provincial bores. Tatiana eagerly awaits Onegin's response to her letter. When he finally approaches her and proceeds to tear it up in her face, her horrified reaction only makes Onegin more disdainful.

Among the guests at the party is Prince Gremin, an older relative of the family, who is clearly enamored of Tatiana. The girl is, however, oblivious to him. Meanwhile, Onegin, deciding to alleviate his ennui, shamelessly flirts with Olga. By her innocent responses, she unwittingly serves as his accomplice. Onegin achieves his purpose when Lensky becomes enraged with jealousy. Realizing too late that his friend is in deadly earnest, Onegin must accept Lensky's challenge to a duel.

Scene 2 takes place in an isolated area of the countryside at dawn. Frightened and desperate, the sisters beg Lensky to call off the duel. But the idealistic poet is now ruled by his romantic fantasies of betrayal. Onegin arrives and, for the first time, seems to be aware that his actions have real consequences. Although Onegin has no heart for the duel, his friend insists that it take place and the two go off into the distance. Shots are heard and Lensky is killed. Onegin awakens to the tragic consequences of his heartlessness, as Tatiana, torn by her shattered illusions, rushes away.

Act III is set in St. Petersburg many years later. Onegin is older, perhaps wiser, but mostly weary from his endless search to find meaning for his life. At a resplendent ball in the palace of Prince Gremin, Onegin watches as the guests perform a sweeping, kaleidoscopic waltz. In the midst of the dancing, Prince Gremin introduces his new wife, an elegant and regal woman. To his utter shock, Onegin recognizes the Princess Gremin as Tatiana. Aware of his thoughtless cruelty of former years, he is also struck by her mature beauty.

In the last scene, Tatiana is alone in her lavish boudoir. With a tormented expression, she reads a letter from Onegin. He appears and for a moment Tatiana succumbs to his newly awakened ardor. They dance a passionate duet in which he shows all the romantic fervor that Tatiana desired, but did not receive, in her youth. Recovering her maturity and wisdom, she tells Onegin that the possibility of their love has passed and orders him to leave her forever. Onegin fails to alter her resolve and sadly departs. Tatiana stands proudly alone, yet obviously torn by suppressed anguish, as the curtain falls.

Eugene Onegin, *Stuttgart Ballet: above, Marcia Haydée and Richard Cragun; overleaf, Vladimir Klos and Birgit Keil*

Marcia Haydée and Richard Cragun in Eugene Onegin. *Stuttgart Ballet*

HARBINGER

1967 ◆ Music by Sergei Prokofiev ◆ Choreography by Eliot Feld

Although the 1960s were certainly not the only decade to be characterized by unrest among the young, the collective voice of youth has rarely been heard so clamorously as in those years. One of the most restless young voices in the field of dance was Brooklyn-born Eliot Feld, who had joined American Ballet Theatre in 1963 after studying at the School of American Ballet and dancing with the New York City Ballet and in the Broadway and film productions of Jerome Robbins's *West Side Story.*

Feld had been known as something of a "bad boy of ballet," but the second time he worked with Robbins—on the 1965 American Ballet Theatre production of *Les Noces* —the young dancer seems to have realized both Robbins's choreographic genius and the profundity of the choreographic art. The twenty-three-year-old Feld had never put two steps together and was, in fact, noted as a singular dramatic performer rather than a classical dancer; yet he set himself the task of choreographing a short duet to the third movement of Prokofiev's Concerto no. 5 in G Major for Piano and Orchestra.

The neophyte choreographer worked for two months on the two-minute *pas de deux* before it approached his vision. He then moved on to the fourth movement to create a trio, and when that was completed he asked Robbins for his opinion. Robbins was so enthusiastic that he went directly to Lucia Chase, director of American Ballet Theatre, with the suggestion that the company produce Feld's ballet. Robbins's opinion was obviously not to be taken lightly, and so Feld's ballet, *Harbinger,* was announced for American Ballet Theatre's 1967 spring season.

Harbinger was given its world premiere by the company during its American tour in Miami, Florida, and its first New York performance, on May 11, 1967, was a triumphant success. Feld was acclaimed by the critics as the greatest force in American choreography since Robbins burst upon the scene with his *Fancy Free* in 1944. It was nothing short of wondrous that Feld, with no previous choreographic experience, should have created a ballet that not only vividly expressed the feelings of American youth but conveyed them in balletic terms that were undeniably and totally original. In discussing the work, Feld stated, "I'm talking about myself and the people I know. It's like showing some of the kinds of personal games we play." Finding his source of musical inspiration in Prokofiev's jagged classicism, Feld constructed a contemporary dance work that retained its bal-

letic intonation while skillfully blending elements of jazz, modern, and improvisational movement.

In 1968, Feld withdrew from American Ballet Theatre, taking with him a number of its leading soloists, including Christine Sarry, John Sowinski, Naomi Sorkin, and Edward Verso. He formed a company of fifteen dancers called the American Ballet Company, which made its debut in 1969 at the Festival of Two Worlds, Spoleto, Italy. This company was considered among the most important in contemporary dance; while the fortunes of his subsequent troupes have fluctuated, their artistic prestige has remained steady because of the quality of Feld's works and of the dancers performing them. *Harbinger* was indeed just that — an initial statement of promise by one of the brightest choreographic lights in our time.

THE BALLET

All the dancers are dressed in nondescript rehearsal attire and wear soft ballet slippers. In the first movement, *Allegro con Brio,* a man performs a solo that expresses, in the choreographer's words, the experience of "being by yourself and having fantasies." His internal monologue is revealed through contractions and stretchings of his body. Six women, who enter and dance around him, portray fanciful images which he senses, but can never take hold of.

The second movement, the march-like *Moderato,* is a chase between a man and a woman in which she never allows him to take hold of her for long. At its end, she leaps into the air and is caught in a fetal position in his arms. The third movement, the brief *Toccata: Allegro con Fuoco,* has a frenzied pace, yet is shot through with an air of melancholy. The patterns of a leading couple are echoed by a group of seven dancers, who repeatedly come together and disperse. The section concludes with an image of hope in which all huddle together and slowly lift their heads toward a glowing amber light.

The fourth movement, *Larghetto,* is about competition. Two men and a woman engage in a game of complex designs, reflecting the contractions and stretching releases of the opening solo. The entire ensemble gathers together for the final section, *Vivo.* The movement motifs developed throughout the work are recapitulated in continually inventive structural configurations until, in the final moments, the women leap into the air and are caught suspended there by the men.

Overleaf: Michaela Hughes in Harbinger. *Eliot Feld Ballet*

181

JEWELS

1967 ◆ Music by Gabriel Fauré, Igor Stravinsky, Peter Ilyich Tchaikovsky ◆ Choreography by George Balanchine

By 1967, Balanchine had been creating ballets for forty-five years and had more than one hundred works to his credit; yet there were no signs that this extraordinary outpouring of genius might be running dry. That year, two Balanchine works were announced for the New York City Ballet's spring season at the New York State Theater, its official home since 1964. The first would be set to orchestrated piano pieces by Chabrier (*Trois Valses Romantiques*), and the second, as yet untitled, would be based on the unique qualities of precious gems.

The idea for a ballet with dancers dressed as jewels originated in Europe in the early 1950s, when Claude Arpels of the world-famous jewelry firm, Van Cleef & Arpels, suggested it to Balanchine. Fifteen years later, when the choreographer visited the jeweler's New York salon, he decided the time had come for the ballet. At first, Balanchine intended to capture the radiance of four gems—emeralds, rubies, diamonds, and sapphires—but he decided that the particular quality of the last was too elusive to convey. For the score, he selected three composers whose music was as inimitable as the gems they would reflect: Fauré, Stravinsky, and Tchaikovsky.

As it turned out, Balanchine created three separate ballets held together by a unifying theme. After its premiere on April 13, 1967, *Jewels* (a title which was at first tentative but then retained) was reviewed as "history's first full-length three-act abstract ballet"; the public was intrigued and flocked to the box office in droves. Although the critical voice was not universal in its praise, the work's immense popular success no doubt arose from its visual splendor and the stunning impact of an evening-long cumulation of abstract virtuoso dance.

Jewels has never been out of the repertoire of the New York City Ballet. For over a decade, the critics and the public have debated which of the three sections is the best. This controversy is perhaps more an indication of an inability to absorb the work's complex synthesis of Balanchinean esthetics than a judgment on the success of what the choreographer intended to convey. The fact remains that the ballets constituting *Jewels* are indeed the products of a master and, furthermore, that the dancers who perform in them are certainly his most precious gems.

THE BALLET

EMERALDS: The caressing prelude to Fauré's *Pelléas et Méli-*

sande has barely begun when the curtain rises to reveal a soft romantic tableau bathed in shimmering sea-green light. Suspended high in the air are coolly glowing green gems; beneath them, a group of women in calf-length green tutus encircle a woman and a man posed in a poetic embrace. As the women move in rhythmic patterns, the ballerina bends in an elegant *révérence*. The couple meet and part throughout the dance, as if in a revery of remembered love.

To the spinning *La Fileuse*, the ballerina performs her solo. Her arms move in seamless, fast-flowing gestures, then her whole body follows their flowing impetus. She skims about and executes gentle backbends until finally she kneels and her arms whisper into repose. The lilting *Sicilienne* accompanies the solo danced by a ballerina who now appears for the first time. Her variation is a breathless construction of waltzing curtsies in which she appears to dance with an imaginary partner.

To music from Fauré's *Shylock*, two women and a man dance in tandem and in canon. A virtuosic solo for the man precedes solos for the two women: the first a fleet, running impromptu, the second a whirl of sustained *piqué* turns. All three dance an exuberant coda, then, with linked arms, breeze off. Another *pas de deux* (added by Balanchine in 1976) for the first ballerina and her cavalier is characterized by mysterious back-to-back rapports—even their exit is a backward-directed walk.

The next *pas de deux*, for the second ballerina and a partner, is one of the most unusual of Balanchine's creations. With the support of her cavalier, the ballerina performs what is essentially a crossover from one side of the stage to the other. She walks on *pointe* in continually changing directions, and occasionally halts to extend her leg with accompanying *ports de bras* in a disquieting time-lapse sequence of execution.

After an effervescent coda by the entire ensemble, a kind of postlude finds the seven principals performing a haunting farewell in patterns expressing yearning. The men watch as the women vanish and the curtain falls.

RUBIES: The three menacing orchestral chords that open Stravinsky's Capriccio for Piano and Orchestra are heard. On stage a tiara of thirteen figures in blood-red costumes stand frozen with their hands joined and arms uplifted to form sharp peaks. The music explodes into pounding rhythms as the dancers launch into forward and backward pelvic thrusts and

Opposite: Adam Lüders and Merrill Ashley in "Diamonds" from Jewels. *New York City Ballet*
Overleaf: Bart Cook and Heather Watts in "Rubies" from Jewels. *New York City Ballet*

contrapuntal jabbings of their feet. The statuesque woman at their center (the female soloist) moves forward and soon the quirky steps take on a witty, fanciful character. A man and woman rush into the fray and briefly perform a sensual yet playful dance.

Four men then come forward; each grasps an ankle or wrist of the female soloist and proceeds to revolve her limbs in extravagant contortions. After the men and women all execute a contrapuntal sequence of peculiar crouched, cross-legged positions, they lope off with hunched-over backs, rhythmically stamping feet, and swaying arms. Their leader departs in the opposite direction, supporting herself in contorted extensions and wide, deep *pliés à la seconde* and a final overextended *penché* as a fillip.

The second movement of the Capriccio opens with blurry coils of music. The ballerina and the *danseur* enter to perform the central *pas de deux*, characterized by repeated entwinings of their arms and the woman's slinky *glissades* to the floor. The music becomes more insistently pounding, as the *danseur's* brief, inventive solo is followed by the ballerina's jazzy one punctuated with high kicks and amusing skyward glances. With rhythmically pumping arms, the man enters backward and the ballerina joins him in a jaunty takeoff of a cakewalk. As the music shifts to a sort of tango, the ballerina echoes it with her rapid flat and pointed footwork. She spins into a dangerous lunge and is caught only at the last moment by her partner. The music finally subsides into a rippling trill; as the couple entwine arms, the woman rests one hand on his and the man kisses it in a gallant gesture.

The last movement, *Allegro capriccioso*, is danced with a combination of euphoria and hysteria. At one point, four men form a diagonal and fling the female soloist into the air, while eight women prance in place in phalanxes. The ballerina performs a variation which the other women accompany with a peculiar motion of undulating hips and arms pawing the air. Amid endless rushing entrances and flying exits, the female soloist leads the other women in a sexy passage in which they step from side to side like chorines, then lunge forward with one leg kicked high in the air behind them. During an antic chase between the men and the principal male, he soars spinning in the air, then exits with whirling *emboîté* turns executed at breakneck speed. The ballerina performs another variation highlighted by whirlwind *piqué* turns and quirky arms flexed tightly at her sides.

In the last moments, the entire ensemble unites with a syncopated revolution in place. In time with the racing music, the dancers form two oblique phalanxes and repeatedly step over their own feet with punctuating kicks. Everyone flies into the air and lands on one knee as the curtain falls.

DIAMONDS: This section, set to the last four movements of Tchaikovsky's Symphony no. 3 in D Major (*The Polish*), opens on a stage ablaze with white light. Twelve women in jeweled white tutus are poised in a classical grouping under a sky of translucent diamonds. In a lilting waltz, *Alla tedesca*, the dancers move gently in alternating canonic groups, led at one point by two female soloists.

The dancers flow back into their opening tableau as the soulful measures of the *Andante elegiaco* introduce the ballerina and the *danseur*. Their *pas de deux*, the quintessence of the Petipa style, is a discourse in which the ballerina prances delicately on *pointe*, swoons back into the arms of her cavalier, and is borne aloft by his floating lifts. It concludes as the *danseur* falls to one knee in homage to his ballerina and places a kiss upon her hand. The *Scherzo*, performed by four female and two male soloists and the two principals, is a series of rapid and unresolved searchings. Moments of Slavic intonation in the music are echoed by the women's czardaslike movements and *ports de bras*.

To the symphony's last movement, *Allegro con Fuoco*, a resounding polonaise is performed by the entire corps, with partners, and the ballerina and her cavalier. The choreography's myriad configurations, crystalline classicism, and perfect musical visualization produce the effect of a bursting, radiant energy. The ensemble becomes a kind of kaleidoscope converging in and out of itself until, after one last burgeoning out, it strikes a tableau of dazzling resolution as the curtain falls.

Daniel Duell, Karin von Aroldingen, and Sean Lavery in "Emeralds" from Jewels. *New York City Ballet*

ASTARTE

1967 ◆ Music by the Crome Syrcus rock band ◆ Choreography by Robert Joffrey

The March 15, 1968, cover of *Time* magazine featured a psyche-delic photocollage showing the face of a hypnotically beau-tiful woman superimposed on the bodies of a young couple: the same woman and an unclad, magnetically virile man. The caption read, "Joffrey Ballet's *Astarte*," and the story inside was entitled "The Great Leap Forward." After more than a decade of cross-country touring, mostly by station wagon, Robert Jof-frey—and this latest of his ballet companies—had arrived.

Almost from the beginning of his career, Joffrey, a Seattle-born dancer-choreographer, had been recognized as an impor-tant and singular voice in American choreography, and the companies that performed his works and those of his co-direc-tor, Gerald Arpino, were highly esteemed. Nevertheless, sur-vival was a constant struggle until 1962, when the Rebekah Harkness Foundation offered to underwrite the Robert Joffrey Ballet for an engagement at the Festival of Two Worlds, Spoleto, Italy, and later that year, for a tour of the Near East sponsored by the State Department. The next year, the company toured the Soviet Union to great acclaim, but soon after its return from abroad, the association between Joffrey and the Harkness Foun-dation dissolved, and the fundless Joffrey Ballet disbanded. Robert Joffrey was nothing if not determined, and within a year he garnered funds from the Ford Foundation to form yet another company. By 1966, that company became the resident dance troupe of the New York City Center, under the name of the City Center Joffrey Ballet.

By the second half of the 1960s, the optimism of the Kennedy years had given way to an era of social reevaluation, protest, and revolution. Since Joffrey himself was still a young man and his company had always identified with youth, he responded to this cultural upheaval by creating *Astarte*, a ballet intended, in his own words, to "attack the senses." Joffrey chose the rather obscure Semitic goddess of sensual abandon as the focus of an extended *pas de deux* which proved to be a relentlessly aggressive multimedia experience. Evidently the time was ripe for *Astarte*: audiences went in droves to this "tuned-in, turned-on, dropped-out and flipped-out" spectacle.

Astarte was not the first exploration into multimedia in dance, but at the time it captured perfectly the rebellious and self-involved sentiments of American youth. Immediacy was the work's prime virtue and because it was so immediate a response to a cultural need, it has almost become a period piece.

Still, its total fusion of choreography, music, lighting, set, and film produced an engrossing spectacle of startling impact, enhanced by the vital interpretations of its original dancers, Trinette Singleton and Maximiliano Zomosa.

THE BALLET

The blaring, acid-rock music of Crome Syrcus begins, and the audience is assaulted by harsh, flickering strobe lights. Spot-lights are played over the audience, with an intentionally hypnotic effect. The stage is slowly lit, and a taut scrim of white fabric serves as a screen upon which a film featuring birds and a blatantly erotic female figure is projected. As the spotlights focus on a young male member of the audience, on the screen the enlarged eye of the woman winks. Entranced, the young man leaves his seat and slowly walks down the aisle and onto the stage, drawn to the figure of the woman. She is the goddess Astarte, and she suddenly appears in person, wearing a multi-colored unitard and with a flower-child tattoo on her face.

Standing face to face with her, and clearly mesmerized, the young man begins to remove his clothing, stopping at his briefs. There now begins a *pas de deux* that is at once sensual and detached, its gestures and movements anticipated, echoed, or distorted by film fragments projected on the screen. The dancers are totally engulfed in their mixed-media world, where in contrast to the pounding music the dance itself proceeds with a cool, measured pace. Aroused by the aloof goddess, the man expresses his idolatry with choreographically intricate manipu-lations of her body. In response, a phallic protrusion is outlined behind the screen, and the film projected on it shows the young man marked with the tattoo of the goddess. Subdued, he becomes the victim of the unconquerable Astarte. He falls in spasms at her feet, and in the film he rolls, anguished, head over heels. The climax comes when he lifts Astarte on his shoulders, her legs wound around his neck, and she arches seductively. Lowering her to the ground, he releases her and she vanishes.

The huge, engulfing screen rises and, still in a trance, the man walks toward the back wall of the theater, seen beyond the stage. Two doors open, and he walks through them out of the theater and onto the street. A final projection shows Astarte's dazed initiate moving through the traffic in the street. In the theater itself, the audience has, ideally, experienced some of the mental and sensual stimulations of a hallucinogenic "trip."

Trinette Singleton and Maximiliano Zomosa in Astarte. *The Joffrey Ballet*

191

SPARTACUS

1968 ◆ *Music by Aram Khachaturian* ◆ *Choreography by Yuri Grigorovich*

The revolution of 1917 changed the course of Russian ballet in two major ways. First, it precluded the return of those illustrious artists —like Pavlova, Nijinsky, Karsavina, Fokine, and Massine —who had frequently left Russia to perform in the West. As the years went by, the exodus of Russian dance artists dwindled to a mere trickle (among the most notable of the last émigrés was Balanchine, who left Russia in 1924).

Second, since the revolution isolated the Soviet Union from outside influences on the ballet, any new stylistic developments could come only from within its own borders. While Leningrad's Kirov Ballet upheld the classical tradition in productions of the Petipa and Ivanov masterworks, the Bolshoi Theater in Moscow (the other major center of Soviet ballet) experimented with a new style that came to be labeled Socialist Realism. The first ballet of lasting merit in this revolutionary style, *The Red Poppy*, choreographed by Lev Lashchilin and Vassili Tikhomirov to music of Reinhold Glière, was first performed by the Bolshoi Ballet on June 14, 1927.

Despite the Bolshoi's position as the leading exponent of Socialist Realist ballet in the intervening years, it was for the Kirov, in 1956, that Leonid Jacobson, one of the Soviet Union's leading choreographers, created the first version of a work that would come to epitomize that esthetic. Based on stories from Plutarch, Jacobson's *Spartacus* had a score by Aram Khachaturian and was disappointingly unsuccessful. Two years later, another, even more unsuccessful, version was choreographed by Igor Moiseyev for the Bolshoi Ballet. A revised production by Jacobson, which was seen in the United States in 1962, also failed.

Success came finally in 1968 when Yuri Grigorovich, who had become ballet master of the Bolshoi after his outstanding productions of *Legend of Love* (1961) and *The Stone Flower* (1962), choreographed his version of *Spartacus* for that company. Hailed as the greatest Soviet work of this generation, the ballet portrays the dramatic spectacle of the Roman slaves' heroic rebellion against imperialistic oppressors through a series of finely conceived scenes of emotional intensity which flow one into the other to vividly mounting impact. Though still retaining some undercurrents of socialist "propaganda," the work gains power through its sweeping choreographic structure, and freshness through its economy of pantomimic gesture. Furthermore, Gri-

gorovich's choreography, with its neoclassic intonation, was a departure from the athletically oriented Bolshoi style and revealed that the company was headed in a new, more enlightened direction. The acclaim accorded *Spartacus* outside the Soviet Union indicates that the Soviet tradition has overcome a kind of stagnation and has regained its place in the spectrum of world ballet.

THE BALLET

The curtain rises to reveal the cold-blooded Roman general Crassus surrounded by Roman shields, his arm lifted victoriously. The shields separate and the Roman soldiers who carry them perform a dance of victory to celebrate their latest conquest, Thrace. Among the Thracians to be brought back to Rome as slaves are Spartacus and his wife, Phrygia. Spartacus is already rankling under the yoke of captivity and it is obvious that he will not endure it for long. At the slave market in the second scene, Spartacus is separated from Phrygia. Phrygia's anguish over being torn from the side of her husband is heightened by the fact that she has been bought by the ruthless Crassus. In the third scene, the desolate Phrygia is mocked by Aegina, Crassus's lustful mistress, at his villa in Rome. The virtuous wife is then subjected to the debauchery of an orgy, the climax of which is a fight between two blindfolded gladiators. The tense conflict ends when one is slain, and the victor, removing his blindfold, is revealed as Spartacus. Horrified over having been forced to murder one of his own kind, Spartacus is determined to throw off his subjugation. In the fourth scene, he resolutely spurs on his fellow slaves as they vanquish their guards and escape.

The Act II curtain rises on the Appian Way at night. Spartacus and his followers convince a group of shepherds to join them in the revolt against Rome, and soon others join the rebel forces. Spartacus is elected their leader, but in a meditative dance soliloquy, he struggles within himself over whether to accept that role. He decides to accept because of his strong desire to free his fellow men and to release his wife from her captivity.

Spartacus finds his way back to the villa and discovers Phrygia; after an ecstatic dance of reunion, they flee. In the next scene, Spartacus and his troops return to the villa and seize it.

Vladimir Vasiliev and Nina Sorokina in Spartacus. *The Bolshoi Ballet*

However, Crassus, Aegina, and their followers escape. Another soliloquy finds Spartacus ruminating on the corruption of the Romans and how he can use it to his own ends. In the last scene, Crassus has been captured, and Spartacus, rather than killing him outright, subjects him to the same test he has undergone. Spartacus himself fights Crassus, easily overpowering him, but again, instead of executing him, Spartacus listens to the villain's cowardly pleas and disdainfully lets him go free.

In the opening scene of Act III, Crassus plans his revenge against Spartacus. Aegina, even more vengeful than her lover, plots her own punishment for Spartacus. Scene 2 takes place at Spartacus's camp at night. Crassus and his army are advancing, and Spartacus has a strategy that is thought too dangerous by his less confident followers. Even Phrygia is frightened. But Spartacus draws from his followers a vow of allegiance. When they take their leave, he performs a final introspective dance in which he questions the courage of his men. That night, Aegina and a group of Roman whores steal into the camp and seduce the rebels with their sexual favors and with drink. In their weakened condition, the rebels are easily defeated by the Romans. Crassus rewards the treacherous Aegina and then declares that Spartacus and his remaining forces must be utterly destroyed. In the last scene, Spartacus knows that defeat is near but fights valiantly to the last. Finally, surrounded by the soldiers of Crassus, he is lifted mercilessly on the points of their spears. Phrygia finds the body of her dead husband and, in a last tragic tableau, she is lifted into the air by the few remaining rebels and as his body and shield are raised up to her, she mourns pitifully over the fallen hero.

Spartacus, *The Bolshoi Ballet: opposite, Vyacheslav Gordeyev as Spartacus; above, Mikhail Gabovich as Crassus*

THE TAMING OF THE SHREW

1969 ◆ *Music by Kurt-Heinz Stolze, after Domenico Scarlatti* ◆ *Choreography by John Cranko*

In the four years since *Eugene Onegin* was premiered by the Stuttgart Ballet, John Cranko created nearly a dozen new works which, except for his version of *The Nutcracker*, were all one-act abstract ballets. A choreographer unparalleled as the maker of full-length dramatic works, Cranko returned to that form in 1969 and went to Shakespeare for inspiration as he had before. His *Romeo and Juliet* of 1962 was a masterful essay in poetic dance tragedy, but this time Cranko turned to a comedy, *The Taming of the Shrew*. As with *Onegin*, Cranko needed a musical score that would perfectly suit his balletic conception, and once again he asked composer-arranger Kurt-Heinz Stolze to find it for him. The composer immersed himself in Domenico Scarlatti's outpouring of keyboard sonatas, and from this prodigious source gleaned themes and musical motifs that he subsequently arranged and orchestrated. The final score proved to be a vibrant musical background that was perfect for the uproarious spectacle on stage.

Cranko's *Taming of the Shrew* was premiered in Stuttgart on March 16, 1969, and was also included in the repertoire of the company when it made its debut at New York's Metropolitan Opera House in the late spring of that year. This lusty romp revealed the full range and power of Cranko's choreographic genius, while providing a wonderful vehicle for the comic talents as well as the virtuosity of Cranko's stars, Marcia Haydée and Richard Cragun. The work was undoubtedly among the primary reasons that the American public immediately took Cranko, his star dancers, and the entire Stuttgart Ballet to its heart. Many have considered this work the twentieth-century equivalent of *Coppélia*, and its enduring popularity gives credence to this assertion.

THE BALLET

The first scene of Act I takes place outside Baptista's house, where his younger daughter, Bianca, is being serenaded by three ill-matched suitors—Hortensio, a fop; Lucentio, a student; and Gremio, an aged *roué*. Their wooing is rudely interrupted by Baptista's elder daughter, Katharina, who, Baptista tells them, must be married before he can give the hand of his younger daughter to anyone. The commotion in the street rouses Baptista's neighbors, who chase away the three suitors.

A tavern is the setting for the next scene. Petruchio, a swarthy gentleman of limited means, swaggers in and orders drink. He is soon set upon by two ladies of easy virtue; before the drunkenly good-natured swain realizes what has happened, they rob most of his clothes and all of the last few lire in his

Richard Cragun and Marcia Haydée in The Taming of the Shrew. *Stuttgart Ballet*

196

pocket. When the three thwarted suitors come into the tavern, Gremio challenges Petruchio to woo and win Katharina and the fortune that comes with her. With little to lose, Petruchio accepts the challenge.

Back at Baptista's house, the beautiful Bianca cannot decide which of her three suitors she prefers. The obstreperous Kate berates her for what she considers outright coquetry, something she herself disdains. Their squabble is cut short by the arrival of Gremio, Lucentio, and Hortensio, who have come disguised as Masters of Singing, Dancing, and Music. With them is Petruchio, who sees at once that in Kate he has met his match. Although Kate rejects his amorous advances, even becoming physically violent, she cannot resist his proposal of marriage.

Very soon, word of Kate's wedding has reached the townspeople, and everyone hastens to view what they consider a ludicrous spectacle. Among the crowd are Gremio, Lucentio, and Hortensio, still plotting their separate conquests of Bianca.

The final scene of Act I is the wedding of Kate and Petruchio. Kate, in her wedding gown, is clearly distressed that Petruchio seems to have jilted her. But he soon arrives and proceeds to shock the gathering and his bride by his outlandish attire and rude treatment of the guests and even the priest. Immediately after the ceremony, Petruchio picks Kate up and whisks her away before the wedding celebration can take place.

As the curtain rises on Act II, Petruchio is taking his already somewhat battered bride to their home. Kate is seated on the back of an ass and it is an effort for her to keep from falling off. Petruchio behaves impossibly, even cutting short their hasty meal before Kate can get a bite.

In the meantime, a carnival is taking place. Gremio and Hortensio, among the revelers, are approached by two women in disguises. Each thinks that Bianca has come to him to be secreted away and to be married. After two weddings take place, the duped suitors discover that they each have married one of the harlots who cheated Petruchio in the tavern. To their chagrin, Gremio and Hortensio find that the women were instructed in their deception by the wily student, Lucentio, who is now free to marry Bianca.

Petruchio and Kate have finally reached their home, and Kate endures still more humiliation at the hands of her husband. Unable to fight any longer, she succumbs to his will. At that, he

is transformed into an affectionate, protective lover, and they dance together in mutual adoration. In the next scene, Petruchio and Kate have set out to attend Bianca's wedding. Petruchio is still prankish, but Kate is now a willing accomplice.

By the next scene, Bianca's wedding has taken place, and Lucentio has already begun to suspect that Bianca may not be a much better bargain than the ladies of easy virtue he foisted upon Hortensio and Gremio. In contrast, Kate and Petruchio reveal that they are a match made in heaven. Having found the meaning of true love, Kate instructs her sister and the other two brides to honor and obey the men they love.

Egon Madsen as Gremio in The Taming of the Shrew. *Stuttgart Ballet*

DANCES AT A GATHERING

1969 ◆ *Music by Frédéric Chopin* ◆ *Choreography by Jerome Robbins*

In 1969, Jerome Robbins rejoined the New York City Ballet as ballet master after an absence of more than twelve years. In that time, Robbins had choreographed and directed two landmarks of the American musical theater, *West Side Story* (1957) and *Fiddler on the Roof* (1964), had formed his own company, Ballets: U.S.A., and had created for American Ballet Theatre his own version of Stravinsky's monumental work, *Les Noces*. Robbins then withdrew to a large extent from public view, becoming involved in a government-funded exploration of aspects of the American theater. But, after attending a performance of his own *Afternoon of a Faun* danced by Edward Villella and Patricia McBride, he was so taken with the dancers that he decided to choreograph a *pas de deux* especially for them to the music of Chopin.

As rehearsals progressed, Robbins listened to more and more Chopin and decided to add another two dancers to the work. The number of dancers soon increased to six, but since all three couples were not always available for rehearsals at the same time, four more dancers were added so that Robbins could keep on creating. When the choreographer invited Balanchine to view the work-in-progress, Balanchine, rather than agreeing with Robbins that the work might be getting too long, told him to make even more dances. The resulting work, *Dances at a Gathering*, for ten dancers, set to eighteen piano pieces by Chopin, was from its first public viewing on May 22, 1969, an unqualified triumph, perhaps the most unanimously heralded ballet of the decade.

Robbins's masterpiece expresses the harmony among a group of individuals who have reached understanding through experiencing life. Its inventive choreography reflects a consummate rapport, both physical and emotional, among the dancers. It seems that in his years of secluded experimentation, Robbins set aside his prior concern with the restlessness and alienation of youth to immerse himself instead in the essence of human movement. Upon the premiere of the ballet, Robbins said that the work was something of a "revolt from the faddism of today. In the period since my last ballet, I have been around looking at dance—seeing a lot of the stuff at Judson Church and the rest of the avant-garde. And I find myself feeling, just what is the matter with connecting, what's the matter with love, what's the matter with celebrating positive things?"

THE BALLET

The curtain rises in silence on an empty stage and a backdrop suggesting gentle clouds floating across a warm afternoon sky. A man dressed in brown tights, soft boots, and a loose white shirt enters on the right. He looks about him as if recalling previous visits to the place. A mazurka is heard, and the man flows easily into full, bounding dance movements until he suddenly comes to a halt. With a flickering lift of his hand to his brow, he affirms the certainty of his memory before leaving.

Two dancers, a man in green and a woman in mauve, now begin to dance, in unison, to the lilting "Wind Waltz," in which their arms constantly complement their wafting torsos, as if gently urged on by a breeze. In brief solos, the man spins and the woman springs in *pas de chat*. Finally, the man spins the woman upside down around his arm to sit on his shoulder and rushes off with her.

Another mazurka is heard as a man in mauve and a woman in pink enter. To its subtle tempo, the man supports his partner in *développés* and traveling lifts, promenades her, and lifts her high in the air. Their movements have a slow-motion, underwater quality as they savor every moment of their dance. The man then lifts the woman upside down and carries her off with her legs high over his head and her head almost brushing the ground.

A garland of mazurkas forms the next section. The first, by a woman in yellow, has a definite folk quality. The man in mauve dances another folklike solo of heel and toe stamping and double *tours en l'air* finishing in deep *pliés*. Next, the man in brown, a woman in pink, and a woman in blue dance a frolicsome *pas de trois* in which the women are alternately partnered and lifted, then lifted together simultaneously in flicking jumps by the man. Two other men join in; all three link their arms like a bridge, and the women dance under it and support themselves on it. The dance becomes more robust as the five swagger, side by side, with punctuating thrusts of their heels and with their hands on their hips. They then strike a series of amusing poses, as if for informal snapshots. While all wonder which two of the three men the women will choose, the woman in mauve arrives, chooses a partner, and all three women kneel to their men.

To a more luxurious mazurka, the man in green and the woman in mauve begin to dance with a certain folk quality,

Stephanie Saland and Peter Martins in Dances at a Gathering. *New York City Ballet*

bobbing lightly, each with one hand on a hip and the other behind the head. Soon, all three couples are dancing; the men partner the women in crossing patterns of alternating slides across the floor and floating lifts. First the women, and then the men, kneel as their partners dance with hopping steps around them. All three couples join hands and move in waltzing steps until, in the last, emphatic moments of the music, the first couple make a bridge with their arms and the two other couples exit under it, followed swiftly by the first.

The breathless trilling of a waltz brings on a woman in yellow and a man in brick, who launch into a competitive, playful game of catch. Circling each other with sweeping arms, they alternately strike abrupt poses and bows. The two play tag, and the man breezes around the woman as she executes rapid *échappés passés*. After more playful posing and rushing about, the man swiftly pulls his partner into the air to rest across the back of his neck and shoulders. Later, they pose in *piqué attitude*, then launch into a sweeping waltz. Finally, holding both her hands, he swings her in a circle, skimming the ground, then flings her into his arms before they exit.

The next waltz is wistful, almost melancholy. Three women, in pink, blue, and mauve, enter; the one in mauve kneels alone as the other two waltz and walk together. The man in green appears and lifts the woman in mauve; the other two withdraw. The couple perform a hesitant waltz marked by lifts in which the woman's legs move as if she were swimming, then the man disappears. She reaches back after him, not realizing he is gone. The woman in mauve rejoins her two dancing friends in their legato movements and poses, one of which is reminiscent of the Three Graces. Each walks alone for a while with her thoughts; then they reunite and, with linked arms, depart.

Entering from diagonally opposite corners, to the music of a robust mazurka, the man in mauve and the man in brown skip backward in a large circle which grows smaller and smaller until they are shoulder to shoulder, facing away from each other. They spin each other around in supported high-flying arcs, then play a game of follow-the-leader, in which the smaller man in brown mimics his tall partner in turns, heel-clicking jumps, and folk poses. Their exit is the reverse of their entrance: beginning shoulder to shoulder, they skip backward in an ever-enlarging circle, and then off.

The woman in green next executes a highly articulated solo of Slavic flavor. During this essay in exquisite musicality, she starts and then checks every movement of her body with, over, and under the music's staccato pace.

To a glorious grand waltz, three couples (the women in yellow, mauve, and blue; the men in green, mauve, and blue) rush in and gently mark time with the infectious music. Soon they whirl into interweaving waltz patterns and, in canon,

crisscross in flying *tours jetés*. In one brief, ecstatic moment, the men toss the women spinning into the air; during a quieter interlude, all canter in a wide circle in single file. Later, the men form a diagonal and in sequence lift, toss, and catch the women in ever more astounding feats of execution; they catch hold of the women's hands and spin them in swift, low circles that skim the ground. The music mounts ecstatically as the dancers leap in *pas de papillon*. As the music subsides, the dancers, with wide-open arms, again bob gently in time to it. After floating lifts for the women, all pose briefly before the women gleefully rush off, pursued by the ardent men.

Dances at a Gathering, *New York City Ballet: opposite, Edward Villella and Patricia McBride; above, Peter Martins*

To a more pensive waltz, the woman in green enters with the man in brick, she dancing coquettishly around him. As he leaves and the man in mauve enters, the woman begins to flirt with the newcomer. She waltzes, turns, executes *piqués relevés* and *développés*, but her exertions are for naught. Her second chance gone, she catches sight of the man in green. She stands before him and flutters her hands like a bird, but he too lingers only briefly before he departs, acknowledging her with a courtly *balancé*. When no other man appears, she dances alone for herself, then, opening her arms in a gesture of wry resignation, leaves.

To a terse, staccato tempo, the woman in pink and the man in brown dance together with constantly shifting lifts and rapid *coupés jetés*, seeming to chatter with their arm and head movements. As the mood suddenly shifts with a rippling interlude in the music, the two embrace; she leans backward yearningly and moves with trembling *bourrées*. But the staccato tempo returns, and the two resume their flippant gestures, with alternating lifts and supported *cabrioles*. Facing each other, they pause, step-stamp emphatically, and then link arms. In the last liquid rippling of the music, the woman revolves over her partner's arm and rests her full body across his shoulder as they withdraw.

The man in brown performs a swift solo marked by *emboîtés* and *coupés jetés*, turns *à la seconde*, and quick, abrupt poses. Then, to the stark, ominous opening chord of a scherzo, the woman in mauve enters, leaping and spinning, reaching out and back, with an urgency that suggests fear. The women in pink and yellow enter, and then the one in yellow remains as the other two leave; she dances a brief solo of frenzied *relevés* and lunges. Two men pass through and one remains to dance with the woman in yellow — he carries her in soaring lifts but also desperately drags her along the floor. They rush away, and after

Antoinette Sibley, Lynn Seymour, and Laura Connor. The Royal Ballet

various entrances and exits of these five dancers, the man in mauve lifts the woman in pink high into the air, where she perches like a delicate bird.

To music of exquisite calm and beauty, the couple kneel together, lost in revery. Then, in dance passages of ravishing simplicity, the woman *bourrées* or promenades with the tender urging of the man. In a moment of tenderness, he rests his head upon her hand. She falls into his arms, and he revolves her in a circle in the air.

As the opening scherzo is reprised, the mood of desperation slowly mounts. The couple spin away from each other; as the woman in pink leaps and is caught horizontally in her partner's arms, the woman in yellow echoes the movement with the man in green. The four dancers place one arm behind their backs and stretch the other one out to the side. The men turn their heads in one direction, then another, and begin to hop, as do the women, and the hops become alternating *sissonnes*. As the man in blue and the woman in mauve join the others, the men rush around the women, who execute *développés à la seconde*. The six dancers next form a semicircle and begin to lunge, in canon, thrusting their arms, turning, and leaping. The men rush together, pulling the women, who lean back in their arms, until all at once the couples embrace passionately, kiss, and abruptly scatter.

To a contemplative nocturne, all the dancers gradually enter the clearing. The woman in mauve sits delicately on the ground as the man in brown bends to place a hand on the earth in a gesture of gratitude. There is more quiet walking until, as the music seems to echo distant thunder, the dancers all look to one side of the clearing. Their gaze follows a slow trajectory across the sky and comes to rest at the opposite side. In unison, each executes a slow side sweep of one arm across the torso and finishes in a pose with upturned palm. They run together into the distance, opening their arms wide. After the men bow to the women and the women curtsy in response, they form couples and begin to promenade romantically as the curtain falls.

Judith Fugate, Kyra Nichols, Sean Lavery, Daniel Duell, and Robert Maiorano. New York City Ballet

TRINITY

1969 ◆ *Music by Alan Raph and Lee Holdridge* ◆ *Choreography by Gerald Arpino*

From its inception, the Joffrey Ballet featured a young Staten Island–born dancer named Gerald Arpino. Arpino had come to ballet only in his late teens, when he began studies with Mary Ann Wells while stationed with the United States Coast Guard in Seattle, Washington. There, he met Robert Joffrey and began an association which has lasted over three decades. While dancing with the Joffrey Ballet, Arpino continued to study modern dance and became co-director of Robert Joffrey's school, the American Ballet Center. In 1961, he made his first attempts at choreography, creating *Partita for Four* and *Ropes* for the Joffrey company.

It was immediately clear from the disparate qualities of these two works that Arpino had a choreographic vision that embraced all modes of dance, from classicism to free-style contemporary movement. In the next several years, he produced a number of distinguished and highly popular works for the Joffrey, no two of which were stylistically alike: *Sea Shadow*, *Incubus*, *Viva Vivaldi!*, *Olympics*, *Nightwings*, *The Clowns*, and *Secret Places*. Arpino's works unquestionably gave the Joffrey Ballet its identity and profile as the company which best expressed the voice of young America in dance. Reflected in his works and in the dancers who performed them were all the elements that constituted contemporary American youth: passion, torment, and alienation as well as discipline, athleticism, romance, and *joie de vivre*.

In 1969, Arpino responded once more to this sensibility in a ballet called *Trinity*, a work in three parts for thirteen dancers. The choreographer himself called it his "Aquarius ballet" to indicate his belief that the outward-directed protest of the late sixties was about to make the transition to the individual's investigation of the spiritual self. In the ballet, Arpino combined the pulsating sound of rock music with the incantatory intonations of liturgical chants. At its premiere on October 9, 1969, *Trinity* was an instantaneous success, and soon became the Joffrey Ballet's signature piece.

Trinity is one of the works in the Joffrey Ballet repertoire which audiences most hunger to see, for rarely has a ballet so totally engulfed its spectators in an aura of celebration. Although Arpino has encountered a large share of critical barbs, none can deny that he does have a certain genius for capturing in movement the essense of contemporaneity. One might say that of all present-day choreographers, Arpino is most vulnera-

bly alive to today's culture. The appellation "Everyman's choreographer" could be applied to him in that he frequently creates ballets which in their range and expression give voice to the thoughts and feelings of the "man in the street."

THE BALLET

Before the curtain rises on the first section, Sunday, there is a resounding brass fanfare. Then the dancers, in richly colored, sleeveless unitards, slowly enter. Soon the rock music breaks forth with all its pulsating power and the dancers respond with celebratory exuberance, performing in small groups, solos, and en masse. A particularly vivid moment occurs when the group links arms at the shoulders, forms a circle, and revolves with measured rising and falling cadence to the throbbing beat; a leading male dancer stands in the center of the circle and gyrates with sinuous, abandoned movements. In the final moments of this section, the dancers, still in their circle, leap toward each other with arms thrown ecstatically upward and then, spent, fling themselves back onto the floor.

The mood and atmosphere alter for Summerland, the second section. Quietly, the dancers rise, some leave the stage, and others remain to begin a passage filled with tender meetings and rapturous gestures. One couple perform an extended duet, while the others celebrate with soaring lifts in which the woman is suspended from one of her partner's arms. The feeling is at once spiritual, euphoric, and sensual. As resounding chimes conclude the section, the men carry the women off in floating lifts.

As its title, Saturday (the ancient Sabbath), suggests, the last movement is ritualistic. Two men enter from opposite sides carrying lighted candles which flicker in the shadows of the darkened stage. The other dancers follow in solemn procession, each one also bearing a candle. After the ensemble departs, the lights come up and the leading male dancer from the first section bursts into a frenzied solo to the insistent, pounding rhythm of a rock version of the "Ite, missa est" of the Roman Catholic Mass. He is joined by his male followers, and the propelling, repetitive beat becomes increasingly erotic. The music soars deafeningly and at its climax, the dancers momentarily depart. They then return, each with two votive candles; as the music and stage lights diminish, they place the candles reverently on the ground and depart with measured gait. The stage is left illuminated by a glowing symbol of inner spiritual light.

Opposite: Rebecca Wright in Trinity. *The Joffrey Ballet*
Overleaf: Dancers of the Joffrey Ballet in Trinity

DEUCE COUPE

1973 ◆ Music by the Beach Boys ◆ Choreography by Twyla Tharp

In 1973, a representative of the most avant-garde faction of modern dance, Twyla Tharp, was invited to create a new work for the Joffrey Ballet—what it might be would be anybody's guess. Born in Indiana and raised in California, Tharp had studied both ballet and modern dance with such acknowledged masters as Merce Cunningham, Margaret Craske, Richard Thomas, and Alwin Nikolais. After dancing in Paul Taylor's company between 1963 and 1965, she left to form her own group and to choreograph. Her first work, *Tank Dive* (1965), immediately earned her a reputation as an iconoclast which peaked with *Dancing in the Streets of Paris and London, Continued in Stockholm and Sometimes Madrid* (1969), a work performed simultaneously in various spaces and viewed by a mobile audience on closed-circuit television.

Less than two years later, Tharp and her small company took on a new identity. With consummate skill and masterful discipline, the choreographer drew together her previously diffuse investigations of unstructured movement. Applying the results to music by American jazz musicians, she created *The Fugue*, *Eight Jelly Rolls*, and *The Bix Pieces*, works that contained images of controlled nonchalance and repressed hysteria, highly organized body noodling, and simple reflections of contemporary movements. Riding the crest of the popularity that she attained with these works, Tharp choreographed *Deuce Coupe* for the Joffrey, its title taken from a song by the Beach Boys, a leading pop group of the 1960s. A selection of the same group's hit tunes constituted the score, and the Joffrey company danced alongside members of Tharp's company, who appeared as guest artists. Tharp commissioned a set from the United Graffiti Artists (whose works had previously been most widely exhibited on the New York City subways), and at each performance they created a different, extemporaneous backdrop.

Deuce Coupe was an essay in movement that seemed at once absurd and meaningful, contrived and inventive, crazy and logical—a lesson in structural clarity and choreographic surprises. Despite its huge success and stunning effect on audiences, the work was probably too much grounded in its own time; within two years of its creation, the work was no longer performed in its original form. Tharp withdrew her own dancers from the work, but for the Joffrey she made a new version entitled *Deuce Coupe II* (with a new set by the Pop artist James

Rosenquist), which was more balletic and serene.

After *Deuce Coupe*, Tharp choreographed a stream of brilliant, innovative works for her own company as well as for other troupes, most notable among the latter being the Joffrey's *As Time Goes By* (1973), a glowing synthesis of the Tharp esthetic, and American Ballet Theatre's production of *Push Comes to Shove* (1976), one of the most innovative of the works created especially for Mikhail Baryshnikov.

THE BALLET

From the outset, *Deuce Coupe* expresses two divergent but not mutually exclusive themes which will, at its conclusion, merge into something of a resolution. As the curtain rises, one of these themes is represented by a ballerina dressed in white chiffon, and the other by a couple in casual, brightly colored summer attire, typical of the California beach set of the 1960s. Their initial movements reveal that this is a ballet about the exploration of dance styles: the ballerina begins to execute a lexicon of classical dance steps; the other two begin a delicious, loose-limbed excursion into seemingly improvisational dance.

Throughout the work, other dancers enter and depart in groups, couples, trios, or singly. While never impinging upon the balletic discourse of the ballerina, they reveal in their own free way some marvelous truths about movement—how a deep-seated restlessness propels the young; how a quick, impatient intelligence is bound to break rules; that dancing is also about letting off steam; and, best of all, that real style isn't something you casually decide on, but something that emerges out of conscious and unconscious probing, encountering, and experimenting. All the while, the Beach Boys' songs, paeans to a simplistic yet vibrant vision of life, play on, and at the rear of the stage, the young graffiti artists stand with spray-paint cans in hand, filling three large white pieces of paper which roll up, carrying their contemporary iconography higher and higher.

The construction of the ballet is so incredibly diverse, yet precisely directed, that the following listing of song titles, ballet steps performed by the ballerina, and dancers in each of the nineteen sections only scratches the surface:

"Matrix I," *ailes de pigeon* through *attitude*, the ballerina and two dancers.

"Little Deuce Coupe," *balancé* through *ballon*, the ballerina

and eighteen dancers.

"Honda I," *ballonné battu* through *déboulés*, the ballerina and three dancers.

"Honda II," *changement de pieds* through *dégagé à la quatrième devant en l'air*, the ballerina and two dancers.

"Devoted to You," *dégagé en tournant* through *failli*, the ballerina and two couples.

"How She Boogalooed It," *faux* through *manège*, the ballerina and full, scattered ensemble.

"Matrix II," *pas de basque sur les pointes* through *pas de chat*, the ballerina and six dancers.

"Alley Oop," *pas de cheval* through *répétition*, the ballerina and eight dancers.

"Take a Load Off Your Feet," *retiré* through *sissonne tombée*, three women and two men.

"Long Tall Texan," *six* through *suite*, three ambling, gyrating women.

"Papa ooh Mau Mau," six marijuana-smoking dancers frugging into spasmodic frenzy (the ballerina has departed).

"Catch a Wave," five dancers.

"Got to Know the Woman," *temps de cuisse* through *temps lié*, the ballerina and another woman in free-style form.

"Matrix III," *temps lié grand* through *voyagé*, the ballerina.

"Don't Go Near the Water," six women "swimming" into frantic spasms.

"Matrix IV," a woman (Twyla Tharp in the original production) and a man, who finally becalms her ceaseless noodling.

"Mama Says—'Eat a Lot, Never Be Lazy,'" one woman leading five men.

"Wouldn't It Be Nice," easy ambling for ten dancers.

"Cuddle Up," the ballerina and entire ensemble execute patterns in which previous motifs are restated in a more controlled manner than before. All form a concluding tableau as the curtain falls.

Above: Christine Uchida and members of the Joffrey Ballet in Deuce Coupe
Overleaf: Deuce Coupe. *The Joffrey Ballet*

VOLUNTARIES

1973 ◆ Music by Francis Poulenc ◆ Choreography by Glen Tetley

In June, 1973, the entire ballet community was shocked by the sudden death of John Cranko, choreographer and director of the Stuttgart Ballet. His company, perhaps finding inspiration from Cranko's own great courage and tenacity, vowed to survive and to preserve Cranko's goals. They chose Glen Tetley, an American choreographer of international repute, as their new director because they believed that by temperament, experience, and sensitivity, he was the best man to carry on Cranko's work.

Having left the study of medicine for dance, Tetley trained with such masters as Hanya Holm, Margaret Craske, Antony Tudor, and Martha Graham, and performed in several companies, including Holm's, John Butler's, the Joffrey, Graham's, American Ballet Theatre, and Robbins's Ballets: U.S.A. In 1962, he joined the Netherlands Dance Theatre, where for nearly a decade he danced and choreographed ballets, and was appointed co-director with Hans Van Manen of that company. Tetley's choreographic style developed into one which subtly fused elements of modern and classical dance to produce works of lean and astringent power. His first major choreographic effort was the enigmatic *Pierrot Lunaire* (1962), and in such works as *Sargasso*, *Ricercare*, *Mythical Hunters*, *Mutations*, *Gemini*, *Field Figures*, and *Laborintus*, Tetley proved himself to be a master of construction, musicality, and understated psychological power.

Cranko had commissioned a work from Tetley for the Stuttgart Ballet shortly before he died. Set to Poulenc's Concerto for Organ, Strings and Timpani, the ballet was conceived as "a linked series of voluntaries" (free-ranging organ or trumpet improvisations often played at religious services). Going to the Latin root of the word, the title also implies "flight" or "desire." After the tragedy, the work became Tetley's homage to Cranko: a work brimming with ecstasy and love and performed by its principals with a fervor that testified to a strong attachment to their late mentor and friend.

THE BALLET

The curtain rises in silence. Upstage center stand a man and woman silhouetted against a glowing pastel backdrop of pointillist pattern. The woman faces the backdrop; the man faces front, his right arm around her waist. Still in silence, the woman

bourrées and both dancers move forward. Suddenly, the woman soars into the air and is held there by her partner in a full-arm press-lift, as a resonant organ chord is heard.

A musical dialogue begins among the organ, strings, and timpani, and the couple perform an extended *pas de deux* in which the man supports the woman in searching gestures and swooning falls. Soon, the leading couple are joined by two men and a woman; the two groups gradually commingle as the women are alternately carried by the men of each group. The others rush off, and the leading man remains to perform a bravura solo of multiple pirouettes and leaps. After he leaves, the other two men dance a vibrant duet, first in canon and then in unison, before they rush off. The music persists in its explosive momentum as six more men soar onto the scene in a series of flying *cabrioles*. Soon, six women join them to perform a lengthy, complex dance in fugal patterns.

The six couples then depart before a *pas de deux* and *pas de trois* are simultaneously performed; the *pas de trois*, with its series of celestial overhead lifts, continues after the duet is completed. The principal couple return and dance a quiet, desperate *pas de deux* punctuated by flying *tours jetés* by six men. Their dance is followed by a *pas de six* for the men and another one for six women who execute a series of soaring jumps, *tours jetés*, *jetés en avant*, and pirouettes.

The principal couple return for a *pas de deux* which counterpoints floor-directed movements against upward extensions, both reflected by ecstatic shifts in the music. After a complex *pas de douze* and *pas de trois*, the leading couple return and restate the press-lift which began the ballet. Upon releasing her, the man tenderly touches his partner before she performs a brief solo, then returns to him and is once again lifted in a horizontal position. One at a time, the six couples *bourrée* on and, very quietly, the men lift the women and carry them far upstage as the leading couple remain far forward. The six couples depart, and their *bourrées* and lifts are then echoed by a trio. The two principals remain alone on stage, the man supporting the ballerina in a series of arabesques, pirouettes, and *promenades*. To a final rapturous organ burst, the man lifts the woman high above him in a gesture of affirmation and, holding her aloft, walks slowly backward as the curtain falls.

Marcia Haydée and Richard Cragun in Voluntaries. *Stuttgart Ballet*

ESPLANADE

1975 ◆ *Music by Johann Sebastian Bach* ◆ *Choreography by Paul Taylor*

Some thirty years ago, Paul Taylor, a young Syracuse University art student possessed of a sunny disposition and an imposing, athletic physique, appeared for an audition at the Juilliard School of Music dance department. Despite his minimal dance training, he won a scholarship to Juilliard and continued his dance studies at the Metropolitan Opera Ballet School and the Martha Graham School. Soon after his first dance appearances, with Pearl Lang and Merce Cunningham, Taylor organized a concert of his own choreography at the Henry Street Playhouse in New York. For the next twenty years, he continued to be in the forefront of American modern dance both as choreographer (with his own company since 1954) and dancer. Especially notable in his dance career were his work as featured male soloist with Graham's company and an unforgettable appearance in Balanchine's *Episodes* in 1959.

Although some of Taylor's earliest works were aggressively avant-garde, he gradually emerged as one of the most classically oriented modern dance choreographers. His *Aureole* (1962) was taken into the repertoire of the Royal Danish Ballet and has been danced by Rudolf Nureyev. Works like *Three Epitaphs* (1953), *Insects and Heroes* (1961), *From Sea to Shining Sea* (1965), *Big Bertha* (1971), and *American Genesis* (1974) bear the idiosyncratic Taylor stamp of free-flowing movement, sardonic humor, and bizarre atmosphere. More times than not, his works have distinguished contemporary American artists as scenic designers, among them, Robert Rauschenberg and Alex Katz.

In 1975, when Taylor announced that he would no longer appear as a dancer, some feared his creativity as a choreographer would be affected. However, in that same year he created what many consider to be his masterpiece —*Esplanade*. Utilizing two violin concertos by Johann Sebastian Bach, this work consisted of no dance steps whatsoever, being instead a celebration of natural, everyday movements. Simple walks, runs, jumps, slides, and falls were miraculously transmuted by Taylor into a masterpiece of dance. His secret was, in a word coined by himself, "zunch," the quality of total commitment that makes a dancer out of a pedestrian —"the ability to focus on what may be only an infinitesimal gesture and hurl it splatch from one soul to another." To the question, "Just how far can we go as dancers?" Taylor answered, "I do not think we want to settle on a comfortable limit." In *Esplanade*, Taylor came close to attaining his ideal: to transform simple movement from locomotion to illumination.

THE BALLET

To the joyous opening *Allegro* movement of Bach's Violin Concerto no. 2 in E Major, dancers in simple attire enter with a bouncy, spirited walk. As they travel in sharply angled patterns, their pace turns to skipping, and then they hold hands and run. Throughout a series of solos, trios, and quartets, the dancers rush in crisscrossing paths and circles. At one point, six dancers lie on their stomachs in a diagonal on the floor, and one spirited woman hops over them one by one. Rising again, the dancers weave to and fro, then leave in a bouncy, intersecting march.

To the *Adagio* and *Allegro assai* movements of the concerto, the dancers walk gently in a circle, kneel, and stand holding hands. The women place their arms tenderly about the necks of the men, who lift them and cradle them in their arms. Always with warm humanity, the dancers form lines and split, kneel and rise and move in more lines, and reverse directions that flow into themselves, until finally the intersecting lines vanish.

To the second movement, the *Largo*, of Bach's Concerto for Two Violins in D Minor, a more dramatic mood unfolds. Three dancers —a statuesque woman, a solicitous man, and another, smaller woman —enter and move together. Another woman runs in briefly, then departs as a fourth woman comes in and separates the members of the first trio. The man and the smaller woman exit, leaving the tall woman and the last to arrive to perform a mysteriously sensual duet. During this, the man rushes in with a sense of urgency, but the smaller woman returns to take him away again. The tall, solemn woman then performs a moving solo, which concludes with her crawling on hands and knees in a small circle, suggesting emotional withdrawal.

In the concerto's final movement, *Allegro*, bright, contrapuntal configurations propel the dancers into increasingly accelerated walks, runs, and jumps. Soon all the dancers are covering the stage, flinging themselves at dazzling speed in interweaving patterns and into full body slides, falls, and rolls. Carried away by their exuberance, the men play catch, energetically tossing the women back and forth into each other's arms. Suddenly, all the dancers scatter, and one woman is left alone. She looks around briefly, opens her arms wide in a loving salutation to the audience, and remains standing that way as the curtain falls.

Preceding pages: Lila York and members of the Paul Taylor Dance Company in Esplanade

Linda Kent and Nicholas Gunn in Esplanade. *The Paul Taylor Dance Company*

UNTITLED

1975 ◆ *Music by Robert Dennis* ◆ *Choreography by Pilobolus Dance Theater*

In December, 1971, a new dance group gave its first professional performances in New York City. Unlike most dance companies, which are named after a dancer, choreographer, city, or country, this group derived its name from a fungus: Pilobolus. Their name gave only a clue to the new dance experience they offered, for the group's dancers, as if transfigured by haunting and hypnotic forces, interlocked, interacted, separated, and reunited in what was clearly a reflection of organic growth. It was as if the dramas of cellular or biomorphic life, normally seen only under a microscope, were magically magnified into an unfolding sequence of theatrical events. Certainly the most innovative dance group to emerge in the 1970s, Pilobolus offered nothing less than a new art form which was a mysterious fusion of dance, acrobatics, mime, and stylized movement.

The company sprang from no dance heritage, and those doing the springing were not dancers in the traditional sense. Pilobolus was founded in 1971 at Dartmouth College by two young men, Moses Pendleton and Jonathan Wolken, who met as undergraduates in the choreography classes of faculty member Alison Chase. The two soon became four when Lee Harris and Robby Barnett, two other students of Chase, joined the group. Together, they conceived, choreographed, and danced their works and also managed and publicized the company. In 1973, Alison Chase herself joined Pilobolus and with her, Martha Clarke. By that time, the group had already captured the imagination of critics and audiences, and had found a place in the forefront of American modern dance.

In 1975, for a work commissioned by the American Dance Festival at Connecticut College, New London, the company abandoned its rarefied calesthenics and biological references, and produced instead a dance that was as much a haunting riddle as a witty, rich theatrical experience. Describing this disturbing, dreamlike vision, Pendleton says, "It started out as a solo, became a duet, escalated to a quartet and finally a sextet. It's basically a duet with six people involved. It's about two women, their relationship with each other—their repressed sexuality, their fantasies and their realities. The tall women was a device to convey a theatrical image. It's quite ambiguous, with layers of meaning. The naked men were essential in that we used them as a juxtaposition to the fully clothed men. That makes a statement in itself, because there is so much beautiful Victorian clothing, and to see the fully naked men against that is a shock, and the shock value is essential."

The piece is still a puzzle to the members of Pilobolus. Jonathan Wolken states, "There is no single mind that can express anything clear about it. It's a piece that hangs together by God-knows-what and yet is very powerful for us all. It's suspended parts of all our psyches, and has very elemental things in it: women, men, relationships and combat between the sexes, birth. It's a journey of its own and there is no way to characterize it." Whatever its meaning—and as atypical as it is of Pilobolus's usual style—*Untitled* has become something of a signature piece for the company. The work was premiered without a title in August, 1975, and it has remained so ever since.

THE BALLET

As the piece begins, we see two women in long Victorian dresses. One woman combs the other's hair. Suddenly, as they begin to walk, they rise to a height of ten feet. The reason is readily apparent: from beneath the hem of each woman's skirt protrude two legs that are naked, hairy, and clearly masculine. For what seems like an exhaustingly long time, these androgynous creatures promenade hither and yon to comic effect. But, eventually, comedy yields to disquieting drama.

The two giantesses are pursued by two male suitors, also in Victorian attire, who look dwarfed and hapless beside them. After a while, two men emerge from beneath the women's skirts. They are naked as the day they were born and, indeed, they appear to *be* newly born, either from the wombs or the imaginations of the women. As they mingle with the other characters, a bizarre charade unfolds, one that defies meaning or sense, but is nonetheless riveting. The action continues in a serenity that is disturbing—all the more so because no tangible dramatic resolution is produced. After a time, the curtain merely falls.

Alison Chase and Martha Clarke in Untitled. *Pilobolus Dance Theater*

NOTRE FAUST

1975 ◆ *Music by Johann Sebastian Bach, Ludwig Minkus, Harry Warren; Argentinian tangos* ◆ *Choreography by Maurice Béjart*

Maurice Béjart, the Marseilles-born son of a philosopher, had a fairly conventional ballet training in the 1940s with such noted teachers as Léo Staats, Lubov Egorova, and Vera Volkova. But, from the very beginning, his choreographic works evinced an imagination that was nothing if not outré. There was *Symphonie pour un Homme Seul* (1955), in which a man struggles between the forces of technology and sex. There was *Haut Voltage* (1956), in which, after two young lovers are electrocuted through the will of a woman with supernatural powers, the young man revives and kills her. And there was *Sonate à Trois* (1957), based upon Jean-Paul Sartre's existentialist vision of hell, *No Exit*.

These early ballets brought Béjart glaringly to the public eye and, in 1959, he was commissioned by the director of the Théatre Royal de la Monnaie in Brussels to create a version of Stravinsky's *Le Sacre du Printemps*. About this work, the choreographer wrote: "Let this ballet then be stripped of all the artifices of the picturesque in a hymn to this union of Man and Woman in the innermost depths of the flesh, a union of heaven and earth, a dance of life and death, as eternal as Spring." Evidently, there must have been something universal in Béjart's message, for his *Sacre* was such a triumph that he was invited to form a company in Brussels. In 1960 the Ballet du XXe Siècle (Ballet of the 20th Century) came into being; in the ensuing years, its eclectic forays into the realms of theater, music, literature, and dance would become quasi-religious experiences for young Europeans while being rejected by many critics as desecrations.

No hostile critical voices were heard more loudly than in the United States, where the Béjart company made its debut at the Brooklyn Academy of Music in New York in 1971. But the public remained fascinated, scandalized, titillated, and, more to the point, hugely entertained. Béjart's works defied any absolute definition: there were spectacular biographical montage portraits (*Nijinsky, Clown of God*); expressions of Eastern philosophy (*Bhakti*); iconoclastic interpretations of classics (*Romeo and Juliet*); celebrations of male encounters (*Songs of a Wayfarer*); abstract studies of narcissism (*Stimmung*); and mammoth symphonic works (*Ninth Symphony*).

In 1975, Béjart created a full-evening poetic extravaganza based on the Faust legend, rendered in terms of a ritualistic black Mass. Entitled *Notre Faust*, the work elicited the usual controversial and conflicting responses, especially when it was performed in New York in 1977. While acknowledging the narrative and spirit of Goethe's *Faust*, Béjart's dance also incorporates elements from the lives of Goethe and Bach and from the choreographer's own life. Béjart saw a conflict in Goethe's work between the solemn ritual and spirituality of religion and the amusingly wicked and sometimes erotic figure of Mephistopheles. To embody this division, he contrasted Bach's B Minor Mass—in his own words, "the voice of God"—with the enticing sensuality of Argentinian tangos. Describing his ballet, Béjart has said, "My *Faust* is a popular work, not an esoteric work; a very spectacular and popular work. I think it ... could be shown to a very general audience, and if they're not familiar with Goethe, they can enjoy the fairy tale, because it's a fairy tale at the same time!"

THE BALLET

Since the choreography of *Notre Faust* relies less on structure than on impact, the sequence of its thirteen episodes can only be summarized.

At the ballet's opening, the aged Faust (usually performed by Béjart himself) speaks quotations from Goethe's poem into a microphone. He encounters the young Mephistopheles, and the two make a contract: Faust will be granted youth and happiness if, following Faust's death, the two exchange identities. Soon, they have exchanged roles and forms—Mephistopheles taking on the form of the old Faust, and Faust the figure of the young Mephistopheles. Together they travel the world as the three Archangels of Darkness—Lucifer, Satan, and Beelzebub—oversee their adventures.

The young Faust is smitten with the innocent Marguerite, whose vision haunts him during the debauchery of Walpurgisnacht. Marguerite, victimized by Faust's seduction, recedes into madness and dies disgraced in prison. The image of Helen of Troy is conjured up for Faust's delectation; he and Helen have a son, Euphorion, a new Icarus, who also dies in his attempt at flight. After Helen's death, Faust is left alone once more in the company of Mephistopheles. They find themselves

Jorge Donn in Notre Faust. *Ballet du XXe Siècle*

by the sea, the mother of all creation, and Faust, visited by childhood memories of his mother, dies in rapture. To Mephis- topheles's declaration, "All is over!" the voice of Faust as a young boy responds, "Everything begins again."

Yann Le Gac, Maurice Béjart, and members of Ballet du XXe Siècle in Notre Faust

A MONTH IN THE COUNTRY

1976 ◆ Music by Frédéric Chopin, arranged by John Lanchbery ◆ Choreography by Frederick Ashton

In 1970, Frederick Ashton retired from his position as director and chief choreographer of London's Royal Ballet, and in the ensuing years withdrew somewhat from public view. Fears that his creative powers might be on the wane, however, were refuted when, in 1975, it was announced that he would choreograph a new ballet inspired by Ivan Turgenev's play *A Month in the Country*, a work he had treasured since seeing it performed in the 1930s.

As always, finding an appropriate score was a crucial problem for Ashton. For various reasons, none of the music of a number of seemingly apt Russian composers satisfied him. Then, Isaiah Berlin suggested that Chopin's music would be perfect for the ballet, and Ashton agreed, selecting some of the composer's early pieces for piano and orchestra: the "Là Ci Darem" Variations, *Fantasy on Polish Airs*, *Andante Spianato* and Grand Polonaise in E-flat. After consulting with conductor-orchestrator John Lanchbery, who would meld these works into a unified score, Ashton embarked on *A Month in the Country*, his first major dramatic work for the Royal Ballet since *Enigma Variations* in 1968.

Ashton had the advantage of having at his disposal the perfect dancer to portray Turgenev's heroine, the superb dramatic ballerina Lynn Seymour, as well as the dramatic and virtuosic talents of a number of Royal Ballet artists, including Anthony Dowell, Alexander Grant, Derek Rencher, Wayne Sleep, Denise Nunn, and Marguerite Porter. The finished work is another example of Ashton's ability to convey a complex dramatic narrative through seamless choreography, without sacrificing any of the original's insightful characterizations, wit, and passion. A triumph upon its premiere in February, 1976, *A Month in the Country* is dedicated by Ashton, with humility and love, "to the memory of Sophie Fedorovitch and Bronislava Nijinska, Chopin's compatriots and my mentors."

THE BALLET

After a soft, atmospheric orchestral introduction echoed by a solo piano, the curtain rises on the sumptuous interior of the Yslaevs' summer home in 1850. French doors at the center of the room open onto a veranda and garden. Reclining on a chaise at the right is Natalia Petrovna, Yslaevs' wife, a warmly beautiful woman in her late twenties. Rakitin, her admirer, is seated on a footstool beside her. At a desk on the other side of the room, Kolia, the young son of Yslaev and Natalia Petrovna, works on his lessons. Yslaev himself, a man of middle age, sits in a comfortable, highbacked chair quietly perusing a newspaper. All are listening as Vera, the Yslaevs' adolescent ward, plays Chopin's music on the piano. Soon, Yslaev is called away on business by Katia, the maid, and a footman enters to serve drinks. Natalia then performs a dance that expresses her joy at being the object of adoration and her anticipation of a happy, serene month in the country.

Vera leaves her piano next to dance a youthful, exuberant solo which brims over with rapid jumps, *pas de chat*, and skimming *batterie*. When Yslaev returns looking for his keys, there follows a delightful pantomimic sequence in which everyone searches the room. Finally, Natalia finds them and gaily hands them to her husband. There is general relief as he departs and the gathering returns to the leisure of the summer afternoon.

Kolia, playing with a ball, now performs a spirited solo replete with *coupés jetés*, double *tours en l'air*, *assemblés*, whirring beats, and *pirouettes à la seconde*. As Kolia finishes this fast, furious virtuosic dance, his young tutor, Beliaev, comes in from the veranda carrying a large white kite as a present for his pupil. From the beginning, it is clear that Vera is fascinated by the handsome tutor, and Natalia also reveals her interest by her warm welcome.

As if he were alone, Beliaev dances a pensive solo of slowly executed *assemblés*, *piqués arabesques*, *chassés*, *chaîné* turns, and legato lunges. He asks Natalia to dance a spirited mazurka with him; Vera and Kolia eventually join them in a vivacious *pas de quatre* of folkish exuberance. The room becomes quiet again, but an undercurrent of strong emotions remains. Alone with Natalia, Rakitin speaks tenderly to her before they perform a brief yet romantic *pas de deux*. To Rakitin's dismay, Natalia confesses that she loves Beliaev, and when Yslaev comes into the room, the turmoil in her heart overwhelms her and she runs crying from the room. Rakitin takes Yslaev aside to cover up his wife's surprising behavior as both men leave.

Vera then enters and dances a solo expressing her adolescent passion for Beliaev, who, in a moment, himself appears. While courtly with Vera, he is clearly playful rather than serious. To

223

amuse her, Beliaev joins her in a quiet, lilting *pas de deux* in which he partners the young girl closely, lifts her gently, and supports her dreamy backbends. Encouraged by his affection, Vera embraces him passionately at the end of their dance. At that moment, Natalia Petrovna returns, and angrily berates both young people, particularly Vera. Beliaev tactfully withdraws. Natalia goes to sit in the highbacked chair and Vera flies to her side, confessing that she loves the tutor. Although the older woman tries to be understanding, her own amorous feelings for Beliaev hold sway and an argument ensues. Her emotions beyond control, Natalia slaps the girl in the face, regretting it at once. Vera, refusing to be consoled, rushes weeping from the room.

Rakitin comes into the room and, although the consolation he offers is not what Natalia desires, she accepts his invitation to stroll in the garden. Beliaev returns to the empty room, and in his moments of solitude ponders the events and the emotions his presence has elicited. For a moment he sits alone in a chair, but soon Katia comes in. The maid's vivaciousness is a relief to the confused tutor, and together they perform a robust peasant dance. Katia too seems to have fallen madly in love with the handsome Beliaev, and she rushes off full of joy.

Once more alone, Beliaev reveals that Natalia Petrovna is the one he loves. Picking up a scarf she has left on the chair, he looks at it adoringly as Natalia herself comes in from the garden and sees this sign of his affection. She now reveals her own infatuation with him by pinning a rose to his jacket, and to the haunting *Andante Spianato*, they perform an impassioned statement of their mutual love which concludes in an embrace.

This time, the wounded Vera catches them in this romantic pose. Seeking revenge, she calls everyone into the room and accuses Natalia Petrovna. At this, Natalia suddenly behaves as though nothing had happened. Chattering and smiling, she laughs off Vera's accusations. The young girl becomes increasingly agitated and rushes off, with Natalia and Yslaev in pursuit. Rakitin, who has seen the rose pinned to Beliaev's jacket, tells

the tutor that for the sake of peace, they must both depart.

The room clears, and Natalia Petrovna returns dressed in a white lace peignoir from which hang two long blue ribbons at the back. In a ravishing solo, she reveals her sadness, longing, and despair. She walks to the chair and weeps, resting her head on its back. A moment later, Beliaev, unseen by Natalia, enters from the garden to steal one last moment with her. Seeing her great sadness, he decides not to prolong their parting. By way of a last adieu, he kneels, takes one of the flowing ribbons in his hands, and places an impassioned kiss on it as Natalia remains lost in grief. Beliaev lays the rose she had given him on the floor and then withdraws. The woman, slowly emerging from her despair, turns from the chair. Seeing the rose, she bends to pick it up and immediately rushes to the open doors, hoping to catch a last glimpse of her beloved, perhaps even to call him to her. But he has gone. Alone, she moves back into the room, the rose in her hand; lifting it to her lips, she kisses it, then lets it drop to the ground as the curtain falls.

Opposite and above: Anthony Dowell and Lynn Seymour in A Month in the Country. *The Royal Ballet*

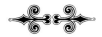

VIENNA WALTZES

1977 ◆ *Music by Johann Strauss (the Younger), Franz Lehár, and Richard Strauss* ◆ *Choreography by George Balanchine*

In 1976, the year of the American Bicentennial, Balanchine paid indirect tribute to the American spirit with an enormous, full-company spectacle entitled *Union Jack*, a celebration of America's mother country, Great Britain. It seems that, at the time, Balanchine was fascinated by such large-scale works, because just as audiences were responding to the overwhelming experience of *Union Jack*, he choreographed another tribute, this time to the beloved waltzes of Imperial Vienna. *Vienna Waltzes*, a dazzling, opulent journey through the land of the waltz, was an immediate success from its premiere on June 23, 1977.

From his youth in Imperial St. Petersburg, Balanchine had been exposed to balletic as well as ballroom interpretations of Viennese dances, which he evidently loved from the first. Almost from the beginning of his choreographic career, he created works reflecting the endless balletic possibilities of three-quarter time: *Les Valses de Beethoven*, created for Les Ballets 1933; *The Bat* (to music from Strauss's *Die Fledermaus*) for the American Ballet, in 1936; *Waltz Academy* for Ballet Theatre, in 1944; and for the New York City Ballet, in 1951, that profoundly disturbing masterpiece *La Valse*. Later works on the same theme were set to music by Glinka (*Valse Fantaisie*; 1953), Brahms (*Liebeslieder Walzer*; 1960), and Emmanuel Chabrier (*Trois Valses Romantiques*; 1967).

However, it is in *Vienna Waltzes*, with its myriad waltz patterns and brilliant construction, that Balanchine has achieved the ultimate in this form. Never has the ballet stage seen an abstraction treated in such lavish yet reverential terms. The seventy-odd New York City Ballet dancers who perform the work seldom look more radiantly elegant or beautiful in the sweep of their dancing, set off by richly evocative costumes and decor. In *Vienna Waltzes*, Balanchine, to quote Lincoln Kirstein, "has jumped backwards in time, and has made from the almost over-familiar melodies of the ballroom, a strong and novel statement of the waltz, its structure and ambiance."

THE BALLET

The familiar opening strains of Johann Strauss's *Tales from the Vienna Woods* are heard before the rise of the curtain. As the music ebbs, the curtain rises on a quiet corner of the Vienna Woods. Arm in arm, a couple slowly stroll into the clearing. The woman, in an elegant gown of pastel pink, nestles at the side of her escort, a dignified man in military uniform. They turn to face each other, he bows and she curtsies; then they embrace tenderly and begin to waltz.

A sudden flourish by the full orchestra warns the two that they may not be alone, and soon four couples rush in, then immediately depart and return again, as the music now flows into the famous theme of "The Vienna Woods." In various combinations, everyone waltzes as if the dance would never end, while the leading couple alternately disappear into the woods and return to join the others. In the penultimate moments of ecstatic music, all the men and women, side by side, form two lines and waltz backward, then unite in couples for a last few turns before leaving. The shadows grow deeper as the leading couple stroll together. To one final surge in the music, they pause and look at each other as if imprinting the moment upon their minds, then nestling together once more, they wander into the shadows.

The thrilling opening rush of Johann Strauss's *Voices of Spring* instantly transforms the clearing into an enchanted glade, and into it springs a ravishing dryad. With spinning *chaîné* turns, she fills the glade with her own waltzing joy, but soon she is joined by her exuberant counterpart, a man in bucolic attire, who bounds on in effortless *sautés*, with light forward flicks of one leg. Eight more dryads in gossamer tutus of various pastel shades appear; like the leading couple, they never seem to alight very long on the ground. Their aerial configurations continue until, in a more luxurious, sweeping tempo, the leading couple dance together in complex yet light partnerings. The ballerina next performs a brief solo in which delight is mingled with yearning rapture. Her partner then returns for a bounding solo highlighted by *coupés jetés* in a tight circle. Everyone takes part in more sylvan playfulness until the melody of the waltz is reiterated and, with quicksilver lightness, they all form a final tableau.

Suddenly, to the opening burst of Johann Strauss's *Explosion Polka*, a couple of most unexpected appearance bound in. The woman has her hair in a pompadour style and is wearing an abbreviated corseted costume, while the man is a caricature of a fop, with striped tights and his hair piled higher than his lady's. They fling themselves through the glade in a hip-wiggling,

Vienna Waltzes, New York City Ballet: opposite, Suzanne Farrell; overleaf, the finale

227

and the woman in black have danced together before.

He approaches and bends to kiss her proffered hand. Suddenly and decisively, she tosses the boa from her shoulders, the officer takes her in his arms, and the two whirl around the ballroom. The reunited lovers withdraw for a moment as the others dance in an elegant pattern of concentric circles. Then the couples stand back as the lovers waltz alone, gliding in a circle and shifting seamlessly from dancing face to face to dancing back to back. As the lights dim, the officer and the woman in black are romantically silhouetted against a glowing background.

With the exuberant opening of the first waltz sequence from Richard Strauss's opera *Der Rosenkavalier*, the *fin-de-siècle* decor rises and transmutes into a seductively muted ballroom, its back wall one vast mirror and its chandeliers suspended high in the air. The room is not long deserted, for men in black tails and women in flowing white ballgowns and long white evening gloves stroll in couples once across the room, and then vanish.

As the music subsides, a solitary woman enters. Appearing pensive and disquieted, she wistfully positions her arms as if embracing a remembered suitor, and then slowly moves into a waltzed revery. As if in answer to her memory, the figure of a man appears; she senses his presence behind her, but he soon disappears. Almost imperceptibly, the melody of the best-known *Rosenkavalier* waltz begins, and the woman's movements become more swooningly abandoned, her skirt wafting around her extended leg. As the man reappears behind her, she lifts the hem of her skirt to cover her face and, as if in a trance, she waltzes hesitantly with him.

All at once the pair is joined by couples who whirl through the ballroom as both the music and the chandeliers brighten. The couples and the woman's partner soon depart; once more alone, she dances and recalls her memories. With a final rapturous backward swoon, she withdraws. The lights then blaze up and the ballroom streams with waltzing couples; their reflections in the ballroom mirror make them appear to be a countless dancing multitude. All the leading couples from the previous waltzes appear, now attired in the same tails and white ballgowns. The music swells ecstatically and the euphoric dancing seems never-ending. In the final instant, this dazzling blur freezes in a tableau of courteously formal elegance as the curtain falls.

licentious polka. Three more couples in identical attire then rush in to disport themselves in the same fashion. The music races as the men toss their women into the air and pounce after them with wide-open legs. Everyone prances saucily together until, in the last moments, the women gather in a small circle facing each other and the men creep up behind them, crouching and leering. The women suddenly turn around and with a pelvic thrust propel the men head over heels onto the ground.

To a quiet tinkling, the pastoral forest setting rises into the air and, magically, the scene is transformed into a *fin-de-siècle* ballroom. Couples in sumptuous costumes enter and begin to dance to the lilting *Gold and Silver Waltz* of Franz Lehár. An imposing officer in a white jacket and bright red trousers strolls, aloof, across the room. Soon, an elegant woman in a startling black gown, a black feather boa, and a glittering diadem adorning her hair walks slowly into the room. From their reticent acknowledgment of each other, it becomes clear that the officer

Vienna Waltzes, New York City Ballet: above, Kay Mazzo and Peter Martins; opposite, Patricia McBride and Helgi Tomasson

GLAGOLITIC MASS

1979 ◆ *Music by Leoš Janáček* ◆ *Choreography by Jiří Kylián*

On the evening of June 26, 1979, at New York's Metropolitan Opera House, the Stuttgart Ballet presented the American premiere of *Return to the Strange Land*, set to piano music by Leoš Janáček by a choreographer named Jiří Kylián. This sequence of two *pas de trois* and two *pas de deux* was conceived with such economy and originality and contained images of such startling beauty that, as a *New York Times* dance critic wrote, "Rarely has a public burst forth with such intensity of irrepressible applause. A dam had broken and enthusiasm spilled forth as naturally as Mr. Kylián's daring choreography." Any mystery that might have lingered concerning the identity and work of this stunning new choreographic talent was solved when, less than two weeks later, the Dutch-based Netherlands Dance Theatre opened a season at the New York City Center. The rapturous acclaim accorded the company by the public and critics alike was due largely to the eight extraordinary ballets (including *Symphony of Psalms*, *Sinfonietta*, *Transfigured Night*, and *November Steps*) choreographed by Kylián, the company's artistic director.

Kylián's background was not what one would expect. He was born in Prague, Czechoslovakia, on March 21, 1947, the son of a Czech ballerina and a banker. At nine, he gave up acrobatics to enroll as a dance student in the Prague National Theater Ballet School. In his teens, he attended the Prague Conservatory, where he studied folk dancing, theater, modern dance in the Graham style, and classical ballet (with the noted Czech ballerina, Zora Semberová), until the British consul in Prague recognized young Kylián's talent and offered him a scholarship to London's Royal Ballet School.

For seven years, from 1968 to 1975, Kylián was soloist and fledgling choreographer with the Stuttgart Ballet, under John Cranko's guidance. (His *Return to the Strange Land* was a homage to his late mentor.) Within a year after being invited to create a work for the Netherlands Dance Theatre, the tall, lithe, poetic young Czech became their resident choreographer and, by 1978, artistic director. In June of 1979, he traveled with the company to Florence, Italy, for the world premiere of his latest work, set to Janáček's *Glagolitic Mass* of 1926.

Beyond question, Kylián had, from the first, felt the closest attachment to the music and artistry of his compatriot Janáček, for both choreographer and composer express passionate reverence for their homeland and an axiomatic awe for the traditional. Janáček's composition, one of his last major works, was a perfect expression of these dual sentiments: the Glagolitic, or Old Church Slavonic, Mass is seen as celebrating a faith based more on a love of the Czech homeland and people (and, by extension, all mankind) than on the specific adoration of God.

THE BALLET

Janáček's fifty-minute choral and orchestral Mass is divided into eight sections, as is Kylián's grand and passionate dance. The celebrants are twenty-two dancers who move with such abandoned energy that they seem held together only by centrifugal force. Their movements—spectacular leaps, whirling turns, searing slides to the floor, sweeping linear patterns—are rooted in elements of modern and classical dance; yet in their originality they defy any description other than "human." Space seems to be limitless, and the eye cannot focus on any specifics but can only absorb the impression of a universal celebration. The physical expressivity of the dancers is awesome in its unconfined energy and flexibility, and their exultant unity is, in effect, both a specific and a general affirmation of humanity. The work fulfills entirely Kylián's precept that dance should capture "the fleeting moments of beauty that pass so quickly and are never repeated."

Opposite: Roslyn Anderson and Gerald Tibbs in Glagolitic Mass. *Netherlands Dance Theatre*
Overleaf: Netherlands Dance Theatre in Glagolitic Mass

ROBERT SCHUMANN'S DAVIDSBÜNDLERTÄNZE

1980 ◆ *Music by Robert Schumann* ◆ *Choreography by George Balanchine*

In 1980 George Balanchine had officially been creating ballets for fifty-five years. At the age of seventy-six, he again drew upon his miraculous choreographic fertility to produce a work as startling in its neo-Romanticism as was his *Apollo* in its neoclassicism. *Robert Schumann's Davidsbündlertänze* was not only structurally a work of consummate balletic craft, but it also contained a disquieting emotional depth that had not been present in Balanchine's other recent ballets, *Ballo della Regina*, *Kammermusik No. 2*, and *Ballade*.

Davidsbündlertänze was inspired by Robert Schumann's well-known set of eighteen piano pieces of the same name, composed in 1837. This twilit piano work, named after a secret fraternity which, in the composer's words, "existed only in the brain of its founder," represents Schumann's alter egos, Eusebius, Florestan, Raro, Serpentinius, and Juvenalis, a group of imaginary artists and composers who banded together against the philistine critics of the day. Schumann ascribed a number of the separate pieces to either Eusebius or Florestan (the principal members of the group), sometimes to both. The ballet itself only hints at this aspect of Schumann's inner life, for its central concerns are the various phases of the composer's relationship with his wife, Clara, and his progressive descent into derangement. *Davidsbündlertänze* is a constant flow of emotional dualities and contrasts that continually ride the music's poetically evocative crests and draw one ever more deeply into Schumann's interior landscape, both musical and psychological.

So close to the emotional source of the original music was this work that some imagined that Balanchine himself was entering a final artistic phase and that his ballet was a kind of poignant leave-taking, in which the various strands of his own creative life seemed to meld into one transcendental farewell. But Balanchine himself denies any parallel; he insists, instead, that the ballet is about atmosphere. "It's better to tell the audience not to analyze," he has said. "If you start to analyze, you'll miss the dancing...words are not supposed to describe music. Words cannot describe. You cannot explain a flower."

THE BALLET

The curtain rises on a nineteenth-century ballroom, framed by a series of billowing white draperies; in the distance there is a seascape surmounted by the suggestion of a Gothic cathedral in the style of Caspar David Friedrich. To the side, at a grand piano, sits a pianist in Romantic period attire. As he plays, the ballet's dramas begin to unfold. While there is no overt narrative, the successive *pas de deux* and other pairings reflect the sentiments expressed in the music.

The first couple rush onto the scene. The woman turns away from him and then toward him with slight waltzing steps, as he catches her around the waist. Fervently pursuing his partner, he holds his hand to his heart until he can place his hands in hers. Finally, she whirls out of his entwined arms and runs off, as he follows.

Another couple walk slowly into the ballroom; the woman's head rests on her own hand, which is placed on his shoulder. It is clear that they are the central couple, representing Schumann and Clara at their most disquieted—the mad composer comforted by his beloved wife. She touches his face, then pulls him to her; he circles her. The couple waltz in a melancholy manner, each reaching out yearningly. They repeat their initial slow walk and then exit with his hand resting on her waist and her hand covering his.

To a restless, buoyant waltz, a third couple fly into the room in *tours jetés*, skips, hops, *sauts de basque*, *sautés*, and abrupt poses. Suddenly, they rush away, as if driven by the wind. The final, fourth couple sweep on in a series of fast, clasping embraces, and rush off in different directions, as the first couple reappear. They dance together in complex partnerings of unusual *promenades* and floating lifts, walks, and little skips, until she *bourrées* away and he walks off in the other direction.

With frantic urgency, the central couple return. They run and leap, rushing about, rarely touching. As they run one way and then the other, he comes to her for a moment or two, but they cross paths in a series of leaps and then disappear in different directions.

A *pas de quatre* danced by the third and fourth couples follows. The women pose in a kind of languorous lunge, and each man, holding his partner's hand, crosses in front of her and covers her eyes with his arms. The dance is replete with shielded

Suzanne Farrell in Robert Schumann's Davidsbündlertänze. *New York City Ballet*

glances, back-to-back supports, and embracing, summoning, and weeping gestures.

A rondo with a gypsy air brings back the first couple. She prances playfully on *pointe* and both leap off as the central couple return for a passionate encounter. With anguished movements, they lunge toward and then away from each other. They spin and leap into *tours jetés* and rise on *demi-pointe* with arms thrust upward. Finally, entwined in each other's arms, they vanish.

The third couple run into the ballroom for a dance that is a series of myriad *promenades* in arabesque; *attitudes* which enwrap him; backbends; and supported turns in *attitude* on her flat foot. After she leaps into his arms and is suspended there for a moment, they cover the room in leaps, then, whirling, run off.

Next the fourth couple return, the man leading the woman, who *bourrées* into the room. They perform a sort of minuet, during which he walks her in a circle as she bends backward over his arm. There are effortless lifts, and finally she *bourrées* from the room as he follows.

Then, with a certain abandon, the woman from the first couple performs a lively, prancing allegro solo. Spinning and leaping in *pas de chat*, she finishes in an abrupt *soussus* and a sharply extended arm gesture with pointed finger.

Next, there is a lively *pas de trois* for all the men except the man of the central couple. They circle each other with leaps and restless rushing, and spin in and out from the center of the circle. The men stop suddenly as their partners enter. In a courtly dance, the ladies are supported in reversed *promenades*. As the dance nears an end, the women *piqué* in *arabesque* with arms *en couronne* and rush off, with the men after them.

After a meditative solo for the central woman, her partner rushes on and begins a frenzied solo. Suddenly, to rippling music, long shadows appear and the white draperies begin to billow; from their midst come five silhouetted, black-caped figures in top hats, holding huge quills and writing tablets. These are the philistine critics who have persecuted the composer. The Schumann figure spins with flailing arms and then as his partner rushes consolingly to him, the critics withdraw. The lovers dance passionately together and are joined by the three other couples. All exchange partners briefly before withdrawing, and the central couple link arms and waltz off.

The third and fourth couples then perform an undulating *pas de quatre* of *chassés*, arrested poses, and *promenades*. The man of the third couple lifts his partner with her back pressed against his chest, and her extended arms fall caressingly over his. As the fourth couple leave, the others rush about until the woman is lifted in *attitude*, a pose echoed by the first couple, who now enter. Soon the first couple are alone, and their separate spinning motions become frenzied. They leave a haunting image as the woman is lifted off stage draped over the man's shoulders.

With urgent encouragement, the central woman pulls her partner into the room. She places his arms about her in a waltz-partnering position, and they begin to dance. They bend back and forth, toward and away from each other. In their waltzing, her arm crosses in front of her face. He bends low to kiss her hand and then begins to walk backward, away from her toward the distant waters which threaten to engulf him. Each reaches an arm out to the other, and the helpless woman bends slowly toward her hand, as if weeping, as her lover goes into the dark.

Davidsbündlertänze, *New York City Ballet: above, Karin von Aroldingen and Adam Lüders; opposite,*
Peter Martins and Heather Watts; overleaf, Kay Mazzo and Ib Andersen

APPENDIX OF SIGNIFICANT FIRST PERFORMANCES

LA FILLE MAL GARDÉE

Ballet in two acts and three scenes. Choreography by Jean Dauberval. First performed in Bordeaux, France, July 1, 1789, to a selection of French popular songs. Later, music by Ferdinand Hérold (1828 Paris Opéra production) and Peter Ludwig Hertel (1864 Berlin production). Revived by Mikhail Mordkin for his Mordkin Ballet, Alvin Theatre, New York, Nov. 12, 1938, with Lucia Chase as Lizette, Dimitri Romanoff as Colin, and Mikhail Mordkin as Widow Simone. Restaged by Dimitri Romanoff and Bronislava Nijinska for Ballet Theatre, Center Theatre, New York, Jan. 19, 1940, with Patricia Bowman, Yurek Shabelevsky, and Edward Caton. New version choreographed by Sir Frederick Ashton with music reorchestrated and augmented by John Lanchbery for the Royal Ballet, Royal Opera House, Covent Garden, London, Jan. 28, 1960, with Nadia Nerina, David Blair, Stanley Holden, and Alexander Grant.

LA SYLPHIDE

Ballet in two acts. Music by Jean Schneitzhoeffer. Choreography by Filippo Taglioni. Book by Adolphe Nourrit. Scenery by Pierre Ciceri. Costumes by Eugène Lami. First performed at the Théâtre de l'Académie Royale de Musique, Paris, Mar. 12, 1832, with Marie Taglioni as La Sylphide and Joseph Mazilier as James. Choreographed by August Bournonville with music by Herman Løvenskjold for the Royal Danish Ballet, Copenhagen, Nov. 28, 1836, with Lucile Grahn as La Sylphide and Bournonville as James. Restaged by Harald Lander for American Ballet Theatre, San Antonio, Texas, Nov. 11, 1964, with Toni Lander and Royes Fernandez. New version choreographed by Erik Bruhn for the National Ballet of Canada, Toronto, Dec. 31, 1964, with Lois Smith and Bruhn. The Bruhn version was mounted for American Ballet Theatre and first performed in New York, July 7, 1971, with Carla Fracci and Ted Kivitt.

GISELLE

Ballet in two acts. Music by Adolphe Adam. Choreography by Jules Perrot and Jean Coralli. Book by H. Vernoy de Saint-Georges, Théophile Gautier, and Jean Coralli. Scenery by Pierre Ciceri. Costumes by Paul Lormier. First performed at the Théâtre de l'Académie Royale de Musique, Paris, June 28, 1841, with Carlotta Grisi as Giselle, Lucien Petipa as Albrecht, Adèle Dumilâtre as Myrtha, and Jean Coralli as Hilarion. First presented in America at the Howard Atheneum, Boston, Jan. 1, 1846, with Mary Ann Lee as Giselle and George Washington Smith as Albrecht. First performed by Ballet Theatre with choreography by Anton Dolin at the Center Theatre, New York, Jan. 12, 1940, with Annabelle Lyon, Anton Dolin, Nina Strogonova, and Harold Haskin. New production for American Ballet Theatre, with choreography by David Blair, premiered at the Carter Barron Amphitheatre, Washington, D.C., July 4, 1968, with Lupe Serrano, Royes Fernandez, Cynthia Gregory, and Paul Nickel. New staging for American Ballet Theatre by Mikhail Baryshnikov, after Coralli, Perrot, and Petipa, premiered at Kennedy Center for the Performing Arts, Washington, D.C., Dec. 16, 1980, with Marianna Tcherkassky and Baryshnikov.

NAPOLI, or THE FISHERMAN AND HIS BRIDE

Ballet in three acts. Music by H. S. Paulli, E. Helsted, N. V. Gade, and H. C. Lumbye. Choreography and book by August Bournonville. Scenery by C. F. Christensen. First performed at the Royal Theater, Copenhagen, Mar. 29, 1842, by the Royal Danish Ballet with August Bournonville as Gennaro and Caroline Fjeldsted as Teresina. First performed in America by the Royal Danish Ballet, New York, Sept. 18, 1956. Divertissements from Act III have been staged by Harald Lander for the London Festival Ballet, 1954, and for Ballet Theatre Workshop, 1963; Erik Bruhn for the Royal Ballet, London, 1962; Hans Brenaa for American Ballet Theatre, 1974; and Stanley Williams for the New York City Ballet, 1977.

THE FLOWER FESTIVAL AT GENZANO

Ballet in one act. Music by E. Helsted and H. S. Paulli. Choreography by August Bournonville. Book by Bournonville after a story by Alexandre Dumas, père. First performed at the Royal Theater, Copenhagen, Dec. 19, 1858, by the Royal Danish Ballet. Staged for London's Royal Ballet by Erik Bruhn, May 3, 1962, with Bruhn and Nadia Nerina. Staged for Ballet Theatre Workshop by Harald Lander, Lisner Auditorium, Washington, D.C., Feb. 20, 1963, with Royes Fernandez and Toni Lander. Staged by Stanley Williams, as part of *Bournonville Divertissements*, for the New York City Ballet, New York State Theater, Feb. 3, 1977, with Peter Martins and Suzanne Farrell.

DON QUIXOTE

Ballet in four acts, eight scenes, with a prologue. Music by Ludwig Minkus. Choreography by Marius Petipa. Book by Petipa after the novel by Miguel de Cervantes. Scenery and costumes by Pavel Isakov, F. Shenian, and I. Shagin. First performed at the Bolshoi Theater, Moscow, Dec. 14, 1869, with Anna Sobeshchanskaya as Kitri and Sergei Sokolov as Basil. Revised version by Petipa in five acts and eleven scenes, first performed at the Maryinsky Theater, St. Petersburg, Nov. 21, 1871, with Alexandra Vergina, Lev Ivanov, and T. A. Stukolkine as Don Quixote. New version after Petipa by Alexander Gorsky, with scenery by Konstantin Korovin, Alexander Golovine, and Baron Klodt and costumes by Korovin. First performed Bolshoi Theater, Moscow, Dec. 6, 1900, with Lyubov Roslavleva as Kitri and Vassily Tikhomirov as Basil. First presented in the United States in a revised version by Rostislav Zakharov after Gorsky by the Bolshoi Ballet, Metropolitan Opera House, New York, Apr. 21, 1966, with Maya Plisetskaya as Kitri, Vladimir Tikhonov as Basil, and Piotr Khomutuv as Don Quixote. Staged by Rudolf Nureyev for the Vienna State Opera Ballet, Vienna, Dec. 1, 1966, and for the Australian Ballet, 1970, the film of which was released in 1973. Staged and choreographed for American Ballet Theatre by Mikhail Baryshnikov, with scenery and costumes by Santo Loquasto. First performed, Opera House, Kennedy Center for the Performing Arts, Washington, D.C., Mar. 23, 1978, with Gelsey Kirkland as Kitri, Baryshnikov as Basil, and Alexander Minz as Don Quixote. Other unique versions include those by Franz Hilverding (Vienna, 1740); Jean-Georges Noverre, with music by Josef Starzer (Vienna, 1768); Ninette de Valois, with music by Roberto

Gerhard and scenery and costumes by Edward Burra, Sadler's Wells, Covent Garden, London, Feb. 20, 1950, with Margot Fonteyn as Dulcinea, Robert Helpmann as Don Quixote, and Alexander Grant as Sancho Panza; and George Balanchine, with music by Nicolas Nabokov, scenery, costumes, and lighting by Esteban Frances, New York City Ballet, New York State Theater, May 28, 1965, with Suzanne Farrell as Dulcinea, Richard Rapp as Don Quixote, and Deni Lamont as Sancho Panza.

COPPÉLIA, or THE GIRL WITH THE ENAMEL EYES
Ballet in three acts. Music by Léo Delibes. Choreography by Arthur Saint-Léon. Book by Charles Nuitter and Arthur Saint-Léon, after the tale Der Sandmann by E. T. A. Hoffmann. Scenery by Charles Cambon, Édouard Despléchin, and Antoine Lavastre. Costumes by Paul Lormier. First performed at the Théâtre Impérial de l'Opéra, Paris, May 25, 1870, with Giuseppina Bozzacchi as Swanilda and Eugénie Fiocre as Franz. New full-length production for American Ballet Theatre with choreography by Enrique Martinez after Saint-Léon and scenery and costumes by William Pitkin, first performed at the Brooklyn Academy of Music, Dec. 24, 1968, with Carla Fracci, Erik Bruhn, and Enrique Martinez as Coppélius. First performed by the New York City Ballet, with choreography by George Balanchine and Alexandra Danilova (one of the greatest Swanildas of our time), with decor by Rouben Ter-Arutunian, Saratoga Performing Arts Center, Saratoga Springs, N.Y., July 17, 1974, with Patricia McBride, Helgi Tomasson, and Shaun O'Brien. New production for the National Ballet of Canada, with choreography by Erik Bruhn and decor by M. Strike, O'Keefe Centre, Toronto, Feb. 8, 1975, with Veronica Tennant, Tomas Schramek, and Jacques Gorrissen.

LA BAYADÈRE
Ballet in four acts. Music by Ludwig Minkus. Choreography by Marius Petipa. Book by Sergei Khudekov and Petipa. First performed at the Maryinsky Theater, St. Petersburg, Feb. 4, 1877, with Ekaterina Vazem as Nikiya, Lev Ivanov (miming) and Pavel Gerdt (dancing) as Solor, and Maria Gorshenkova as Gamzatti. New Soviet version with choreography by Alexander Gorsky and Vassily Tikhomirov, with decor by Konstantin Korovin. First performed by the Bolshoi Ballet, Moscow, Jan. 31, 1923. New version with choreography by Agrippina Vaganova, with decor by Konstantin Ivanov, Piotr Lambin, Orest Allegri, and Adolf Kvapp. First performed by the Kirov Ballet, Leningrad, Dec. 13, 1932. New version with choreography by Natalia Makarova after Marius Petipa, with scenery by Pier Luigi Samaritani and costumes by Theoni V. Aldredge, first performed by American Ballet Theatre, Metropolitan Opera House, New York, May 21, 1980, with Makarova, Anthony Dowell, and Cynthia Harvey.

THE SLEEPING BEAUTY
Ballet in three acts with prologue. Music by Peter Ilyich Tchaikovsky. Choreography by Marius Petipa. Book by Petipa and Ivan Vsevolozhsky after Charles Perrault. Scenery by Ivan Andreyev, Mikhail Bocharov, Constantine Ivanov, Henryk Levot, and Matvei Shishkov. Costumes by Vsevolozhsky. First performed at the Maryinsky Theater,

St. Petersburg, Jan. 15, 1890, with Carlotta Brianza as Princess Aurora, Pavel Gerdt as Prince Florimund, Marie Petipa as the Lilac Fairy, Enrico Cecchetti as Carabosse, Varvara Nikitina as Princess Florine, and Cecchetti as the Bluebird. Staged by Nicholas Sergeyev after Petipa, with additional choreography by Bronislava Nijinska and decor by Leon Bakst, for Diaghilev's Ballets Russes, first performed in Western Europe at the Alhambra Theatre, London, Nov. 2, 1921, with Olga Spessivtseva, Pierre Vladimiroff, Lydia Lopokova, Carlotta Brianza, and Stanislas Idzikowski. Revived in a new production by Sergeyev, with additional choreography by Frederick Ashton and Ninette de Valois and decor by Oliver Messel, for the Sadler's Wells Ballet, Royal Opera House, Covent Garden, London, Feb. 20, 1946, with Margot Fonteyn, Robert Helpmann, Beryl Grey, Pamela May, and Alexis Rassine. First performed in America with choreography by Catherine Littlefield for the Philadelphia Ballet, Academy of Music, Philadelphia, Feb. 12, 1937. Sadler's Wells production first seen in America at the Metropolitan Opera House, New York, Oct. 9, 1949, with Fonteyn, Helpmann, Grey, Moira Shearer, and Rassine. Kirov Ballet version with choreography by Konstantin Sergeyev and decor by Simon Virsaladze first performed in America at the Metropolitan Opera House, New York, Sept. 22, 1961, with Alla Sizova and Yuri Soloviev. New version choreographed by Rudolf Nureyev with decor by Nicholas Georgiadis for the National Ballet of Canada, National Arts Centre, Ottawa, Sept. 1, 1972, with Veronica Tennant and Nureyev. Staged by Mary Skeaping after Sergeyev, with decor by Oliver Messel, for American Ballet Theatre, Metropolitan Opera House, New York, June 15, 1976, with Natalia Makarova, Mikhail Baryshnikov, Martine van Hamel, Dennis Nahat, Fernando Bujones, and Yoko Morishita.

THE NUTCRACKER
Ballet in two acts. Music by Peter Ilyich Tchaikovsky. Choreography by Lev Ivanov. Book by Ivanov after adaptation by Dumas, fils, of E. T. A. Hoffmann's tale The Nutcracker and the Mouse King. Decor by M. I. Bocharov, Constantine Ivanov, and Ivan Vsevolozhsky. First performed at the Maryinsky Theater, St. Petersburg, Dec. 18, 1892, with Antonietta Dell'Era as the Sugar Plum Fairy and Pavel Gerdt as the Cavalier. First performed in Western Europe, in a staging by Nicholas Sergeyev after Ivanov, by Sadler's Wells Ballet, Sadler's Wells Theatre, London, Jan. 30, 1934, with Alicia Markova and Harold Turner. First full-length version in the United States choreographed by Willem Christensen for the San Francisco Ballet, 1944. New version choreographed by George Balanchine, with scenery by Horace Armistead and costumes by Karinska, for the New York City Ballet, New York City Center, Feb. 2, 1954, with Maria Tallchief, Nicholas Magallanes, and Tanaquil LeClercq. New Balanchine production for the New York City Ballet, with scenery by Rouben Ter-Arutunian and costumes by Karinska, New York State Theater, Dec. 11, 1964, with Allegra Kent, Jacques d'Amboise, and Patricia McBride. New version choreographed by Rudolf Nureyev (Prince's Act II variation by Vassily Vainonen), decor by Nicholas Georgiadis, for the Royal Swedish Ballet, Royal Swedish Opera House, Stockholm, Nov. 17, 1967. New staging choreographed by Mikhail Baryshnikov, scenery by Boris Aronson and costumes by Frank Thompson, for American Ballet Theatre, Opera

House, Kennedy Center for the Performing Arts, Washington, D.C., Dec. 21, 1976, with Marianna Tcherkassky as Clara, Mikhail Baryshnikov as the Nutcracker Prince, and Alexander Minz as Drosselmeyer.

SWAN LAKE

Ballet in four acts. Original version, with choreography by Julius Reisinger, music by Peter Ilyich Tchaikovsky, book by V. P. Begichev and Vasily Geltzer, and decor by H. Shangin, K. Valtz, and H. Gropius, first produced Mar. 4, 1877, Bolshoi Theater, Moscow. Revived in 1880 and 1882 at the Bolshoi by Olaf Hansen. Second version, with choreography by Marius Petipa and Lev Ivanov, music by Tchaikovsky, book by Begichev and Geltzer, scenery by M. Botcharov and H. Levogt, first performed at the Maryinsky Theater, St. Petersburg, Jan. 27, 1895, with Pierina Legnani as Odette/Odile and Pavel Gerdt as Prince Siegfried. First performed in Western Europe with choreography by Achille Viscusi in Prague, Czechoslovakia, June 27, 1907. Performed in two acts by Diaghilev's Ballets Russes, Royal Opera House, Covent Garden, London, Nov., 1911, with Mathilde Kschessinska and Vaslav Nijinsky. First staged in the United States by Mikhail Mordkin after Petipa/Ivanov, with scenery by James Fox, at the Metropolitan Opera House, New York, Dec. 20, 1911, with Catherine Geltzer and Mordkin. First staging in England in its entirety by Nicholas Sergeyev after Petipa/Ivanov, with decor by Hugh Stevenson, for the Sadler's Wells Ballet, Sadler's Wells Theatre, London, Nov. 29, 1934, with Alicia Markova and Robert Helpmann. Revised production for the Sadler's Wells Ballet, with decor by Leslie Hurry, first performed in the United States at the Metropolitan Opera House, New York, Oct. 20, 1949, with Margot Fonteyn and Robert Helpmann. One-act version, with original choreography by George Balanchine and decor by Cecil Beaton, first performed by the New York City Ballet, New York City Center, Nov. 20, 1951, with Maria Tallchief and André Eglevsky. First performed by the Stuttgart Ballet with choreography by John Cranko and decor by Jürgen Rose, at the Württembergische Staatstheater, Stuttgart, Germany, Nov. 14, 1963. Staged by Rudolf Nureyev after Ivanov, with decor by Nicholas Georgiadis, for the Vienna State Opera, Oct. 15, 1964, with Margot Fonteyn and Nureyev. First performed by American Ballet Theatre, staged by David Blair after Ivanov, costumes by Freddy Wittop and scenery by Oliver Smith, Civic Opera House, Chicago, Feb. 16, 1967, with Nadia Nerina and Royes Fernandez (New York premiere, New York State Theater, May 9, 1967, with Toni Lander and Bruce Marks). New production with choreography by Erik Bruhn and decor by Desmond Heeley, first performed by the National Ballet of Canada, O'Keefe Centre, Toronto, Mar. 27, 1967, with Lois Smith and Earl Kraul. Staged by Mikhail Baryshnikov for American Ballet Theatre, Kennedy Center for the Performing Arts, Washington, D.C., Mar. 27, 1981, with Martine van Hamel and Kevin McKenzie.

LE CORSAIRE

Ballet in three acts and five scenes, based on Lord Byron's poem *The Corsair*. First version: Music by Robert Bochsa. Choreography by François Decombe Albert. First performed at the King's Theatre, London, June 29, 1837, with Albert as Conrad, Hermine Elssler as Medora, and Pauline Duvernay as Gulnare. Second version: Music by Adolphe Adam and others. Choreography by Joseph Mazilier. Book by H. Vernoy de Saint-Georges and Mazilier. Scenery by Martin, Despléchin, Cambon, and Thierry. Costumes by A. Albert. Technical effects by Victor Sacré. First performed at the Théâtre Impérial de l'Opéra, Paris, Jan. 23, 1856, with D. Segarelli as Conrad, Carolina Rosati as Medora, and Mlle. Couqui as Gulnare. Third version: Music by Riccardo Drigo. Choreography by Marius Petipa. First performed at the Maryinsky Theater, St. Petersburg, Jan. 25, 1899, with Pierina Legnani as Medora. The *pas de deux* from the Petipa version first presented in America by the Kirov Ballet in New York, 1961, with Alla Sizova and Yuri Soloviev, and in London by the Royal Ballet, Covent Garden, Nov. 3, 1962, with Margot Fonteyn and Rudolf Nureyev.

LES SYLPHIDES

Ballet in one act. Music by Frédéric Chopin (Prelude in A op. 28 no. 7; Nocturne in A Flat op. 32 no. 2; Waltz in G Flat op. 70 no. 1; Mazurka in C op. 67 no. 3; Mazurka in D op. 33 no. 2; Waltz in C Sharp Minor op. 64 no. 2; Waltz in E Flat op. 18 no. 1), orchestrated variously by Glazunov, Tcherepnine, Stravinsky, and Liadov. Choreography by Michel Fokine. Decor by Alexandre Benois. After various early versions, presented at a charity performance, as *Chopiniana*, Maryinsky Theater, St. Petersburg, Mar. 8, 1908, with Olga Preobrajenska, Anna Pavlova, Tamara Karsavina, Vera Fokina, and Vaslav Nijinsky. First performed by Diaghilev's Ballets Russes at the Théâtre du Châtelet, Paris, June 2, 1909, with Pavlova, Karsavina, Alexandra Baldina, and Nijinsky. First performed by Ballet Theatre, Center Theatre, New York, Jan. 11, 1940, with Karen Conrad, Nina Stroganova, Lucia Chase, and William Dollar. Staged by Alexandra Danilova to the piano score and danced in rehearsal costumes as *Chopiniana* for the New York City Ballet, New York State Theater, Jan. 20, 1972, with Kay Mazzo, Karin von Aroldingen, Susan Hendl, and Peter Martins.

THE FIREBIRD

Ballet in one act and three scenes. Music by Igor Stravinsky. Choreography and book by Michel Fokine, based on Russian folk tales by A. Afanasiev. Scenery by Alexander Golovine and costumes by Golovine and Leon Bakst. First performed at the Paris Opéra, June 25, 1910, by Diaghilev's Ballets Russes with Tamara Karsavina as the Firebird, Michel Fokine as Ivan Tsarevich, Alexis Bulgakov as Kastchei, and Vera Fokina as the Tsarevna. Revived by Diaghilev's Ballets Russes, with new decor by Natalia Goncharova, Lyceum Theatre, London, Nov. 25, 1926, with Lydia Lopokova, Serge Lifar, and Lubov Tchernicheva. New version for Ballet Theatre with choreography by Adolph Bolm and decor by Marc Chagall, first performed Metropolitan Opera House, New York, Oct. 24, 1945, with Alicia Markova, Anton Dolin, John Taras, and Diana Adams. Staged by Serge Grigoriev, Lubov Tchernicheva, and Tamara Karsavina for the Sadler's Wells Ballet, Edinburgh Festival, Aug. 23, 1954, with Margot Fonteyn, Michael Somes, Frederick Ashton, and Svetlana Beriosova. New version choreographed by George Balanchine, with decor by Chagall, for the New York City Ballet, New York City Center, Nov. 27, 1949, with Maria Tallchief, Francisco Moncion, Edward Bigelow, and Pat McBride. New version choreographed by Maurice Béjart, with costumes by Joelle Roustan, first performed by the Paris Opéra Ballet, Palais des Sports, Paris, Oct. 31, 1970, with Paolo Bortoluzzi as the Firebird. Revived by American Ballet Theatre, with choreography after Fokine by Christopher Newton and decor after Goncharova, Dorothy Chandler Pavilion, Los Angeles, Feb. 21, 1977, with Natalia Makarova, Clark Tippet, Marcos Paredes, and Marie Johansson. First New York performance by American Ballet Theatre, Metropolitan Opera House, Apr. 26, 1977, with Makarova, Ivan Nagy, Paredes, and Karena Brock.

LE SPECTRE DE LA ROSE
Ballet in one act. Music by Carl Maria von Weber. Choreography by Michel Fokine. Book by Jean-Louis Vaudoyer. Set and costumes by Leon Bakst. First performed by Diaghilev's Ballets Russes, Théâtre de Monte Carlo, Apr. 19, 1911, with Vaslav Nijinsky and Tamara Karsavina. First presented at the Théâtre du Châtelet, Paris, June 6, 1911, with Nijinsky and Karsavina. First American performance by Diaghilev's Ballets Russes, Metropolitan Opera House, New York, Apr. 3, 1916, with Alexandre Gavriloff and Lydia Lopokova. First performed by Ballet Theatre, Palacio de Bellas Artes, Mexico City, Oct. 31, 1941, with Ian Gibson and Annabelle Lyon. Performed at the Hamburg Ballet Festival, Germany, June 22, 1975, with Mikhail Baryshnikov and Lynn Seymour. Presented in a new concept by Maurice Béjart, with sets and costumes by Joelle Roustan and Roger Barnard, Ballet du XXe Siècle, Brussels, 1978, with Judith Jamison and Patrice Touron. First performed by the Joffrey Ballet, Mark Hellinger Theatre, New York, Mar. 6, 1979, with Rudolf Nureyev and Denise Jackson.

PETROUCHKA
Ballet in one act and four scenes. Music by Igor Stravinsky. Choreography by Michel Fokine. Book by Stravinsky and Alexandre Benois. Scenery and costumes by Benois. First performed by Diaghilev's Ballets Russes, Théâtre du Châtelet, Paris, June 13, 1911, with Vaslav Nijinsky as Petrouchka, Tamara Karsavina as the Ballerina, Alexandre Orlov as the Blackamoor, and Enrico Cecchetti as the Charlatan. First presented by Diaghilev's Ballets Russes, Century Theater, New York, Jan. 24, 1916, with Léonide Massine, Lydia Lopokova, and Adolph Bolm. First performed by Ballet Theatre, Palacio de Bellas Artes, Mexico City, Aug. 27, 1942, with Yurek Lazowski, Irina Baronova, David Nillo, and Simon Semenoff. Revived by American Ballet Theatre, New York State Theater, June 19, 1970, with Ted Kivitt, Eleanor D'Antuono, Bruce Marks, and Dennis Nahat. First performed by the City Center Joffrey Ballet, New York City Center, New York, Mar. 12, 1970, with Edward Verso, Erika Goodman, Christian Holder, and Yurek Lazowski.

L'APRÈS-MIDI D'UN FAUNE
Choreographic poem in one act. Music by Claude Debussy. Choreography by Vaslav Nijinsky. Scenery and costumes by Leon Bakst. First performed by Diaghilev's Ballets Russes, Théâtre du Châtelet, Paris, May 29, 1912, with Vaslav Nijinsky as the Faun and Lydia Nelidova as the First Nymph. First presented by Col. W. de Basil's Ballets Russes, Metropolitan Opera House, New York, Nov. 1, 1936, with David

Lichine and Tamara Grigorieva. First performed by Ballet Theatre, Palacio de Bellas Artes, Mexico City, Nov. 4, 1941, with George Skibine and Jeanette Lauret. First performed by the Joffrey Ballet, Mark Hellinger Theatre, New York, Mar. 6, 1979, with Rudolf Nureyev and Charlene Gehm.

LE SACRE DU PRINTEMPS
A tableau of pagan Russia in two acts. Music by Igor Stravinsky. Choreography by Vaslav Nijinsky. Decor by Nicholas Roerich. Book by Stravinsky and Roerich. First performed by Diaghilev's Ballets Russes, Théâtre des Champs-Élysées, Paris, May 29, 1913, with Maria Piltz as the Chosen Maiden. Revised version for the Ballets Russes with choreography by Léonide Massine first performed at the Paris Opéra, Dec. 15, 1920, with Lydia Sokolova. New version by Massine first performed at the Academy of Music, Philadelphia, Apr. 11, 1930, with Martha Graham. Staged for the Municipal Opera, Berlin, by Mary Wigman, Sept. 24, 1957. First performed by the Royal Ballet, London, with choreography by Kenneth MacMillan and decor by Sidney Nolan, Royal Opera House, Covent Garden, May 3, 1962, with Monica Mason. First performed by the Ballet du XXe Siècle with choreography by Maurice Béjart, Théâtre Royal de la Monnaie, Brussels, Dec., 1959. First performed by the Munich Opera Ballet with choreography by Glen Tetley, decor by Nadine Baylis, Bavarian State Opera House, Munich, Apr. 17, 1974, with Ferenc Barbay. First performance of the Tetley version by American Ballet Theatre, Metropolitan Opera House, New York, June 21, 1976, with Mikhail Baryshnikov.

PARADE
Realist ballet in one act. Music by Erik Satie. Choreography by Léonide Massine. Book by Jean Cocteau. Decor by Pablo Picasso. First performed by Diaghilev's Ballets Russes, Théâtre du Châtelet, Paris, May 18, 1917, with Léonide Massine as the Chinese Conjurer, Maria Chabelska as the American Girl, Lydia Lopokova and Nicholas Zverev as the Acrobats, and Leon Woizikowsky as the Manager in Evening Dress. First presented in the United States by the City Center Joffrey Ballet, City Center, New York, Mar. 22, 1973, with Gary Chryst, Eileen Brady, Gregory Huffman, Donna Cowen, and Robert Talmadge.

THE THREE-CORNERED HAT
Ballet in one act. Music by Manuel de Falla. Choreography by Léonide Massine. Book by Gregorio Martínez Sierra, after the novel by Pedro Antonio de Alarcón. Decor by Pablo Picasso. First performed by Diaghilev's Ballets Russes, Alhambra Theatre, London, July 22, 1919, with Léonide Massine as the Miller, Tamara Karsavina as the Miller's Wife, Leon Woizikowsky as the Corregidor, and Stanislas Idzikowski as the Dandy. First performed in the United States by Col. W. de Basil's Ballets Russes de Monte Carlo, St. James Theatre, New York, Mar. 9, 1934, with Massine, Tamara Toumanova, David Lichine, and Michel Katcharoff. First performed by Ballet Theatre, Metropolitan Opera House, New York, Apr. 11, 1943, with Massine, Argentinita, Simon Semenoff, and Michael Kidd. First performed by the City Center Joffrey Ballet, City Center, New York, Sept. 25, 1969, with Luis Fuente, Barbara Remington, Basil Thompson, and Frank Bays.

APOLLO

Ballet in two scenes. Music by Igor Stravinsky. Choreography by George Balanchine. Book by Stravinsky. Decor by André Bauchant (later by Gabrielle "Coco" Chanel). First performed by Diaghilev's Ballets Russes at the Théatre Sarah Bernhardt, Paris, June 12, 1928, with Serge Lifar as Apollo, Alice Nikitina (alternating with Alexandra Danilova) as Terpsichore, Lubov Tchernicheva as Polyhymnia, and Felia Doubrovska as Calliope. First performed in the United States by the American Ballet, with decor by Stewart Chaney, at the Metropolitan Opera House, New York, Apr. 27, 1937, with Lew Christensen, Elise Reiman, Holly Howard, and Daphne Vane. First performed by Ballet Theatre, Metropolitan Opera House, New York, Apr. 25, 1943, with André Eglevsky, Vera Zorina, Nora Kaye, and Rosella Hightower. First performed by the New York City Ballet, New York City Center, Nov. 15, 1951, with André Eglevsky, Maria Tallchief, Tanaquil LeClercq, and Diana Adams.

THE PRODIGAL SON

Ballet in three scenes. Music by Sergei Prokofiev. Choreography by George Balanchine. Book by Boris Kochno. Decor by Georges Rouault. First performed by Diaghilev's Ballets Russes, Théatre Sarah Bernhardt, Paris, May 21, 1929, with Serge Lifar as the Prodigal Son, Felia Doubrovska as the Siren, Michael Federov as the Father, and Leon Woizikowsky and Anton Dolin as the Friends. First American performance, with choreography by David Lichine for the Original Ballet Russe, 51st Street Theater, New York, Nov. 26, 1940, with David Lichine, Sono Osato, Dimitri Rostoff, Boris Belsky, and Lorand Andahazy. Revived for the New York City Ballet with choreography by Balanchine, City Center, New York, Feb. 23, 1950, with Jerome Robbins, Maria Tallchief, Michael Arshansky, Herbert Bliss, and Frank Hobi. Revived for American Ballet Theatre, in a staging by John Taras, Kennedy Center for the Performing Arts, Washington, D.C., Dec. 11, 1980, with Robert La Fosse and Cynthia Gregory.

THE GREEN TABLE

Dance of Death in eight scenes. Music by Frederic (Fritz) Cohen. Choreography by Kurt Jooss. Book by Jooss. Decor by Hein Heckroth. First performed by the Folkwang Tanzbühne, Théatre des Champs-Élysées, Paris, July 3, 1932, with Jooss as Death. Revived for the City Center Joffrey Ballet, City Center, New York, Mar. 9, 1967, with Maximiliano Zomosa as Death.

SERENADE

Ballet in four parts. Music by Peter Ilyich Tchaikovsky. Choreography by George Balanchine. Costumes since 1952 by Karinska. First performed by students of the School of American Ballet, Felix M. Warburg estate, White Plains, N.Y., June 9, 1934. Performed by the School of American Ballet producing company, Avery Memorial Theatre, Hartford, Conn., Dec. 6, 1934, with Kathryn Mullowney, Heidi Vosseler, and Charles Laskey.

JARDIN AUX LILAS

Ballet in one act. Music by Ernest Chausson. Choreography by Antony Tudor. Decor by Hugh Stevenson. First performed by Ballet Rambert, Mercury Theatre, London, Jan. 26, 1936, with Maude Lloyd as Caroline, Hugh Laing as Her Lover, Antony Tudor as The Man She Must Marry, and Peggy van Praagh as An Episode in His Past. First performed by Ballet Theatre, Center Theatre, New York, Jan. 15, 1940, with Viola Essen, Hugh Laing, Antony Tudor, and Karen Conrad. First performed by the New York City Ballet, City Center, New York, Nov. 30, 1951, with Nora Kaye, Hugh Laing, Antony Tudor, and Tanaquil LeClercq.

LES PATINEURS

Ballet *divertissement* in one act. Music by Giacomo Meyerbeer (from the operas *Le Prophète* and *L'Étoile du Nord*), arranged by Constant Lambert. Choreography by Frederick Ashton. Decor by William Chappell. First performed by the Vic-Wells Ballet, Sadler's Wells Theatre, London, Feb. 16, 1937, with Harold Turner as the Boy in Blue, Mary Honer, Elizabeth Miller, June Brae, and Pamela May as solo girl friends, and Margot Fonteyn and Robert Helpmann as the White Couple. First performed by Ballet Theatre, with decor by Cecil Beaton, Broadway Theater, New York, Oct. 2, 1946, with John Kriza, Barbara Fallis, Cynthia Riseley, Diana Adams, Anna Cheselka, Nora Kaye, and Hugh Laing. First performed by the Joffrey Ballet, with reconstruction of the original decor by Chappell, City Center, New York, Nov. 2, 1977, with Mark Goldweber, Francesca Corkle, Ann Marie De Angelo, Cynthia Anderson, Patricia Miller, Denise Jackson, and Gregory Huffman.

FRANKIE AND JOHNNY

Ballet in one act. Music by Jerome Moross. Choreography by Ruth Page and Bentley Stone. Book by Michael Blandford and Moross. Decor by Paul Dupont. First performed by the Page-Stone Ballet, Great Northern Theater, Chicago, June 19, 1938, with Ruth Page as Frankie, Bentley Stone as Johnny, Ann Devine as Nelly Bly, and Sean Marino as the Bartender. First performed with new scenery by Clive Rickabaugh by the Ballet Russe de Monte Carlo, City Center, New York, Feb. 28, 1945, with Page and Stone (later, Ruthanna Boris and Frederic Franklin).

BILLY THE KID

Ballet in one act. Music by Aaron Copland. Choreography by Eugene Loring. Book by Lincoln Kirstein. Decor by Jared French. First performed by Ballet Caravan at the Chicago Opera House, Oct. 16, 1938, with Loring as Billy, Marie-Jeanne as the Mother/Sweetheart, Lew Christensen as Pat Garrett, and Todd Bolender as Alias. First performed by Ballet Theatre, Civic Opera House, Chicago, Dec. 8, 1940, with Loring, Alicia Alonso, Richard Reed, and David Nillo.

RODEO, or THE COURTING AT BURNT RANCH

Ballet in one act. Music by Aaron Copland. Choreography by Agnes de Mille. Book by De Mille. Scenery by Oliver Smith. Costumes by Kermit Love. First performed by the Ballet Russe de Monte Carlo, Metropolitan Opera House, New York, Oct. 16, 1942, with De Mille as the Cowgirl, Frederic Franklin as the Champion Roper, Casimir Kokitch as the Head Wrangler, and Milada Mladova as the Ranch

Owner's Daughter. First performed by Ballet Theatre, Hessisches Staadtstheater, Wiesbaden, Germany, Aug. 14, 1950, with Allyn Ann McLerie, John Kriza, James Mitchell, and Charlyne Baker. First performed by the Joffrey Ballet, City Center, New York, Oct. 28, 1976, with Beatriz Rodriguez, Russell Sultzbach, Robert Thomas, and Jan Hanniford.

FANCY FREE
Ballet in one act. Music by Leonard Bernstein. Choreography by Jerome Robbins. Scenery by Oliver Smith. Costumes by Kermit Love. First performed by Ballet Theatre, Metropolitan Opera House, New York, Apr. 18, 1944, with John Kriza, Harold Lang, Jerome Robbins, Muriel Bentley, Janet Reed, and Shirley Eckl. First performed by the New York City Ballet, New York State Theater, Jan. 31, 1980, with Peter Martins, Jean-Pierre Frohlich, Bart Cook, Lourdes Lopez, Stephanie Saland, and Florence Fitzgerald.

APPALACHIAN SPRING
Ballet in one act. Music by Aaron Copland. Choreography by Martha Graham. Scenery by Isamu Noguchi. Costumes by Edythe Gilfond. First performed at the Library of Congress, Washington, D.C., Oct. 30, 1944, with Martha Graham as the Bride, Erick Hawkins as the Husbandman, May O'Donnell as the Pioneer Woman, Merce Cunningham as the Preacher, and Nina Fonaroff, Pearl Lang, Marjorie Mazia, and Yuriko as the Followers.

SYMPHONIC VARIATIONS
Abstract classical ballet in one act. Music by César Franck. Choreography by Frederick Ashton. Decor by Sophie Fedorovitch. First performed by the Sadler's Wells Ballet, Royal Opera House, Covent Garden, London, Apr. 24, 1946, with Margot Fonteyn, Michael Somes, Pamela May, Brian Shaw, Moira Shearer, and Henry Danton. First performance in the United States by the Sadler's Wells Ballet, Metropolitan Opera House, New York, Oct. 12, 1949, with Fonteyn, Somes, May, Shaw, Shearer, and John Hart.

THEME AND VARIATIONS
Abstract classical ballet in one act. Music by Peter Ilyich Tchaikovsky. Choreography by George Balanchine. Decor by Woodman Thompson. First performed by Ballet Theatre, City Center, New York, Nov. 26, 1947, with Alicia Alonso and Igor Youskevitch. First performed by the New York City Ballet, with costumes by Karinska, City Center, New York, Feb. 5, 1960, with Violette Verdy and Edward Villella. First performed as the last movement of Suite No. 3, with decor by Nicolas Benois by the New York City Ballet, New York State Theater, Dec. 3, 1970, with Gelsey Kirkland and Edward Villella.

ORPHEUS
Ballet in one act. Music by Igor Stravinsky. Choreography by George Balanchine. Decor by Isamu Noguchi. First performed by Ballet Society, New York City Center, Apr. 28, 1948, with Nicholas Magallanes as Orpheus, Maria Tallchief as Eurydice, Francisco Moncion as the Dark

Angel, Beatrice Tompkins as Leader of the Furies, Tanaquil LeClercq as Leader of the Bacchantes, and Herbert Bliss as Apollo.

CINDERELLA
Ballet in three acts. Music by Sergei Prokofiev. Choreography by Frederick Ashton. Decor by Jean-Denis Malclès. First performed by the Sadler's Wells Ballet, Royal Opera House, Covent Garden, London, Dec. 23, 1948, with Moira Shearer as Cinderella, Michael Somes as Prince Charming, Robert Helpmann and Frederick Ashton as the Ugly Stepsisters, Pamela May as the Fairy Godmother, and Alexander Grant as the Jester. First performed in the United States by the Sadler's Wells Ballet, Metropolitan Opera House, New York, Oct. 18, 1949, with Margot Fonteyn, Somes, Helpmann, Ashton, May, and Grant.

THE MOOR'S PAVANE
Ballet in one act, based on Shakespeare's Othello. Music by Henry Purcell (themes from Abdelazer, or The Moor's Revenge, The Gordian Knot Untied, and Pavane and Chaconne for Strings, arranged by Simon Sadoff). Choreography by José Limón. Costumes by Pauline Lawrence. First performed by the José Limón Company, Palmer Auditorium, Connecticut College, New London, Aug. 17, 1949, with José Limón as the Moor, Betty Jones as the Moor's Wife, Lucas Hoving as His Friend, and Pauline Koner as His Friend's Wife. First performed by American Ballet Theatre, New York State Theater, June 27, 1970, with Bruce Marks, Toni Lander, Royes Fernandez, and Sallie Wilson. First performed by the City Center Joffrey Ballet, City Center, New York, Oct. 13, 1973, with Christian Holder, Jan Hanniford, Burton Taylor, and Beatriz Rodriguez.

AFTERNOON OF A FAUN
Ballet in one act. Music by Claude Debussy. Choreography by Jerome Robbins. Set and lighting by Jean Rosenthal. Costumes by Irene Sharaff. First performed by the New York City Ballet, City Center, New York, May 14, 1953, with Francisco Moncion and Tanaquil LeClercq. First performed by the Royal Ballet, Royal Opera House, Covent Garden, London, Dec. 14, 1971, with Anthony Dowell and Antoinette Sibley.

THE CONCERT, or THE PERILS OF EVERYBODY
A charade in one act. Music by Frédéric Chopin. Choreography by Jerome Robbins. Decor and lighting by Jean Rosenthal. Costumes by Irene Sharaff. First performed by the New York City Ballet, City Center, New York, Mar. 6, 1956, with Tanaquil LeClercq, Todd Bolender, Yvonne Mounsey, Robert Barnett, Wilma Curley, John Mandia, Shaun O'Brien, Patricia Savoia, and Richard Thomas, with Nicholas Kopeikine at the piano. First performed by Robbins's Ballets U.S.A. at the Festival of Two Worlds, Spoleto, Italy, June 8, 1958, with new decor by Saul Steinberg. Revived by the New York City Ballet, New York State Theater, Dec. 2, 1971, with Sara Leland, Anthony Blum, Bettijane Sills, Shaun O'Brien, Robert Weiss, Bart Cook, Steven Caras, Gloriann Hicks, Delia Peters, and Christine Redpath, with Jerry Zimmerman at the piano. First performed by the Royal Ballet, Royal

Opera House, Covent Garden, London, Mar. 4, 1975, with new decor by Edward Gorey, with Lynn Seymour, Michael Coleman, and Georgina Parkinson.

AGON

Abstract ballet in one act. Music by Igor Stravinsky. Choreography by George Balanchine. Lighting by Nananne Porcher. First performed in a preview performance by the New York City Ballet, City Center, New York, Nov. 27, 1957, with Diana Adams, Melissa Hayden, Barbara Walczak, Barbara Milberg, Todd Bolender, Roy Tobias, Jonathan Watts, and Arthur Mitchell. Premiered on Dec. 1, 1957, City Center, New York, with the same cast.

STARS AND STRIPES

Ballet in Five Campaigns. Music by John Philip Sousa, arranged by Hershy Kay. Choreography by George Balanchine. Costumes by Karinska. Decor by David Hays. First performed by the New York City Ballet, City Center, New York, Jan. 17, 1958, with Allegra Kent, Diana Adams, Robert Barnett, Melissa Hayden, and Jacques d'Amboise.

SUMMERSPACE

A Lyric Dance. Music by Morton Feldman (*Ixion*). Choreography by Merce Cunningham. Decor by Robert Rauschenberg. First performed by the Merce Cunningham Dance Company, American Dance Festival, Connecticut College, New London, Aug. 17, 1958, with Merce Cunningham, Carolyn Brown, Viola Farber, Cynthia Stone, Marilyn Wood, and Remy Charlip. First performed by the New York City Ballet, New York State Theater, Apr. 14, 1966, with Anthony Blum, Kay Mazzo, Patricia Neary, Sara Leland, Carol Sumner, and Deni Lamont.

REVELATIONS

A ballet in three parts. Music: traditional Afro-American spirituals. Choreography by Alvin Ailey. Costumes by Lawrence Maldonado. Lighting by Nicola Cernovitch. First performed by the Alvin Ailey American Dance Theater at the 92nd St. YM-YWHA, New York, Jan. 31, 1960, with Joan Derby, Minnie Marshall, Merle Derby, Dorene Richardson, Jay Fletcher, Nathaniel Horne, Carmen Howell, and soloists assisted by the Music Masters Guild Chorus of the Harlem Branch, YMCA.

MARGUERITE AND ARMAND

Ballet in one act. Music by Franz Liszt (Piano Sonata in B Minor), orchestrated by Humphrey Searle, later by Gordon Jacob. Choreography by Frederick Ashton. Decor by Cecil Beaton. First performed by the Royal Ballet, Royal Opera House, Covent Garden, London, Mar. 12, 1963, with Margot Fonteyn as Marguerite, Rudolf Nureyev as Armand, Michael Somes as His Father, and Leslie Edwards as the Duke. First performed in the United States by the Royal Ballet, Metropolitan Opera House, New York, May 1, 1963, with the same cast.

THE DREAM

Ballet in one act. Music by Felix Mendelssohn, arranged by John Lanchbery. Choreography by Frederick Ashton. Scenery by Henry Bardon. Costumes by David Walker. First performed by the Royal Ballet, Royal Opera House, Covent Garden, London, Apr. 2, 1964, with Antoinette Sibley as Titania, Anthony Dowell as Oberon, Keith Martin as Puck, and Alexander Grant as Bottom. First performed in the United States by the Royal Ballet, Metropolitan Opera House, New York, Apr. 30, 1965, with the same cast. First performed by the City Center Joffrey Ballet, Wolf Trap Performing Arts Center, Virginia, Aug. 9, 1973, with Rebecca Wright, Burton Taylor, Russell Sultzbach, and Larry Grenier.

ROMEO AND JULIET

Ballet in three acts, based on Shakespeare's tragedy. Music by Sergei Prokofiev. Choreography by Kenneth MacMillan. Decor by Nicholas Georgiadis. First performed by the Royal Ballet, Royal Opera House, Covent Garden, London, Feb. 9, 1965, with Rudolf Nureyev as Romeo and Margot Fonteyn as Juliet. First performed by the Royal Ballet in the United States, Metropolitan Opera House, New York, Apr. 21, 1965, with the same cast.

EUGENE ONEGIN

Ballet in three acts and six scenes, based on the free-verse novel *Eugene Onegin* by Alexander Pushkin. Music by Peter Ilyich Tchaikovsky, arranged and orchestrated by Kurt-Heinz Stolze. Choreography by John Cranko. Decor by Jürgen Rose. First performed by the Stuttgart Ballet, Württembergische Staatstheater, Stuttgart, Germany, Apr. 13, 1965, with Marcia Haydée as Tatiana, Ray Barra as Onegin, Egon Madsen as Lensky, and Ana Cardus as Olga. First performed in the United States by the Stuttgart Ballet, Metropolitan Opera House, New York, June 10, 1969, with Marcia Haydée, Heinz Clauss, Egon Madsen, and Susanne Hanke.

HARBINGER

Ballet in five movements. Music by Sergei Prokofiev (Piano Concerto no. 5 in G Major). Choreography by Eliot Feld. Decor by Oliver Smith. Costumes by Stanley Simmons. Lighting by Jean Rosenthal. First performed by American Ballet Theatre, Miami, Florida, Mar. 31, 1967, with Christine Sarry, Edward Verso, Janet Mitchell, Cynthia Gregory, Marcos Paredes, and Eliot Feld. First New York performance, New York State Theater, May 11, 1967, by the same company and with the same cast (Paula Tracy replacing Janet Mitchell).

JEWELS

Abstract ballet in three acts. Music by Gabriel Fauré (*Pelléas et Mélisande* and *Shylock*); Igor Stravinsky (Capriccio for Piano and Orchestra); Peter Ilyich Tchaikovsky (Symphony no. 3 in D Major, last four movements). Choreography by George Balanchine. Costumes by Karinska. Scenery by Peter Harvey. First performed by the New York City Ballet, New York State Theater, Apr. 13, 1967, with Violette Verdy, Conrad Ludlow, Mimi Paul, and Francisco Moncion ("Emeralds"); Patricia McBride, Edward Villella, and Patricia Neary ("Rubies"); and Suzanne Farrell and Jacques d'Amboise ("Diamonds").

ASTARTE
A psychedelic ballet. Music composed and performed by Crome Syrcus. Choreographed by Robert Joffrey. Set and lighting by Thomas Skelton. Costumes by Hugh Sherrer. Film by Gardner Compton. First performed by the City Center Joffrey Ballet, City Center, New York, Sept. 20, 1967, with Trinette Singleton and Maximiliano Zomosa.

SPARTACUS
Ballet in three acts. Music by Aram Khachaturian. Choreography by Yuri Grigorovich. Decor by Simon Virsaladze. First performed by the Bolshoi Ballet, Bolshoi Theater, Moscow, Apr. 9, 1968, with Vladimir Vasiliev as Spartacus, Ekaterina Maximova as Phrygia, Maris Liepa as Crassus, and Nina Timofeyeva as Aegina.

THE TAMING OF THE SHREW
Ballet in two acts after the play by Shakespeare. Music by Kurt-Heinz Stolze, after Domenico Scarlatti. Choreography by John Cranko. Decor by Elizabeth Dalton. First performed by the Stuttgart Ballet, Württembergische Staatstheater, Stuttgart, Germany, Mar. 16, 1969, with Marcia Haydée as Kate, Richard Cragun as Petruchio, Susanne Hanke as Bianca, and Egon Madsen as Gremio. First performed by the Stuttgart Ballet in the United States, Metropolitan Opera House, New York, June 12, 1969, with the same cast.

DANCES AT A GATHERING
Ballet in one act. Music by Frédéric Chopin (Mazurka op. 63 no. 3; Waltz op. 69 no. 2; Mazurka op. 33 no. 3; Mazurkas op. 6 nos. 2 and 4; op. 7 nos. 4 and 5; op. 24 no. 2; Waltz op. 42; Waltz op. 34 no. 2; Mazurka op. 56 no. 2; Etude op. 25 no. 4; Waltz op. 34 no. 1; Waltz op. 70 no. 2; Etude op. 25 no. 5; Etude op. 10 no. 2; Scherzo op. 20 no. 1; Nocturne op. 15 no. 1). Choreography by Jerome Robbins. Costumes by Joe Eula. Lighting by Thomas Skelton. First performed by the New York City Ballet, May 8, 1969, and premiered May 22, 1969, New York State Theater, with Allegra Kent, Sara Leland, Kay Mazzo, Patricia McBride, Violette Verdy, Anthony Blum, John Clifford, Robert Maiorano, John Prinz, Edward Villella, and pianist Gordon Boelzner. First performed by the Royal Ballet, Royal Opera House, Covent Garden, London, Oct. 19, 1970, with Laura Connor, Ann Jenner, Monica Mason, Lynn Seymour, Antoinette Sibley, Michael Coleman, Anthony Dowell, Jonathan Kelly, Rudolf Nureyev, and David Wall.

TRINITY
Ballet in three sections. Music by Alan Raph and Lee Holdridge. Choreography by Gerald Arpino. Lighting by Jennifer Tipton. First performed by the City Center Joffrey Ballet, City Center, New York, Oct. 9, 1969, with Christian Holder, Donna Cowen, Starr Danias, Rebecca Wright, Dermot Burke, Gary Chryst, and James Dunne, with the rock group Virgin Wool, Hub Miller at the organ, and the Boys Choir of St. Luke's Chapel.

DEUCE COUPE
Music by the Beach Boys. Choreography by Twyla Tharp. Setting by United Graffiti Artists. Costumes by Scott Barrie. First performed by the City Center Joffrey Ballet, City Center, New York, Mar. 1, 1973, with Erika Goodman as the ballerina, Twyla Tharp, and members of the Joffrey Ballet and the Twyla Tharp Dancers.

VOLUNTARIES
Ballet in one act. Music by Francis Poulenc (Concerto for Organ, Strings and Timpani). Choreography by Glen Tetley. Decor by Rouben Ter-Arutunian. First performed by the Stuttgart Ballet, Württembergische Staatstheater, Stuttgart, Germany, Dec. 22, 1973, with Marcia Haydée and Richard Cragun, Birgit Keil, Reid Anderson, and Jan Stripling. First performed in the United States by the Stuttgart Ballet, Metropolitan Opera House, New York, June 4, 1975, with the same cast. First performed by the American Ballet Theatre, Music Hall, Cleveland, Ohio, Feb. 4, 1977, with Cynthia Gregory and Charles Ward, Martine van Hamel, Michael Owen, and Richard Schafer. First New York performance by American Ballet Theatre, Metropolitan Opera House, May 2, 1977, with Natalia Makarova and Clark Tippet, Leslie Browne, Michael Owen, and Richard Schafer.

ESPLANADE
Music by Johann Sebastian Bach (Violin Concerto no. 2 in E Major and Concerto for Two Violins in D Minor, *Largo* and *Allegro* movements). Choreography by Paul Taylor. Costumes by John Rawlings. First performance by the Paul Taylor Company, Lisner Auditorium, Washington, D.C., Mar. 1, 1975, with Bettie de Jong, Carolyn Adams, Eileen Cropley, Nicholas Gunn, Monica Morris, Elie Chaib, Lila York, Greg Reynolds, and Ruth Andrien. First New York performance, Lyceum Theatre, June 11, 1975, with same cast.

UNTITLED
Music by Robert Dennis. Choreography by Pilobolus Dance Theater (Alison Chase, Moses Pendleton, Robby Barnett, Jonathan Wolken, Martha Clarke, and Michael Tracy). Costumes by William Mickley and Kitty Daly. First performed by Pilobolus at the American Dance Festival, Connecticut College, New London, Aug. 2, 1975.

NOTRE FAUST
Spectacle ballet in two acts and thirteen scenes. Music by Johann Sebastian Bach, Ludwig Minkus, Harry Warren, and Argentinian tangos. Choreography and book by Maurice Béjart. Decor by Thierry Bosquet. First performed by Ballet du XXe Siècle, Théâtre Royale de la Monnaie, Brussels, Dec. 12, 1975, with Béjart as Faust/Mephistopheles, Yann Le Gac as Mephistopheles/Faust, Jorge Donn as Lucifer and Euphorion, Bertrand Pié as Satan, Patrice Touron as Beelzebub, Monet Robier as Marguerite, and Shonach Mirk as Helen of Troy. First performed in the United States by the same company and cast, Uris Theatre, New York, Mar. 29, 1977.

A MONTH IN THE COUNTRY

Ballet in one act. Music by Frédéric Chopin ("Là Ci Darem" Variations, *Fantasy on Polish Airs*, *Andante Spianato* and Grand Polonaise in E Flat for Piano and Orchestra), arranged by John Lanchbery. Choreography by Frederick Ashton. Decor by Julia Trevelyan Oman. First performed by the Royal Ballet, Royal Opera House, Covent Garden, London, Feb. 12, 1976, with Lynn Seymour as Natalia Petrovna, Alexander Grant as Yslaev, Wayne Sleep as Kolia, Derek Rencher as Rakitin, Denise Nunn as Vera, Marguerite Porter as Katia, Anthony Conway as Matvei, and Anthony Dowell as Beliaev. First performed in the United States by the Royal Ballet, Metropolitan Opera House, New York, Apr. 27, 1976, with the same cast.

VIENNA WALTZES

Ballet in five movements. Music by Johann Strauss, Jr. (*Tales from the Vienna Woods*, *Voices of Spring*, and *Explosion Polka*); Franz Lehár (*Gold and Silver Waltz*); and Richard Strauss (first waltz sequence from *Der Rosenkavalier*). Choreography by George Balanchine. Decor by Rouben Ter-Arutunian. Costumes by Karinska. Lighting by Ronald Bates. First performed by the New York City Ballet, New York State Theater, June 23, 1977, with Karin von Aroldingen, Sean Lavery, Patricia McBride, Helgi Tomasson, Sara Leland, Bart Cook, Kay Mazzo, Peter Martins, Suzanne Farrell, and Jorge Donn (performed in the gala preview; subsequent performances by Jean-Pierre Bonnefous).

GLAGOLITIC MASS

Ballet in one act. Music by Leoš Janáček (*Mša Glagolskaja*, 1927). Choreography by Jiří Kylián. Sets by Walter Nobbe. Costumes by Nobbe and Joop Stokvis. Lighting by Joop Caboort. First performed by the Netherlands Dance Theater, Teatro della Pergola, Florence, June 5, 1979. First performed in New York by the same compány, New York City Center, July 16, 1979.

ROBERT SCHUMANN'S DAVIDSBÜNDLERTÄNZE

Ballet in one act. Music by Robert Schumann (*Davidsbündlertänze* op. 6). Choreography by George Balanchine. Decor by Rouben Ter-Arutunian. Lighting by Ronald Bates. First performed by the New York City Ballet, New York State Theater, June 19, 1980 (performed in gala preview, June 12, 1980), with Karin von Aroldingen, Suzanne Farrell, Kay Mazzo, Heather Watts, Adam Lüders, Jacques d'Amboise, Ib Andersen, and Peter Martins; Gordon Boelzner at the piano.

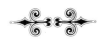

GLOSSARY

Arabesque
A basic ballet posture in which the dancer balances on one leg, the other leg raised and extended behind. There are many variations in arm and body positions. *Arabesque penchée*, an arabesque in which the dancer leans forward, raising the extended leg high and lowering the head and forward arm correspondingly.

Assemblé
A step in which the dancer brushes one foot out along the floor and into the air, springs upward on the supporting foot, brings both feet together off the floor, and lands in fifth position.

Attitude
A ballet posture with one arm raised overhead, back arched, corresponding leg bent at the knee and raised behind the trunk while the body is balanced on the other leg. It is a pose borrowed from Giovanni da Bologna's famous sixteenth-century statue of Mercury.

Balancé
A rocking step in three-quarter time in which weight is shifted from one foot to the other with the knee bending as it receives the weight on the new foot.

Ballabile
A spirited group dance usually performed by the corps de ballet.

Ballet blanc
"White ballet"; usually applied to the nineteenth-century classical ballets in which the female dancers wear romantic white tulle skirts.

Ballet d'action
A dramatic ballet with a plot, either tragic or comic.

Barre
In a ballet classroom, the horizontal wooden railing along the walls which dancers grasp while performing their daily class exercises (*barre* work).

Batterie
Steps in which the legs beat against each other as the dancer springs into the air. *Grande batterie* refers to steps with higher elevation and more beats; *petite batterie*, less elevation and fewer beats.

Bourrée
Small, quick steps—often traveling, sometimes in place—done on *pointe* or *demi-pointe* in fifth position.

Cabriole
The *grande batterie* step in which a leg is thrust straight up and the supporting leg raised forcefully to beat against it before returning to the floor.

Chaîné
Linked steps, usually *tours chaînés*, a chain of small, swift turning steps executed in a straight line or in a large circle.

Chassé
A step on the floor in which one foot slides from a closed position to an open one, the other foot "chasing" it out of its position.

Couronne
Position of the arms raised like a crown above the dancer's head. It is the traditional *port de bras* accompanying the fifth position.

Danseur
Male dancer. *Premier danseur*, a principal male dancer. *Danseur noble*, a male dancer who embodies the noble style of classical ballet.

Demi-caractère
A role which, while still in the classical mode, has elements of folk or character dancing; also applied to a dancer who excels in such roles.

Développé
An unfolding movement of the leg and foot. *Développé à la seconde*, the leg and foot unfold from a closed position into an extension in second position.

Divertissement
A special dance inserted into a ballet or opera. *Grand divertissement*, an elaborate group dance used as a set piece and having little relation to the plot of the ballet.

Emboîté
Literally, "boxed"; most usually, a series of interlocking jumping steps with the feet crossing close together, one in front of the other; may be performed in various directions.

En tournant
Steps performed with the body turning.

En travesti
A female dancer disguised as a male, or a male dancer disguised as a female (Madge the Witch in *La Sylphide*, for example).

Entrechat
One of the *batterie* steps in which the dancer jumps and, while in the air, crosses and recrosses the legs. *Entrechat quatre*, the legs make two distinct movements, crossing rapidly before and behind.

Farruca
A Spanish gypsy dance.

Fouetté (en tournant)
A turn in which the dancer rises on one foot and whips the other, extended leg around for each turn.

Gaillarde
A gay and lively dance popular in the sixteenth and seventeenth centuries.

Galop
A spirited dance to music with two beats to a measure.

Gargouillade

A variation on the *pas de chat* involving a *rond de jambe* action executed by the commencing leg and sometimes by the closing leg.

Glissade

A gliding, traveling movement linking other steps.

Jeté

A step in which the weight is thrown from one leg to the other in a leap. Different from a jump. **Coupé jeté**, a *jeté* in which one leg brushes out and the foot of the other leg comes to the ankle of the supporting, or landing, foot. **Jeté en avant**, a leap forward. **Grand jeté**, a great leap in which the leg is raised at a 90 degree angle as it is thrown forward for high elevation. **Tour jeté**, properly, *grand jeté en tournant*; an interchanging of the legs in a scissorlike motion while in the air.

Pas de chat

A light, catlike spring with knees bent; feet are lifted one at a time and brought back to the floor in fifth position at almost the same time. **Pas de chat en tournant**, the same step executed with a full turn.

Pas de deux

A dance for two performers. **Grand pas de deux**, the showpiece in classical ballet for a ballerina and *danseur*, in five sections: the entrance, the adagio, a bravura solo for each dancer, and a coda.

Piqué

A taken step directly onto one *pointe* or *demi-pointe*. **Piqué arabesque**, an arabesque taken directly onto one *pointe* or *demi-pointe*. **Piqué attitude**, an *attitude* taken directly onto one *pointe* or *demi-pointe*. **Pique relevé**, from one *pointe* or *demi-pointe*, the working leg is lowered to *plié* and then rises again onto *pointe* or *demi-pointe*.

Pirouette

A complete turn in a spinning motion on one foot. **Pirouette à la seconde**, the dancer spins on one foot with the other raised at right angle to the body.

Plié

The knee bend that is often the preparation and the finish of a jump or turn. **Grand plié à la seconde**, with feet turned out in second position and heels firmly on the floor, knees bend simultaneously and then straighten.

Pointe

Tip of the toe. **Demi-pointe**, "half toe" (the ball of the foot). **Pointe tendue**, a position in which one leg, with the toe pointed, is extended on the floor and the weight rests on the other foot.

Port de bras

The arm movements and positions.

Positions of the Feet

First position, legs turned out, feet turned out at 180 degree angle with heels touching. Second position, same as first, but with heels twelve inches apart. Third position, legs and feet turned out with feet crossed close together, heel of forward foot angled outward from instep of other foot. Fourth position, legs and feet turned out and parallel, with front foot about twelve inches forward. Fifth position, legs and feet turned out, close together, one foot crossed exactly in front of the other and parallel to it, toes of one next to heel of other.

Promenade

A dancer *en promenade* turns slowly in place holding his or her pose.

Relevé

The raising of the body onto full *pointe* or *demi-pointe* on one or both feet. **Relevé arabesque**, the raising of the body in an arabesque position. **Relevé passé**, while one foot rises to the *demi-pointe* or full *pointe* from fifth position, the other passes either to the front or to the back of the knee.

Révérence

A curtsy or bow.

Rond de jambe (à terre)

A step in which the working foot, with toe pointed, sweeps in a semicircle on the floor. **Grand rond de jambe**, the supporting leg is bent at the knee while the working foot sweeps in a large semicircle in the air or on the floor. **Rond de jambe en l'air**, the working leg is raised and turned out to second position while the foreleg makes a circle, finishing with the leg extended in the air.

Sarabande

A majestic court dance similar to a minuet.

Saut de basque

A traveling step in which the dancer jumps and turns as one foot is drawn up to the knee of the other leg.

Sauté

Literally, jumping.

Seguidilla

A Spanish regional dance.

Sissonne

A step originated by the Comte de Sissonne with many variations. Basically, the dancer jumps from both feet onto one foot. **Sissonne fermé**, a *sissonne* in which the second foot almost immediately joins the working foot in a closed position.

Soutenu

A turning step in which the legs sustain the fifth position on *demi-pointe*.

Tour

A turn. **Tour en l'air**, from the fifth position the dancer springs up in the air, feet crossed, and executes one or two complete turns, coming down in fifth position on one knee, or in an arabesque or similar pose.

INDEX

All numbers are page references. Italics indicate those pages on which illustrations of the index entries appear.

PHOTO CREDITS

The author and publisher wish to thank the following individuals and institutions who have supplied the photographs on the pages indicated:

BBC Hulton Picture Library: 12, 13 (left and right), 14 (top),
15 (bottom), 86, 121, 124
Bibliothèque Nationale, Opéra, Paris: 5, 73, 83
Candid Illustrators/Andrew Mark Wentink: 108
©Steven Caras: 19, 38, 39, 40, 53, 57, 90, 92, 93, 99, 128, 132–33, 148 (bottom),
151, 152–53, 155, 156, 184, 201, 203, 226, 238, 239
©Costas: 189
Covent Garden/J. B. Debenham, London: 14 (bottom)
© Alan Cunliffe: 60
©Zoë Dominic: 61
©Beverly Gallegos: 26, 131, 192, 225
Vera Krassovskaya, Leningrad, Courtesy of Dance Perspectives Foundation: 6
Photo Lavolé, Paris: 30
Judith Michael: 49
©Herbert Migdoll: 70–71, 74–75, 78–79, 81, 82, 84, 89, 95, 96, 103, 105, 112,
114–15, 116, 123, 140, 158–59, 163, 169, 182–83, 186–87, 190, 204, 206–7, 209,
210–11, 218, 221, 228–29, 234–35
MIRA: 164, 167, 174
© Barbara Morgan: 16
The Museum of London: 9
Tony van Muyden: 17 (bottom)
The Dance Collection, New York Public Library at Lincoln Center:
4 (top and bottom), 10, 11, 68, 76
©Leslie E. Spatt: 42–43, 45, 126, 136–37, 147, 148 (top), 170, 177, 178–79, 180, 196,
197, 202, 212, 224
©Martha Swope: 2–3, 18, 25, 29, 34, 36, 41, 47, 58, 66, 102, 111, 117, 118, 119, 142,
143, 144, 145, 146, 149, 157, 198, 200, 230, 231, 236, 240
The Theatre Museum, London/Gordon Anthony: 15 (top)
©Jack Vartoogian: 17 (top), 20, 22–23, 27, 50–51, 55, 62–63, 80, 97, 100, 109, 129,
161, 173, 175, 195, 214–15, 217
©Linda Vartoogian: 33, 65, 165, 222
Victoria and Albert Museum, Crown Copyright, London: 1
Jennie Walton: 139
©Rosemary Winckley: 31, 32, 56, 59, 171, 195, 232

ACKNOWLEDGMENTS

*I have received invaluable assistance in the preparation of this book from a number of
individuals. My warmest thanks go to Mary Whitney for her diligent and
creative photographic research; to Steven Caras, Herbert Migdoll, Leslie E. Spatt,
Martha Swope, Jack Vartoogian, and Rosemary Winckley
for their vivid and evocative photographs; to Genevieve Oswald and her helpful
staff of the Dance Collection, Performing Arts Research Center,
The New York Public Library at Lincoln Center; and to the many dancers who
furnished information regarding the ballets they have performed.
My very special gratitude to Andrew Mark Wentink for his extraordinary help in
the preparation of the manuscript. His astute observations and precise knowledge of
dance have been instrumental in lending insight to this book.
For his enthusiasm and encouragement, my heartfelt thanks to Paul Gottlieb,
President and Publisher of Harry N. Abrams, Inc. For her unfailing support, my deep
gratitude to Darlene Geis, Project Director. For her extraordinary taste and
understanding of dance, my special thanks to designer Judith Michael.
And for her patience, goodwill, and sensitive attention to the manuscript,
my sincere gratitude to my editor, Margaret Donovan.*